QUESTIONING THE HUMAN

Questioning the Human

Toward a Theological Anthropology
for the Twenty-First Century

Edited by

Lieven Boeve, Yves De Maeseneer,
and Ellen Van Stichel

FORDHAM UNIVERSITY PRESS

New York 2014

Library of Congress Control Number: 2014938148

Printed in the United States of America
16 15 14   5 4 3 2 1
First edition

CONTENTS

QUESTIONING THE HUMAN

Exploring New Questions
for Theological Anthropology

Lieven Boeve, Yves De Maeseneer,
and Ellen Van Stichel

What does it mean to be human? In today's context, this fundamental question lies at the heart of many debates in the Church and the world. Unseen cultural, political, and scientific developments provoke new challenges that can no longer be tackled from traditional perspectives on the human being.[1] The familiar concepts theologians use to make sense of Christian beliefs about the human being have lost much of their purchase. Humanity is said to be created in God's image and likeness, marked by sin but, through God's grace, saved to a new life in Christ. But what do we mean by "human nature," "personhood," "freedom," "soul," "relation," and other concepts that this account traditionally draws on? There is an urgent need to explore the questions that theological anthropology faces in our contemporary context.[2]

This collection is distinctive in several ways. All the authors share a Roman Catholic background, which makes this volume a helpful complement to recent publications that represent views predominantly from other theological traditions.[3] Moreover, nearly fifty years after Vatican II's groundbreaking document *Gaudium et Spes*, it is a timely moment to assess the state and future of theological anthropology. The contributors share a fundamental methodological option for a critical-constructive dialogue with contemporary culture, science, and philosophy. Nevertheless, this commonality does not prevent this collection from integrating a wider range of approaches than is usually found in theological collections. This volume brings together experts in systematic theology and in theological ethics—two disciplines that often seem to think and write in parallel academic universes. Authors come from different American (including black and Latino) and European (including French and German) theological contexts. Moreover, the interdisciplinary insights on which the different contributors draw stem from both the natural sciences (neuroscience, evolutionary biology, ethology, etc.) and the humanities (cultural studies, philosophy, hermeneutics). This does not mean that we can pretend to cover all the important perspectives in one book, but it does indicate the kind of multidisciplinary cooperation that should be provoked by the complexity of the questions at stake.

Each of the essays explores recent literature in theology and other disciplines in order to address a burning question in theological anthropology. To organize the various essays, we clustered them around three anthropological key terms: "nature," "self," and "relationality." Accordingly, the three parts of this book tackle, from a theological perspective, the challenges related to the classical natural-law tradition (Part I), the challenges to the modern conception of the subject (Part II), and the challenges to the postmodern awareness of diversity in a globalizing context (Part III).

In what follows, we briefly sketch the red thread that connects the different essays, bringing to the fore how the different parts present fundamental challenges to the theological heart of Christian anthropology (creation, sin and grace, and salvation).

In Part I, "Human Nature and Science," the authors consider the challenge that scientific developments pose for the classical understanding of the human being as the image of God. Further, they address the ethical implications of this challenge, in particular with respect to the concept of natural law. The evolutionary account of *Homo sapiens* as a descendant of earlier primate species raises questions about our status as beings created in imago Dei, the image of God. It seems to undermine not only any claim about the human being's unique position in relation to other species but also the idea of nature as a God-given teleological order that could serve as a normative standard for moral reflection. The foundational theory of theological ethics as it was developed by Thomas Aquinas presupposed that human creatures, as rational animals, could by their very nature know the natural law, which, as a participation in God's eternal law, grounded universally valid moral insights. Contemporary advocates of natural law still invoke it as the basis of human dignity and of crosscultural moral principles or even norms, hoping to counter moral relativism (particularly when it comes to sexual ethics and human rights). But does it still make sense to appeal to human nature in ethical reflection? And if so, what does contemporary science tell us about an adequate understanding of this nature? To what extent can we still uphold notions such as the universality of morality or the distinctiveness of the human being among the animals?

In Chapter 1, "Theological Anthropology, Science, and Human Flourishing," theological ethicist Stephen J. Pope investigates the possibility of retaining a core affirmation communicated in the old language of imago Dei and natural law—namely, the notion of a universal morality—while giving full credit to evolutionary theory's insights into humanity. After introducing Thomas's traditional interpretation and current Church teachings on evolution, Pope compares recent publications by two prominent moral theologians. Lisa S. Cahill, offering an account of the relationship between imago Dei and natural law, arrives at an inclusive, universal ethic that promotes an equal right to access the conditions necessary for human flourishing, while Jack Mahoney associates the concept of imago Dei with our capacity for altruism, which could be traced back to evolution theory itself. Pope shows how the authors connect an evolutionary perspective on human nature with a reinterpretation of theological anthropology—two distinct approaches to evolutionary theism. With this chapter, Pope lays the groundwork for the rest of this first part, questioning the notion of imago Dei as well as the roots of our human morality.

While Pope focuses on the question of how the natural sciences may alter our notion of human nature, systematic theologian Henri-Jérôme Gagey in "The Concept of Natural Law in the Postmodern Context" situates the issue in a broader cultural setting. The postmodern awareness of cultural plurality and the radical historicity of our moral values render any appeal to nature suspicious. Gagey takes "In Search of a Universal Ethic: A New Look at the Natural Law" (2009), a document of the International Theological Commission, as his starting point for examining to what extent to which, and the conditions under which, this concept can prove relevant in the postmodern context. In the 2009 document this advisory panel to the Vatican distances itself from the "modern rationalist approach" and its essentialist belief in human nature as immutable and ahistorical. It does not, however, go far enough. Gagey formulates a twofold challenge: the move away from a physicalist conception of natural law as identical with biological laws on the one hand calls for more explicit attention for the essentially social and historical character of human nature and, on the other hand, demands an approach which presents natural law thinking less as a scientific enterprise than as an initiation into wisdom. Natural law is a paradoxical concept, he concludes: it is in the first place a theological notion intended to express a fundamental anthropological conviction, and yet its aim is to function as a properly philosophical concept, directed to promote a reasonable ethical debate between different spiritual and religious traditions.

While Gagey voices a hermeneutical concern to safeguard the difference between theology/philosophy and the natural sciences, theological ethicist Johan De Tavernier by contrast seeks to cross these boundaries in his "Personalism and the Natural Roots of Morality." Personalist anthropology emerged as the attempt to overcome a putative physicalism in the natural-law tradition. It asserts that the human being is not reducible to nature but rather a person with spiritual and moral values. De Tavernier suggests that personalism itself tends toward a certain dualism between body and mind, nature and spirit—think, for instance, of its one-sided emphasis on culture over nature. Evolutionary biology challenges this view. In *The Descent of Man*, Charles Darwin already focused on the evolutionary roots of human beings and their morality, claiming that the distinction between human and animal behavior is, in some cases, not so different. For example, animals have a capacity for sympathy, empathy, and group loyalty, to name just a few of their characteristically "human" traits. Morality does not start in culture; its roots are in dispositions that are programmed into our nature by evolution. As a result, good and evil are no longer exclusive theological and philosophical themes and could not be presented as the fruit of socialization (nurture) alone. De Tavernier proposes a renewed integration of natural scientific insights into the personalist tradition, an integration that parallels what Stephen Pope does for the natural-law tradition.

The contribution of systematic theologian (and biologist) Celia Deane-Drummond, "In God's Image and Likeness: From Reason to Revelation in Humans and Other Animals," further elaborates on the issue of whether the human person can claim a unique status in creation. Against a recent theological approach that, by a process of extension, includes other creatures in the honor of bearing the divine image, Deane-Drummond defends the idea of retaining the distinctiveness of human beings in a nuanced way. From Thomas she borrows his interpretation of the terms "image" and "likeness": He used the language of divine "likeness" to describe other animals, thereby expressing a sense of shared creaturely being; with the term "image," Thomas referred to the distinctive character of human beings. Deane-Drummond adopts this distinction but, informed by recent ethological studies on animals, bases the image dimension not on the capacity for freedom that Thomas focused on but rather on the religious capacity. Moreover, she interprets this distinctiveness in terms of the performative, as presenting the particular task of humanity to recognize its divine vocation to serve God and to exist in respectful communion with other beings. Rather than argue that animals display the divine image, the author suggests that the close relationship between humans and other animals clarifies the distinctive features of what it means to be human. If human beings consider every species to have its own telos, they can better understand how to relate to other creatures and how to respect their particular human charism for the living community of both humans and other creatures.

Recent and often polemical debates on faith and science must not blind us to the fact that theological anthropology—a discipline that has developed primarily over the course of the past century—has been centered less on the classical concept of "human nature" than on the modern notion of the "human subject." In recent decades, however, this modern view of the self, defined as an autonomous center of consciousness and agency, has increasingly come under attack. In the second part of this collection, "Christ and the Disputed Self," three systematic theologians explore how we can find alternative visions to what Charles Taylor has called the "buffered self." Each of the three essays enters into dialogue with insights from other disciplines (neuroscience, cultural studies, and postmodern French philosophy) to formulate a diagnosis of the crisis of the modern human subject and to propose alternative theories that might offer a way out of the impasse in which the contemporary world finds itself. They all seek a more comprehensive view, oriented toward overcoming dualist accounts: How can we integrate self and world / other persons, mind and body, freedom and determinism? The three approaches converge remarkably in the retrieval of Christology for an adequate understanding of what it means to be human. All of the three authors explicitly state that renewal in theological anthropology is not a theoretical exercise in Christian doctrine but has ethical implications: It reframes the practical question of what it means to act in Christ.

In his chapter, "Neuroscience, Self, and Jesus Christ," Oliver Davies offers, first, a schematic overview of three major historical periods, with a view to illustrating how developments in science and technology influenced the development of the rationality of theology. For theological anthropology and Christology, a highly significant shift is located in the understanding of the relationships between mind and body and between self and world. More specifically, Davies focuses on the elements of the human (ethical/Christian) act, in dialogue with recent neuroscientific insights into how our cognition of other persons works. Cognition of the other—and the eventual act that is chosen in this encounter—is a matter of thoroughly embodied processes. Davies in his rich, multilayered analysis offers a new understanding of the human self as much more complex, interdependent, and vulnerable than modern philosophy and theology were able to acknowledge. At first glance, this may seem to weaken human freedom, once so strongly secured in the modern subject; however, Davies sees in this renewed, scientifically informed anthropology an opportunity to retrieve natural law (an embodied form of universality), the imago Dei, and the transforming power of Christ and the Spirit at work in Church and society.

In "Incarnation in the Age of the Buffered, Commodified Self," Anthony J. Godzieba, too, proposes a retrieval of personhood but reflects on it in light of cultural developments in which the human person is considered fragmented, secularized, and fully immersed in consumer culture. We have noted Charles Taylor's "buffered self," formed by a modern "social imaginary" to disavow transcendence. Godzieba introduces the claim of American cultural critic Chris Hedges that we not only are living our lives as consumers but find our lives measured over against a commodified celebrity culture that denigrates ordinary life and narrates "authenticity" in terms of material consumption and success. Viewed from a contemporary perspective, Christian theological anthropology has been at times insightful and at times clumsy in dealing with secularization. However, it has largely ignored the capitalist formatting of contemporary experience. Outside theology, the dominant narrative of "person" has changed to the degree that Christian notions of grace and salvation have become literally unthinkable. Theological anthropology must tackle these philosophical, social, and cultural presuppositions directly if it is to speak with any sort of productive force in the twenty-first century. Godzieba argues that Catholicism's incarnational and sacramental imagination, with its emphasis on embodiment and particularity, can be a resource for crafting an anthropology that resists the reductionism of the mainstream narrative and makes grace thinkable again.

In "The Gifted Self: The Challenges of French Thought," Robyn Horner makes explicit the fundamental philosophical question at stake in this second part of the book. Given the diagnosis that the theological anthropology of *Gaudium et Spes* is intrinsically modern in approach, she investigates the fate of the modern subject in the wake of poststructuralist critiques such as that of Jacques Derrida. According to Derrida, our relation to the world and to each other is not based in a subject identical to itself; rather, the subject is characterized by "différance," splitting forever "the self from itself." Horner then asks whether a (post-)phenomenological anthropology such as that of Jean-Luc Marion might be helpful in renewing theological anthropology. Marion's work allows us to think the lost or dissipated self by means of the logic of the gift. Unable ever to be present to itself, the subject can be defined only as radical openness to the givenness of the world and of phenomena in general. In that very openness, Marion argues, the subject appears as radically given to itself, a givenness it realizes only in its responding to, and thus being given to, others. This new, christologically grounded approach to the subject and its relation to the world enables a new theological definition of the human being as given and created by God.

All three authors in the second part of this book agree that a major step beyond the modern subject in anthropology is the growing awareness of the constitutive role of embodied relationality for the human self, which as such cannot be reduced to individual self-consciousness. In the book's third part, "Relating in a Fallen World," three authors explore how the focus on relations among human beings in the world raises further questions: What world are we talking about, and which others? To whom do we feel related, and in what way? At stake is the tension between the theological retrieval of the imago Dei as the image of a triune, relational God and the harsh reality of power, exclusion, and violence. Written from the perspectives of traditionally marginalized groups, the essays sharpen our insight into the often implicit limitations of mainstream theological anthropology. Has the discourse on "human nature" not in fact promoted a particular culturally conditioned view of humanity? Similarly, is the "modern subject" not mirroring the illusion of Western men that they are self-contained autonomous individuals?

In her chapter, "Difference, Body, and Race," Latina theologian Michelle A. Gonzalez points out that a merely Western theological anthropology will not suffice in a world that is multicultural and globalized. There are various anthropolog*ies*, as each generation of Christians reinterprets the meaning of our humanity in the sociocultural, historical, and political context of the day. Non-Western, contextualized anthropologies, rooted in the insights of liberation and constructive theology, bring to the fore the traditionally marginalized concepts of difference, body, and race. The idea of *mestizaje* within Latino/a theologies shows, for example, how hybridity is not merely typical for Latino/a culture but can be seen as a fundamental characteristic of human existence in general and of Christ as the full image of humanity in particular. Black theology highlights the problematic connection between the image of God and embodiment and thematizes how racism relates to the construction of what is and is not human. Theology must critically investigate how its constructions of humanity privilege certain traits of human existence over others, which hinders us in genuinely considering all human beings as created in the image of God.

In "Public Theology: A Feminist Anthropological View of Political Subjectivity and Praxis," Rosemary P. Carbine takes up the challenge of non-Western voices for theology's political relevance, more specifically for elaborating a constructive feminist public theology. She critically analyzes public theology's prevailing anthropology, which often aligns itself with Euro-American modernity's rationalist notion of humanity and its associated modes of political participation. This modern anthropology falsely naturalizes elite gendered, racial, nativist, and corporatist constructs of the human person. To offer a theo-political alternative view of public engagement and personhood, Carbine reconfigures public theology as the praxis of imagining, creating, and sustaining a community, and does so by revisiting Catholic social teaching on the Church's public role in an eschatological and anthropological light. Feminist, womanist, and *mujerista* theological anthropologies propose a relational notion of the person, which Carbine weaves with Catholic social teaching into a religio-political reconceptualization of the imago Dei, beckoning us to live our full humanity in an ever more just community. She argues that effective public theology should subsist in rhetorical, symbolical, and prophetic practices that perform this community-creating work. The concrete implications of Carbine's feminist public theology and theological anthropology are illustrated by examples of dominant and subaltern subjects involved in movements for social and economic justice as well as for the civil rights of immigrants.

Gonzalez and Carbine both consider the capacity to recognize difference and relationality to be the crucial criterion of an adequate theological anthropology. Theological ethicist Wilhelm Guggenberger reminds us in his chapter, "Desire, Mimetic Theory, and Original Sin," that relationality and culture are themselves highly ambiguous phenomena. Drawing on René Girard's attempt to reveal the transcultural foundation of human community and its inherent violence, Guggenberger develops a fundamental dramatic-theological interpretation of original sin and grace. If human beings are mimetic beings by nature, even neurologically hardwired to be so, our desires are formed in our imitation of models. The theological-anthropological question is about the kind of relations we want to foster and about how to break the cultural mechanism whereby rivalry, exclusion, and resentment rule. Our globalizing consumer culture is an important point of reference here. The understanding of original sin as the dynamism of negative mimesis requires a profound process of conversion. In this context, grace must be understood as the occurrence that makes an escape from the vicious cycle of violence possible, opening our desire of becoming receptive to, and of finding fulfillment in, a truly human community.

It may be clear that the present collection does not presume to give a definite answer to the initial question of what it means to be human. It does, however, explore some of the most important challenges faced by theological anthropology today in depth and with a view toward formulating some key theological questions; we have only begun to grasp glimpses of a possible response—glimpses that we hope will invite further reflection and enliven the discussion. In this spirit David G. Kirchhoffer presents some concluding remarks in "Turtles All the Way Down? Pressing Questions for Theological Anthropology in the Twenty-First Century." His point of departure is the insight that human beings are the world (rather than merely live in the world). Relationality thus being the key-word for an up-to-date theological anthropology, Kirchhoffer discusses the main challenges that such an anthropology faces: first, anthropocentrism (as challenged by the ecological crises, the debate on who counts as a person, and technology); second, historicity (as introduced by social-constructivism and as taken more seriously in the Christian tradition in recent decades); third, vulnerability (as a morally neutral consequence of our interdependency); and, finally, language (as a means to engage with diverse discourses ranging from art through to philosophy, business, and cognitive neuropsychology). More than claiming to know the solutions for these different challenges, Kirchhoffer rather encourages theologians to further reflect on them and the way they are discussed in theological and other discourses with a necessary (self-)critical epistemological suspicion. For only in this way will we arrive at a relevant theological discourse on what human beings are, and be a legitimate dialogue partner for other discourses.

PART I

Human Nature and Science

CHAPTER I

Theological Anthropology, Science, and Human Flourishing

Stephen J. Pope

There is no doubt that the human race, *Homo sapiens*, evolved from predecessor hominids around 200,000 to 150,000 years ago. We constitute one class among the great apes and have more genetic similarity to chimpanzees than chimpanzees have with orangutans. We are intelligent, group-living animals. Like other primates, we have a sense of fairness, tend to prefer our own offspring and members of our own groups to outsiders, and generally pursue a policy of punishing cheats and cooperating with those who are trustworthy.

What does an evolutionary view of humanity imply for theology? If we were not created on the "sixth day," does that also mean that we can no longer be considered, as Genesis proclaims, created in the "image and likeness of God" (1:26)? Does an evolutionary view of human origins also suggest that God is not the author of the moral law? What does an honest recognition of the evolutionary roots of morality imply about the long-established Christian claim that God teaches in two "books"—the divine law revealed in scripture and the natural law discovered by reason? What, in short, is the status of the central Christian affirmation that humans are created in the "image of God?" Can we retain an account of the natural moral law while taking seriously that our species is the product of a long process of biological evolution?

This chapter will argue that an account of biological evolution provides a framework within which to think about the meaning of both the imago Dei and natural law. First, it traces the traditional interpretation of these themes in the writings of Thomas Aquinas and briefly summarizes current Church teachings on evolution, imago Dei, and natural law. Then it focuses on the recent theological treatments of imago Dei and natural law in the writings of two prominent contemporary moral theologians, Jack Mahoney and Lisa Sowle Cahill. We argue that reflection on the imago Dei and the natural law would do well to incorporate evolutionary theory. Doing so enables us to develop a viable alternative to two unacceptable extremes: a traditionalist dualism that simply ignores contemporary evolutionary anthropology and piously affirms the truth of the imago Dei and the natural law, and a reductionistic naturalism that takes science seriously but dismisses the imago Dei and natural law as anachronistic holdovers from a prescientific age that can no longer command our respect. Our distinctively human capacities have grown through the evolutionary process in a way that both continues to bear its imprint and that allows us to transcend it in acts of responsible love.

Thomas Aquinas on the Imago Dei and Natural Law

The Christian concept of natural law, notably as developed by Thomas Aquinas, was based on the conviction that the Creator purposefully designed the entire created order with a vast array of particular species whose essences are unchanging. All creatures are created in the "likeness" of God in that they manifest, in remote and analogical ways, something of God's existence, or life, or intelligence, yet human beings alone are said to be created in God's image because we are created with the capacity for the "spiritual operations" of knowing and willing. Nonhuman animals are thus "traces" or "vestiges" of God, but we are the "image" of God. Thomas interpreted the biblical description of our creation in the "image and likeness of God" (Gen. 1:26) as pointing to our rational capacities. Our rational capacities enable us to take responsibility for ourselves and other creatures. It enables us to be both "masters of our own acts" and to exercise "dominion" over other creatures (Gen. 1:26; also Gen. 5:1 and 9:6).[1]

Thomas held that the mind of the Creator governs all of the creation through the eternal law. All creatures are governed by the God-given order of nature, which proceeds through all creatures behaving according to the internal dynamics of their own natures. God acts as primary cause in and through creatures acting on one another as secondary causes. The human person has a special dignity because he or she has a rational soul. According to Thomas, the soul is the "subsistent form" of the human body. As the form of the body, it exists both to animate the body and to order the body and all of its parts in the relation to one another. As "subsistent," the soul can exist independently of the body after death in a separated state prior to the resurrection of the body. The spiritual character of intellectual and volitional acts indicates that the soul is not dependent on the body for its acts. Acts of understanding and willing, that is, are not the activities of any bodily organ, including the brain or the central nervous system. Thomas is not, however, advocating dualism, because he did not understand the soul to be a substance in itself. He regarded the human person as the substance, and the human soul as its subsistent formal principle.

Human beings are unique because we alone are held to the natural law, which Thomas defines as the *rational creature's* "participation" in the eternal law.[2] Other animals are intelligent, but we alone are rational, capable of deliberation, planning, and offering logical arguments for our judgments. Natural law constitutes the framework of ethical norms to which the virtuous person conforms and by which he or she attains some degree of flourishing in this life. As rational creatures we are obligated to conform to the divinely created "order of nature."[3] The precepts of the second table of the Decalogue offer a formulation of the basic norms governing the goods of life, sex, marriage and family, property, and speech. These norms are revealed in divine law for the sake of clarity, Thomas thought, but their importance is evident to any rational person who reflects on the most basic normative requirements of any relatively well-ordered community. The natural law is a way of talking about what counts as appropriate conduct for "rational animals." "Reasonable" in this context refers not to instrumental rationality, the most efficient way to get what one happens to want, but rather to the intelligent pursuit of the human good—i.e., the best way to get what one ought to want given our rational nature.

Thomas's account of both the imago Dei and natural law were obviously rooted in a view of human nature that was formed by biblical, Aristotelian, patristic, and other ancient sources. It assumed a hierarchically structured cosmos with human beings located in a "middle position" between purely spiritual and rational creatures, angels, and purely material and irrational creatures, plants and animals. In this teleological scheme, the lower always exists for the sake of the higher. Plants exist for the sake of animals, and irrational animals were thought to exist the sake of rational animals.

Thomas had no reason to doubt that there was a real Adam and a real Eve who were created by God and placed in paradise to dwell in harmony with God and one another, or that they then sinfully and irrationally disobeyed God, were cast out of the garden, and left the rest of us with the legacy of original sin and concupiscence. This view was consistently maintained by modern Catholicism, with few individual exceptions, up through and beyond the age of Darwin.

Darwinism, Evolution, and the Magisterium

The Darwinian account of *Homo sapiens* as descended from previous primate species raises a host of profound questions for this classic Catholic anthropology. An overwhelmingly strong convergence of evidence from a variety of disciplines uncovered that the earth is much older than the biblical chronology allows. It issued a frontal attack on the Thomistic view of nature as designed by God and populated by unchanging species functioning within a fixed and permanent "order" of nature. It provided an unassailable body of evidence showing that instead of created in a paradise we evolved out of predecessor hominids.

This paradigm shift raises major questions about human dignity. The vision of human beings as descended from predecessor species (but not monkeys) challenged the widespread Christian anthropocentric assumption that we are the primary purpose for the existence of all other animals. Awareness of our continuity with other species called into question the assumption that the world is divided neatly into rational and irrational creatures. Scientific research shows that we are not as rational as once assumed, and that animals are more intelligent than we used to think. Evolutionists regard the differences between species as more a matter of degree than of kind. Rather than created in the image of God, we seem to be just another species of primate (albeit one with special cognitive abilities). As Stephen Jay Gould put it, we are a "tiny twig on an improbable branch of a contingent limb on a fortunate tree."[4]

This view of nature as a scene of constant struggle that is "red in tooth and claw" also called into doubt the assumption that we ought to "conform to" the natural order of nature. In the first place, nature is not so orderly. In the second, only the social Darwinians advise us to conform to it. If anything, ethics struggles against nature. Evolutionary thinking, then, would seem to have left both the imago Dei and the natural law in tatters.

The Catholic Church has had a complex and ambivalent relation to evolutionary theory.[5] In the first half of the twentieth century, the evolutionary explorations of Jesuit paleontologist Teilhard de Chardin were greeted with enthusiasm in some quarters but hostility in others. His works were censored by his Jesuit superiors and banned by the Holy Office. He was required to leave his teaching post and to sign a statement renouncing any suggestion that he rejected the doctrine of original sin.

Pope Pius XII's encyclical *Humani Generis* (1950) offered tentative recognition of the value of evolutionary theorizing. The pope taught that the hypothesis of the evolution of the human body could be entertained by Catholics as long as they acknowledged that, even if the body is understood as emerging from "pre-existent matter," the soul of each person is specially created and "infused" into matter directly by God.[6] The encyclical also insisted that a legitimate interpretation of evolution could not deny the doctrine of "monogenism," the belief that all human beings originated from a single primal couple. Pius assumed that monogenism is entailed in the doctrine of original sin: Universal redemption in Christ (Rom. 5:12–21; 1 Cor. 15:20–23) presumes a prior universal fall in Adam (Gen. 3). Recent authoritative treatments of evolution continue to hold the natural unity of the human race (perhaps in a way that is consistent with a single common ancestor) but have quietly stopped referring to monogenism.[7]

Pope John Paul II's treatment of evolution was shaped in part by his desire to avoid repetition of the Galileo fiasco and the Church's condemnation of Copernicanism. He went further than Pius XII in conceding that evolution is "more than a hypothesis," but he too felt it absolutely necessary to invoke the special divine creation of each soul to provide ontological support for human dignity.[8] One might wonder why the pope did not think that God could have worked equally well to give divine support to human dignity through secondary causality rather than by means of special divine intervention. In Thomas's understanding of causality, after all, God is the primary cause of everything that exists and works through particular secondary causes. God's love creates and gives value to everything that exists, including the human person and his or her dignity. In any case, the pope insisted that human dignity rests on God's having specially created each soul and inserted it into the human body at some point very early in the embryological process.

John Paul II made an important distinction between scientific findings about evolution (what some people call "facts"), scientific theories about evolution (including either weakly, moderately, or strongly supported hypotheses), and philosophical and theological speculation based on either of these other aspects of evolutionary thinking. The pope made a distinction between the indisputable fact that we have evolved and ontological naturalism, which argues that anyone who accepts the fact of evolution cannot also continue to believe in God.

Another key issue concerns the relation between mind and brain. The pope maintains that the naturalist claim that mind emerges from matter without divine influence contains three interrelated mistakes: It confuses a philosophical speculation with an empirically verifiable scientific claim; it fails to support the dignity of the person; and it contradicts the theological claim that we are made in God's image. He insists that we not confuse the different kinds of epistemological claims that come, respectively, from science, philosophy, and theology. Yet it is hard to see why, in itself, the simple claim that mind emerges from matter contradicts the affirmation that we are made in God's image or have a special dignity. After all, the second creation story depicts God as a potter who forms us out of the clay of the earth. It is not the material "out of which" we have come that establishes our dignity but rather the distinctive intellectual, moral, and religious abilities that it produces in us. It is not how we begin that is decisive but where we can end up. It is thus not the material of the brain that has dignity but the human mental and affective capacities that the brain makes possible. The soul is the form of the body, and the mind's activity is what the form does. The pope is best interpreted here as warning us about the dangerous consequences that come from wrongly construing the emergence of mind from matter. Instead of evolutionary theory reducing the mind to matter, Christian theology sees an ascending movement from matter to mind.

The imprint of John Paul II's teaching is also registered in the *Catechism of the Catholic Church*. It explains that "Scripture presents the work of the Creator symbolically as a succession of six days of divine 'work,' concluded by the 'rest' of the seventh day,[9] but 'nothing exists that does not owe its existence to God the Creator.' The world began when God's word drew it out of nothingness; all existent beings, all of nature, and all human history is rooted in this primordial event, the very genesis by which the world was constituted and time begun."[10] Yet for some reason it treats Adam and Eve as historical figures whose sin in paradise constituted the "fall" of the entire human race.[11] While the account of the fall in Genesis 3 uses figurative language, the *Catechism* concedes, it "affirms a primeval event, a deed that took place at the beginning of the history of man. Revelation gives us the certainty of faith that the whole of human history is marked by the original fault freely committed by our first parents."[12]

The *Catechism* continues to invoke both the imago Dei and the natural law as if evolution makes no difference to how we interpret them. Critics might read this as incoherent eclecticism, but proponents might distinguish the job of the magisterium, to teach what is true, from the task of theologians—to provide, as best they can, the reasons why what is taught is in fact the case. The difficulty faced by theology, however, is considerable: how to reinterpret the imago Dei in a way that makes sense in light of an evolutionary view of human origins, and how to make sense of natural law in a contemporary context that thinks of nature in a way that is radically at odds with old Aristotelian-Thomistic conception. The *Catechism* does not help matters when it repeats old formulas—e.g., defining natural law as right reason acting in conformity to nature.[13]

The imago Dei is the basis of the Catholic affirmation of inviolable human rights, including the rights to religious freedom, a just wage, and health care. It also grounds our responsibilities for one another and the world, including the duties of solidarity and stewardship. "All human beings, in as much as they are created in the image of God, have the dignity of a person."[14] As the *Compendium* puts it, "The right to the exercise of freedom belongs to everyone because it is inseparable from his or her dignity as a human person."[15]

The International Theological Commission in 2004 issued an important related document, *Communion and Stewardship: The Human Person as Created in the Image of God.* The document itself is not a product of the magisterium but was drafted to assist the work of the magisterium in the Congregation for the Doctrine of the Faith. The Commission worked on this topic from August 1999 to August 2004 under the supervision of Cardinal Joseph Ratzinger, the ex officio president of the commission.

Communion and Stewardship builds on the Catholic emphasis on the imago Dei as the basis of human dignity. It reaffirms the teaching of Pius XII and John Paul II: "The doctrine of the immediate or special creation of each human soul not only addresses the ontological discontinuity between matter and spirit, but also establishes the basis for a divine intimacy which embraces every single human person from the first moment of his or her existence."[16] It also recalls the teaching of *Gaudium et Spes:* The human person is "the only creature on earth that God willed for his own sake."[17]

Seeking to avoid ecologically irresponsible interpretations of this teaching, however, the document makes a deliberate effort to distance itself from distorted forms of anthropocentrism. It underscores the importance of the interdependence of living creatures and our organic connections to other living creatures, in a way that fosters greater ecological responsibility as well as a more relational conception of our humanity.[18] Stewardship requires that we act as responsible agents within the evolutionary process itself: "Under the guidance of divine providence and acknowledging the sacred character of visible creation, the human race reshapes the natural order, and becomes an agent in the evolution of the universe itself." Indeed, theologians have a special kind of stewardship: "In exercising their stewardship of knowledge, theologians have the responsibility to locate modern scientific understandings within a Christian vision of the created universe."[19]

Communion and Stewardship makes the interesting point that the imago Dei, understood as revealed fully in Christ, can be understood developmentally: The "link between Christology and anthropology . . . [reveals] a deeper understanding of the dynamic character of the *imago Dei*. Without denying the gift of man's original creation in the image of God, theologians want to acknowledge the truth that, in the light of human history and the evolution of human culture, the *imago Dei* can in a real sense be said to be still in the process of becoming."[20] *Communion and Stewardship* also links the imago Dei with natural law: "The theology of the *imago Dei* also links anthropology with moral theology by showing that, in his very being, man possesses a participation in the divine law. This natural law orients human persons to the pursuit of the good in their actions."[21] The International Theological Commission invokes natural law to validate deontological protections for human dignity against consequentialist moralities and to ground cross-cultural moral norms, particularly regarding reproductive ethics, sexual ethics, and human rights.[22]

We will now turn to two scholarly perspectives in theological ethics that address the same nexus of issues in different ways. The writings of John Mahoney and Lisa Sowle Cahill offer distinctive approaches to our thinking about the relevance of human evolution for our interpretation of the imago Dei and natural law.

Jack Mahoney: Imago Dei in an Evolutionary Context

Jack Mahoney, the well-known author of *The Making of Moral Theology: A Study of the Roman Catholic Tradition*,[23] has long sought to recover the significance of the affections, grace, Christ, and the Holy Spirit for moral theology in a tradition that he believes has been much too strongly focused on reason, sin, law, and institutional authority. Mahoney in his major work attempted to elaborate on *Gaudium et Spes*'s personalist retrieval of the imago Dei, in order to correct the uniformity, legalism, and physicalism of modern Catholic moral teachings. Natural law was at the core of the Church's outdated mindset. The council's appreciation for the Church's participation in the dynamic, evolutionary nature of history opened it up to be more creative and responsive to the "signs of the times." Instead of focusing narrowly on the features of special moral acts, Mahoney urges, a dynamic view of the cosmos encourages us both to attend to the totality of values that confront us in personal and social experience and to respond to them in mature, conscientious ways. Mahoney developed his concern for totality into an ethical cosmopolitanism. In his monograph *The Challenge of Human Rights* (2007) he argues that a strong ethic of human rights provides the best normative framework for supporting ethical cosmopolitanism and affirming the moral unity of the human race.[24]

The Making of Moral Theology laments the way in which the magisterium has failed to acknowledge either the religious and moral significance of human evolution or the need to adjust norms to "changing circumstances."[25] Mahoney accepts certain themes of the natural-law tradition—our social interconnectedness, the centrality of the common good, and the person as intelligent, free, and responsible. Yet he abandons natural-law language as hopelessly outmoded and substitutes an ethic of responsibility. Christian ethics seeks to act rightly within nature, he argues, but not to derive moral norms from it.

Mahoney in his new monograph *Christianity in Evolution: An Exploration* (2011) continues this line of thought by examining the broad doctrinal and moral implications of human evolution.[26] We are the product of evolution. We are created in the image of a God who is infinitely altruistic. How we interpret the meaning of what it means to be created in the image of God depends ultimately on who or what we think God is. Mahoney roots anthropology in Christology. Jesus Christ, the image of God (Col. 1:15; also John 1:18, 14:8–9; 2 Cor. 4:4; Heb. 1:3), is the incarnation of divine altruism, the eternal altruism of the triune God. Mahoney proposes a "theology of altruism which finds its origin in the initiative of God who is characterized as an interpersonal total love of mutual altruism within the persons of the Trinity."[27]

Evolutionary theory has dedicated a great deal of attention to the evolution of altruism. Mahoney adopts the language of "altruism" to speak about Christian ideals in a way that makes sense to those who embrace an evolutionary view of the world. The imago Dei suggests that we are best able to manifest who God is when we act altruistically toward one another. Mahoney interprets the imago Dei as revealed in our human capacity to imitate, if only in limited ways, the eternal altruism of the triune God. As created in the image of God, we flourish to the extent that we live altruistically: "For those who want to save their life will lose it, and those who lose their life for my sake will find it" (Matt. 16:25). Divine grace heals the divisions caused by egocentrism, fears, and insecurities.[28] Those seeking to live altruistically need support from friends and community. We need most of all the inspiration of the Holy Spirit and the Christian solidarity, mutual encouragement, and wisdom found in the Church. The Eucharist draws us into a way of life based not on propitiatory sacrifice but on loving self-offering for the sake of fellowship in the new covenant.[29]

Evolutionary thinking, Mahoney maintains, helps us better understand the full context of human life. Consider, for example, sexual behavior:

> We can conjecture that this began in our animal forebears as the instinctive drive to reproduction which became adapted in their case to the need to provide an extended caring environment for offspring which required considerable time to develop. With the progress to hominization, or to becoming fully human, this sustained mutual support of parents for each other, which initially helped them bring up their children together, came to be appreciated as human values in their own right, expanding beyond the physical process of reproduction and upbringing to become a medium of inter-personal communication and sharing within a wide variety of personal and social contexts. Human sexuality was no longer simply animal sexuality. It had evolved into human sexual companionship, which could contribute to the personal and social enhancement of the individual persons involved. Thus, with evolution, this relationship between fully fledged persons is now capable of being exercised in numerous ways in society. This occurs most evidently in still sharing the capacity for the loving reproduction and upbringing of children, but now it is also capable of finding expression in a range of personal and social contexts through other forms of relationship between the sexes which express and are influenced by their mutual interest and attraction.[30]

What help can be provided to moral theology by such an evolutionary context? Mahoney suggests that such a perspective can help us understand the struggle to "humanize" our sexual desires by channeling them into an interpersonal meaning, the context of companionship and human flourishing, and the recognition that sexual behavior and gender identity have both social contexts and social impact. Human sexuality calls forth capacities that transcend the drive for immediate gratification. These realities go beyond a narrow moralistic emphasis on act-governing norms and the virtues that guard conformity to them. It opens up the possibility that in some circumstances couples would use, and in fact be obliged to use, artificial birth control and that a same-sex couple would be morally obliged to pledge fidelity to one another. One does not need a moral theology informed by evolutionary biology to move in this direction, but the evolutionary biology provides a complexifying framework that makes such a move more plausible.

Evolutionary naturalists often argue that we have been programmed by natural selection to be self-seeking animals who cannot really engage in such a process of "humanization." In contrast, Mahoney argues, it is more accurate to describe us as intelligent social animals who have evolved to the point where we are capable of acting altruistically even when doing so runs against our "fitness interests." Culture can take us beyond where our "selfish genes" would want us to go; grace heals and directs the power of both nature and nurture to enable us to act altruistically.

This evolutionary vision of human existence, Mahoney believes, makes it impossible to continue to hold that we are literally "fallen" from an original state of harmony with God and one another. We must, he argues, jettison the Augustinian notion of "original sin" and its picture of humanity as riddled with concupiscence. Mahoney does not deny that we are prone to selfishness and live within a morally damaged world. But, he insists, we have to be intellectually forthright and admit that Genesis 3 is mythological and that death is not the result of a primordial fall but just a fact of life.

Mahoney is especially sensitive to the pastoral damage that has been wreacked by excessive preoccupation with sexual concupiscence. The legacy of Jansenism has not been entirely exhausted by Christian culture. Yet is seems possible to appreciate the created goodness of the human body and our sexual capacities and, indeed, all the created world while at the same time acknowledging of the depth of our disordered affectivity and our own responsibility for it. Indeed, a deeper understanding of the latter can underscore the former. As Karl Rahner pointed out, concupiscence is fundamentally a problem of the spirit and its malformed desires, not the body and its sensitive appetites.[31]

Lisa Sowle Cahill: Imago Dei and Natural Law

Theological ethicist Lisa Cahill is one of the foremost advocates of a revised approach to natural law. Cahill interprets the imago Dei as depicted in Genesis 1:26 as involving our capacity for relationship to God, our neighbors, and the rest of the created world.[32] "The aspect of humanity that constitutes the image is mutual and creative relationship, not intelligence, freedom, or a human soul. Humans, in the image of God, are fulfilled in relationship."[33] She recognizes that we have special cognitive abilities but focuses on how these augment our social capacities to enable us to develop relationships marked by genuine mutuality that respects both similarities and differences. As the image of God, we are called to form affective and social bonds with companions without eliminating their otherness.

Because every person is made equally in the image of God, she argues, all should have an equal right to access to conditions that promote human flourishing. This ethical perspective is "natural" because we share it as part of our common humanity, and it is "law" in that it generates, and needs to be supported by, moral obligations, virtues, and ideals. Particular communities interpret goods in historically specific ways, but, in some version or other, they refer to human goods that are appreciated by people in most cultures. Cahill is opposed to two extremes: In the public realm of moral discourse, she is reserved about the ethic of radical autonomy that attends only to the arbitrary choices of individuals, and in the ecclesial context, she criticizes authoritarian and deductive approaches to natural law that try to dictate right and wrong from abstract perspectives that are unaware of their own ideological biases.

Moral knowledge of the natural law comes from concretely grasping the human good sought by people in particular contexts. Cahill's "inductive" approach to natural law engages in consensus-building conversation on three levels of human nature: species-typical characteristics (particularly embodied capacities for knowing and loving self, others, and community), basic human goods, and fundamental equality. Experience shows us that we all share an inclination to survive and flourish, to reproduce and sustain families, and to live in society and to revere what is sacred. All societies recognize the harmful nature of unjust behavior such as murder, adultery, theft, and lying—these too are "natural" under some circumstances, but not in a normative sense. The process of identifying the human good in concrete situations takes place properly only when all relevant parties exercise mutual respect based on a shared recognition of each party's equal right to be engaged in the conversation.

Equal dignity generates an inclusive ethic focused on empowerment and moral agency. Cahill advocates a universal ethic that recognizes that every person ought to have minimally equal access to the essentials of a good life. She insists that we widen the lens of our moral perspective in a way that gives proper attention to the common good, distributive justice, and the preferential option for the poor. She praises international human-rights discourse for promoting degrees of cross-cultural moral agreement on the basic human needs that must be met if people are to live good lives.

This desire for agreement on the pursuit of human goods opposes both religious sectarians and secular liberal skeptics.

What is the significance of evolution in this theological ethic? Cahill does not give the kind of theological centrality to the evolutionary framework that we find in Mahoney, but she does take it seriously. She agrees with Mahoney that the doctrine of original sin can be interpreted in unhelpful ways. She also recognizes the mythological nature (not her language) of Genesis 3, which she understands to provide an account not of the *origin* of evil but rather of the *dynamic tendency* of evil to take on a life of its own and, once it gains a foothold, even to become unavoidable.

Cahill speaks of the power of sin in a way that Mahoney could accept: "The inevitability of sin is not due to a blot on the soul, a defect inherited through sexual reproduction, or a twist in the wills of individual agents." Human evolution has set conditions that make the sinful distortion of relationships not only possible but inevitable: "the evolved and 'natural' instinct of every living thing (and group) to preserve itself and its advantages, an instinct that is not morally wrong in itself; the social and practical ways in which identity and selfhood necessarily are constituted; the gradual development of moral awareness in all persons; and the de facto pervasiveness of biased social behavior."[34]

These factors all operate because of our evolutionary past, and not because at some moment Adam and Eve made a fateful decision to commit a sin that instantly warped human nature. The myth of Adam and Eve is especially valuable because it symbolizes our solidarity in sin. Chapter 3 of Genesis depicts sin as a willful betrayal of right relationships. The first woman abandons her "vocation to image God's rule" in alliance with her partner. Her turning away from God degrades her thought process: "The crux of the woman's sin is forgetting her own dignity within creation."[35] Rather than an event that happened at a certain moment in the distant past, this sinful process happens in every life: "We develop moral consciousness already within social relations that are dangerous if not already damaging. We understand what is 'good and evil' within contexts that potentially distort our evaluation of goods and of how prioritization of good for ourselves affects others with whom we are in relationship (personally or through social structures)."[36] This sets the context for Cahill's account of how moral evil becomes embedded in social structures.

Cahill reads Genesis 3 as symbolizing a "fall" of the first couple out of their proper relationship to God, one another, and the world of other living creatures. Systems of social domination are the "deplorable result of human betrayal of God's image."[37] Biblical stories of redemption beginning with Abraham and Sarah show the kind of trust necessary to restore proper relationships with God and one another in covenantal love. Jesus shows what it means to create relationships in a way that reflects our "new creation in God's image (Col. 3:10)."[38] Jesus came to teach and to empower us to "live in God's image and under God's rule. . . . In God's image and God's kingdom, the one-flesh partnership of all humans is on the way to renewal."[39] This renewal effectively transforms corporate as well as personal lives.

Cahill's theological anthropology receives some confirmation in evolutionary theory's focus on contingency, diversity, and sociality. Evolutionary accounts of the origin of species underscore that pain and suffering are built into the very structure of nature. Indeed, as she points out, "speaking in purely factual terms, there is a 'natural' human disposition to evil as well as to good."[40] The human sciences, including sociobiology and evolutionary psychology, "help shed explanatory light on the dismal reality of evil as a fact of human life" and underscore our awareness of the "great and complex variety of [human] traits." Many of these traits evolved because they initially promoted survival and reproduction, but then can be redirected to other ends. This view of nature generates realism about the conflict and finitude that characterizes nature generally.

Any plausible account of natural-law ethics takes into account the negative aspects of our evolved human nature—e.g., toward out-group prejudice, exploitation of the weak, etc. We have evolved capacities for dominance, aggression, and violence that must be curbed for the sake of social order. Our evolutionary heritage has also bequeathed us with pro-social capacities for cooperation, reciprocity, affiliation, attachment, empathy, and reconciliation. Natural law in Cahill's perspective does not "conform" to nature, or strive to restore a "lost" integrity, but tries to encourage and develop some of these tendencies while discouraging others. "The central moral challenge posed by the reality of evil is to extend human beings' naturally self-serving emotions and preferences to non-kin, non-members, 'strangers, and even enemies,' and even when it does not serve their immediate success strategy or that of their group."[41] Like Mahoney, Cahill maintains that this kind of extended altruism is promoted in Christian narratives, practices, and symbols, including the universal claim "All are made in the image of God."[42] Those who are seeking to live out this truth cannot do so alone: We "must build reconciling communities that make the plight of the poor a special priority."[43]

Evolutionary consciousness accents our temporality and consequently also our finitude, vulnerability, and weakness. As Cahill explains, "Even in speaking about redemption it is important to recognize that we are placed in a world that is contingent and finite. Conflict in and through the body, in respect of bodily needs, vulnerabilities, and capacities is not only a part of the historical record but inevitable, since our space, resources, and capacity for relationship are abundant but not endless."[44] Cahill deliberately wants to avoid committing the "naturalistic fallacy," improperly inferring moral values from a purely descriptive account of a state of affairs. She clearly differentiates what is simply found in human nature from what we determine to be its morally desirable features.

Conservative critics might charge that what is "right" does not depend on moral consensus and that inferences can at best generate rules of thumb rather than exceptionless moral norms. Cahill does believe that inductive natural law can generate some moral absolutes (e.g., against torture and rape), but she also recognizes that, "to the extent that real social circumstances can present agents with no good solutions to dilemmas, 'objective' morality can require decisions that are far from ideal."[45] She is inclined to sharpen Thomas's well-known (but not always observed) distinction between the universality of the first precepts of the natural law and the variability that marks their secondary specification.[46] The virtue of prudence helps us to determine the relevance of this general knowledge of goods and harms in particular historical contexts.

The imago Dei in this perspective provides theological backing for human dignity, but those who do not accept biblical premises can recognize the value of human dignity on other grounds. Human dignity lies at the core of natural law. The Church's patriarchy and sexism obscures its own affirmation that all human beings are created in the imago Dei. Against communitarian skeptics, she maintains that the language of human dignity can appeal to the deep human aspirations of non-Christians as well as Christians. Human flourishing can be found only to the extent that our evolved social, affective, and cognitive capacities are trained in ways that accord with our intrinsic dignity. Grace invites us to participate in a dynamic process that restores our humanity and allows us more adequately to reflect the image of God as intelligent, social beings living under evolutionary constraints.

Assessment: Evolution, the Imago Dei, and Natural Law

The positions we have just examined provide a selective but important sample of current thinking about the significance of evolution for theological ethics. The magisterium and its theological advisors tend to use old language without attempting to constructively engage evolutionary thinkers. The magisterium provides doctrinal criteria for distinguishing legitimate from illegitimate speculation about the philosophical and theological implications of evolution. Statements by John Paul II and Benedict XVI assume that there can be no real conflict between the fact of human evolution, properly interpreted, and Catholic teachings about either the imago Dei or the natural law.

Mahoney begins *Christianity in Evolution* with a critique of the literalist picture of creation envisioned in popular piety and perpetuated by some documents of the magisterium. He then moves to theological revision. He is convinced that scientific knowledge of evolution requires Christians to drop the doctrine of original sin and stop viewing the death of Jesus as an atoning sacrifice. Prior to his appropriation of biological evolution, Mahoney argued on pastoral and moral grounds that natural-law doctrine is anachronistic and ought to be abandoned. He would like to replace a deontological, rule-focused ethics of natural law with an ethics focused on conscience, responsibility, and virtue, especially love or altruism. His recent assimilation of evolutionary perspectives confirms his earlier rejection of natural law.

Cahill takes evolution seriously but regards it as one source of information for the hermeneutical process of creatively interpreting scripture and tradition, not as the basis for a wholesale rethinking of fundamental Christian beliefs. She agrees with Mahoney that the doctrine of original sin is, in various ways, problematic. He finds it problematic for two reasons: It is based on what we now know to be a grossly inaccurate account of our origins, and it leads to a false and morally pernicious view of Jesus' death as the only way to appease an angry God. Cahill sees the danger of imbalanced readings of the doctrine of original sin and one-sided views of sacrificial atonement, but her corrective strategy seeks to expand and complexify the interpretive lens through which she reads these doctrines rather than jettison them altogether.

The same difference shows up in each author's respective treatment of the natural law. Mahoney finds natural law unsustainable in an evolutionary worldview that no longer recognizes fixed essences, a morally structured natural order, human acts defined by formal and final causes, and a historic "fall" that has rendered us morally deformed. Mahoney rejects natural law for pastoral as well as theoretical reasons, and puts in its place a theological ethics centered on responsible altruism. Cahill concurs with his objections to natural-law ethics as it is presently formulated by the magisterium, but she is committed to rehabilitating rather than rejecting the basic concept. She wants to retain the appeal of the natural-law tradition to human experience, practical reason, and concrete human goods, including basic bodily and social goods.

It is hard to know whether Cahill and Mahoney are actually disagreeing, or just talking past one another, or ultimately concur on the relevance of scientific knowledge of nature for Christian ethics. Their differences in method do not lead to significant differences in moral substance: They clearly agree more than they disagree about the meaning of the imago Dei and the overall message of Christian morality.

One point of comparison concerns the actual meaning of the phrase "natural law." Consider a typical neoscholastic account of the natural law, found in the 1917 edition of the *Catholic Encyclopedia*: "Those actions which conform with [nature's] tendencies, lead to our destined end, and are thereby constituted right and morally good; those at variance with our nature are wrong and immoral," and "actions are wrong if, though subserving the satisfaction of some particular need or tendency, they are at the same time incompatible with that rational harmonious subordination of the lower to the higher which reason should maintain among our conflicting tendencies and desires."[47] Neither Mahoney nor Cahill are willing to accept a version of natural law that requires conformity to the natural order. Neither analyzes the morality of specific acts in terms of their inner teleology or final causality or employ a faculty psychology that subordinates the senses and passions to the will and the will to the intellect.[48] In contrast to the static view of nature assumed by neoscholastics, Cahill describes nature as both developmental and always embedded within particular cultural contexts: We "pursue goods that are specified in different ways at different times. That may be more or less completely realized, and that will vary at the level of particular instantiations."[49]

Pope John Paul II tried to offer a more updated, personalist version of natural law in *Veritatis Splendor*.[50] Yet he insisted that "the morality of the human act depends primarily and fundamentally on the 'object' rationally chosen by the deliberate will."[51] Some objects of acts are, by their very nature, "'incapable of being ordered' to God, because they radically contradict the good of the person made in his image."[52] The natural law prohibits intrinsically evil acts because their objects always, by their very nature, violate the moral order and attack human dignity. This position generates strong deontological absolutes—e.g., that each and every sexual act in which artificial contraception is used is a violation of the natural law and an attack on human dignity.

Obviously neither Mahoney nor Cahill concurs with this ethic. They suggest, on the contrary, that whether concrete behavior promotes or contradicts "the good of the person made in [God's] image" depends on its specific agent and circumstances. Mahoney repudiates, while Cahill revises, the language of natural law, but it is not clear that their methodological differences lead to alternative norms, virtues, or approaches to concrete moral decisions. They both interpret the imago Dei primarily in terms of our capacity for altruistic service and mutuality. They differ over both the value of using the symbolism of "fall" and "original sin" to describe the place of evil in human life and the usefulness of employing the language of "atonement" to describe how God works in and through Jesus' death and resurrection to bring about the redemption and reconciliation of all things in Christ. But they share a conviction that our growing knowledge of our evolutionary origins and biological constitution provides important insights about the human condition that makes us individually and collectively prone to sin and in need of transformation by the power of divine grace.

Conclusion

This chapter has examined the question of how an evolutionary perspective on human nature might influence how we think about the theological claim that we are created in the image of God and morally governed by the natural law. Mahoney and Cahill show how these themes are connected to theological anthropology, Biblical interpretation, and theologies of salvation. They offer two distinct approaches to evolutionary theism that appreciates our characteristically human traits, needs, and capacities while also recognizing our continuity with the rest of life. They take "nature" seriously but always within the context of culture. They see that evolutionary approaches to human nature enrich rather than undermine the Christian description of the person as *imago Dei*. They do not attempt to use information about nature to provide a foundation for a universal moral code for all times and all places. They do not show how knowledge of evolution help us be more aware of the in-built moral challenges as well as the positive capacities that can be cultivated in the pursuit of human flourishing. Knowledge of human evolution can be appropriated to support a theological ethic that understands that we manifest what it means to be created in the image of God when we treat one another with love and understanding.

CHAPTER 2

The Concept of Natural Law in the Postmodern Context

Henri-Jérôme Gagey

In our postmodern culture, which has developed, to an extent never before attained, an awareness of the historicity of human existence, the concepts of human nature and natural law, such as they are given in Catholic doctrine, seem to have lost all means of analyzing the present condition of humanity and are able to represent only the traits of an era that has today disappeared. But the reason for its dismissal is perhaps too quickly assumed. Can we truly come up with concepts that permit us to speak of the universality of the human phenomenon and to engage in a rational dialogue with members of other spiritual or religious traditions, in order to discern the way to reestablish the foundations of a universal ethic? Can we, without any additional details, form our existentialist perspective according to which the human is what he makes of himself, manifesting his liberty in his capacity to tear himself away from the systems that have conditioned him? In our culture today, it is possible to openly reflect on these questions in a truly radical way. Indeed, this is applicable not only to abstract philosophical themes but also to social practices that are at present in the process of breaking up, even to our very own ways of behaving as human beings in the most decisive areas of our existence: in the reproduction of the species, involvement in the distinctiveness of the sexes, in relation to the body, to life, and to death.

For those preoccupied by such questions, food for thought may be found in the statement *In Search of a Universal Ethic: A New Look at the Natural Law*, a recent publication by the International Theological Commission, an advisory organ of the official Roman Catholic magisterium.[1] This important text endeavors to give a renewed credibility to the concepts of human nature and natural law by removing the misunderstandings to which, in the contemporary culture, they have given rise. It ascribes these misunderstandings to what it calls "the modern rationalist model of natural law." This involves, according to our document, an "abstract and maximalist" interpretation of the Catholic tradition that "stands at the threshold of a grave crisis, particularly since, through the rapid development of the human sciences, Western thought became more aware of the historicity of human institutions and of the cultural relativity of numerous behaviors that had once been justified by appealing to the obviousness of natural law" (§33). In this chapter, I would like, in a first phase, to take up these misunderstandings as put forward by this document, in order to subsequently reflect on the challenges that they raise from the perspective of Christian anthropology.[2]

The Misunderstandings Concerning the Concept of Natural Law

According to the Theological Commission, what is problematic about the definition of human nature and natural law according to the "modern rationalistic" model is its ahistoric character. This model is indeed characterized "by the essentialist belief in an immutable and ahistorical human nature, of which reason can perfectly grasp the definition and essential properties" (§33). In reaction, Christian theology has sometimes all too easily "justified some anthropological positions on the basis of the natural law, which subsequently appeared as conditioned by the historical and cultural context" (§10). The quest for a universal moral norm by reference to natural law became, consciously or not, Eurocentric and fed "the clashing of civilizations."

This "essentialist belief" is related to "the idea that it is possible for reason to deduce *a priori* the precepts of the natural law, beginning with the definition of the essence of the human being" (§33). The consequence is that natural law then appears "as a codex of ready-made laws that regulates as it were virtually all behaviour" (§33). This essentialist vision was more and more challenged by modern Western philosophy as well as by histori-

cal and social sciences when they came to disclose the profound historical nature of the most characteristic features of human existence. In this
context, the idea of an immutable and "ahistorical" human nature can only
lose its credibility.

The ahistorical character of this model, in relation to the content of
natural law, stands out particularly where, in the areas of bioethics and sexual morality, natural law evokes no more than "a resigned and completely
passive submission to the physical laws of nature, while the human being,
on the other hand, rightly seeks to master and to order these determinisms
for his own good" (§10). This biological or natural reductionism does not
then recognize the essential spiritual orientation of the human being. "It
presents the natural law as an objective factor that forces itself on the personal conscience from the outside, independent of the workings of reason
or of subjectivity and arouses the suspicion that it introduces a form of het-
eronomy incompatible with the dignity of the free human person" (§10).

In the face of an unprecedented situation, no room remains for a free
personal judgment or for a responsible and innovative ethical discernment.
In particular, no account is taken of "the concrete situation of human persons in the history of salvation, marked by sin and by grace, which has
nonetheless a decisive influence on the knowledge and practice of natural
law" (§33). Nothing can then prevent the determinations of natural law
from being identified with a "scientific" approach analogous to that of the
exact and experimental sciences in which the observer occupies a neutral
position.

Now, as the document expresses a little further on, the search for the
definition of human nature and of natural law is not of this kind. It is, to
the contrary, motivated by an extremely historical and practical purpose:
It aims to support "the elaboration of a universal ethic in a secularized
and pluralistic society such as our own" (§33). The moralist's reflection
proceeds much more in the way of a substantiated wisdom than of an objective scientific demonstration. As such, it necessarily deploys itself in the
framework of a "hermeneutic circle." For, as the Theological Commission
elaborates, a certain number of moral qualities are required to make an
adequate moral reflection (§55):

> To reach a correct evaluation of what should be done, the moral subject
> must be endowed with a certain number of interior dispositions that
> allow him to be both open to the requisites of the natural law, and also
> well informed about the facts of the concrete situation. In the context
> of the pluralism of our time, we are ever more aware of the fact that

> one cannot develop a morality based on the natural law without also
> reflecting on the interior dispositions or virtues that make it possible
> for the moralist to be able to develop an adequate norm of action.

This, according to the document, is what justifies the Church's claim to
exercise the role of "guarantor and interpreter" (§34) in the interpretation
of natural law in historical situations when the definition of the good has
become obscure—a claim that is difficult for many modern pluralist societies to accept. I will come back to that point below.

   With great honesty the International Theological Commission exposes
the many misunderstandings generated by "the modern rationalist model"
of interpretation of natural law. Now the question is how Christian anthropology can get past this model and engage fruitfully with contemporary culture today. The challenge it faces in that context seems to me to be
the following.

   We need to free ourselves from the intellectual reflex that manages, usually in an unconscious way, to objectify natural law by identifying it with
the laws of physical or biological nature. Our document denounces this
rigid identification, but it remains the case that it is often resorted to, and
not only in Catholic milieus.[3] Positively speaking, we have to realize that
the knowledge of natural law is the result not of a hypothetical-deductive
rationally restricting approach but truly of an initiation into wisdom involving the element of an authoritative body of practice and regulation.
This point picks up on one of the a priori's of the modern conscience: How
can the contribution of tradition be assumed in the reception of the truth?
Hence, in this chapter I will first look into how human nature and its relationship to its biological determinants is conceived within the document in
order to understand better a new interpretation of natural law. In a second
step, I will discuss the notion of natural law as a "wisdom" approach and its
implications on the role of the magisterium.

Natural Law and Biology

THE HUMAN BEING: SPIRITUAL CREATURE AND FINITE FREEDOM

Against the excesses of the modern rationalist conception of natural law,
the true historic character of Christian anthropology should be emphasized, particularly as developed in *Gaudium et Spes*, which finds its source in
the definition of the human being as a spiritual creature made in the image
and likeness of God. Indeed, defining the human being as a spiritual crea-

ture and therefore as a finite freedom is to affirm that his infinite dignity is to not be submitted to a blind determinism (either biological, familial, or social—see *GS* 17). This also means that his activities fall within a horizon of promise and command that frame his destiny in historicized terms. Moreover, in the biblical account, the historical vocation of humanity— "to grow, multiply, and rule the earth"—is announced before the account of original sin: It is not therefore the experience of sin that begins history. In the terms to which we have become accustomed through contemporary anthropology, he human's distance from the place of his biological determination can be put in this way: With humans, desire exceeds instinct and historicizes it.[4] Humans accomplish in the realm of desire and works the needs that animals satisfy through the instinct toward certain behaviors for which they are programmed.

Human beings desire what they need. What is typical of human beings, however, is that they attribute meaningfulness to their desires. For example, when they eat to regenerate their cells and to purify themselves of the toxins that they have accumulated, it is through fulfilling their desire by eating a meal and finding pleasure in it. Similarly, the sexual act, necessary for the reproduction of the species, is not sought in an instinctual way (with the male, alerted by certain olfactory, auditory, or visual signals that the female is fertile, coupling with her repeatedly) but rather according to an eminently socialized and erotic modality.

In one way or another, humans satisfy a drive that cannot be extinguished by merely satisfying fundamental physiological needs but that unceasingly seeks satisfaction in new objects. From this perspective, there is a rupture with the animal nature. The desire always exceeds, quantitatively and qualitatively, the instinct for which it is a substitute. For example, we eat more than is biologically necessary, and often this food is prepared artistically, and its consummation is surrounded by ceremonies, reasoned discourse, and symbols. This excess of desire over instinct implies that even the functional basis of these activities, the biological needs that they satisfy, can sometimes be radically ignored. So, in the adventures of Tintin and Snowy, one of Captain Haddock's favorite outcries is "Drink without thirst!"

Drink without thirst: This is an achievement of which animals are generally not capable! Such an activity is within the reach only of the human animal, to the extent that the human being seeks enjoyment in his relation to the objects necessary for the satisfaction of his needs. This search for enjoyment is capable of turning toward substitute objects in whose acquisition the drive is sublimated. This is what initiates the transition from the

sucking of the mother's breast to the sucking of the thumb or to the in-
numerable "security blankets" that infants invent. These processes of sublimation are accomplished under the guidance of the culture that exerts a
decisive role in proposing to the drive accessible and viable objects such as
sport, science, art, politics power, cooking, caring, etc.[5]

However, if this desire always puts the human being in the position of
excess in relation to the satisfaction of his or her needs, the drive needs,
to the contrary, to be restrained through the establishment of structured
prohibitions. Human behavior, then, from this perspective appears to be a
"restricted" behavior (and is no longer in excess) in terms of the dynamic
of its drives. The realm of culture comes into play here and bridles the
dynamic of the desire through the issuing and implementation of prohibitions. The human is then placed in a sort of unstable equilibrium that is
at the same time in excess of what is instinctive and subdued in terms of
drive. These two elements of excess and limitation should be considered
constitutive for human nature.

THE SOCIAL NATURE OF THE HUMAN

As the geneticist Albert Jacquard liked to recall, the human being's offspring is, in infancy, the least autonomous of all living creatures.[6] His point
is that, if human babies are abandoned, they prove unable to survive merely
by following their instincts. For them to reach their fulfillment as persons,
they must belong to the realm of language and of society, which compen-
sate for their instinctual weakness. Hence, language and society are not
merely an added dimension to human nature but a primary part of it. From
the beginning, human beings are social and reasoning animals that cannot
be defined apart from their belonging to a community.

In Christian anthropology, one touches here on the limits of the tradition's recovery of Boethius's definition of the person as an "individual
substance of rational nature"—the definition is limited because it lacks any
reference to the social nature of human beings. The document of the Theological Commission, for instance, takes up this definition of the person
by Boethius but not without completing it by adding: "*On the other hand,*
the person is manifested in his or her capacity to enter into relationships"
(§67, my italics).[7] One might wonder, however, whether this addition, "on
the other hand," is radical enough. Does this not entail a risk to define
the human person as *additionally* "capable of entering into a relationship"?
Should one not go so far as to consider the person to be formed intimately
and originally through the social relationships that preside at the person's

conception, birth, and development? In particular, one emphasizes, then, that it is part of human nature to be begotten and to belong to a genealogy, and not to be born as the product of a technological performance. In a Thomist perspective, perhaps one needs to go as far as to apply the definition that Thomas Aquinas reserved for the divine persons in designating them as "subsistent relationships"—to free ourselves from what is too constraining and limiting in Boethius's definition?[8] A question I leave to those who are more Thomist than myself . . .

TAKING CARE OF THE ANIMALITY AND THE CORPORALITY OF THE HUMAN BEING

So far I have argued for a going beyond, biological determinism as constitutive of being human—for going beyond it through a deeper consideration of desire and sociality as being what defines what is true of the human person. However, at the same time one needs to emphasize that the fulfillment of human desires and projects is in keeping with a corporal existence of which the actual biological level of organization takes place according to its own logic. While some might focus too much on the implication that our biological origin has for human nature, others, representing certain contemporary philosophical currents, deny the meaning and the normativity of these biological determinatives altogether.[9] These latter thinkers do not deny that the laws of nature impose their constraints and conditions on human existence, but they perceive this state of affairs as something that needs to be "surmounted"—that is, denied, in light of a definition of the human as the creator of himself. As the Theological Commission puts it (§71):

> From that point on, some people deemed that human freedom is essentially the power to count as nothing what man is by nature. The subject should therefore not attribute any meaning to that which he has not personally chosen and should decide for himself what it is to be a human being. Man, therefore, comes to understand himself more and more as a "denatured animal", an anti-natural being who affirms himself to the extent to which he opposes himself to nature. Culture, proper to man, is then defined not as a humanization or a transfiguration of nature by the spirit, but as a pure and simple negation of nature.

In the contemporary context, these philosophical trends tend to become dominant and the social practices that they legitimate completely transform how humans relate to their own humanity. This is what may be considered an "anthropological revolution," whose uniqueness is to radically undo the order of the desire and the order of needs and, in this way, to refuse all ethical normativity of biological determinatives that are considered as the contingent limitations from which one needs to be liberated. Thus the philosopher André Gorz described in an amazing way how "techno-science has produced a world that exceeds, opposes, and violates the human body through conduct that demands an acceleration and intensification of the solicited responses."[10] One thinks here, for example, of what can happen to the body of a top athlete in professional sports, where the quest for performance at any price leads to its manipulation, thanks to the assistance of the biotechnologies that have nothing medical about them beyond their name. Note also Sylviane Agacinski's denunciation of the instrumentalization of the bodies of destitute young women in the Third World, involving the practice of what has been euphemistically referred to as gestation surrogacy. These are the phenomena that are in the background of the document when it denounces in contemporary culture "the resurgence of a radical anthropological dualism that opposes body and spirit. . . . Such dualism manifests itself in the refusal to recognize any human or ethical meaning in the natural inclinations that precede the choice of the individual reason" (§74).

In condemning this return of an anthropological dualism in contemporary culture,[11] the Theological Commission invites us to rediscover the profound realism of the definition of the soul, or "forma corporis," as developed by medieval theology. The anthropological dualism of the Hellenistic tradition considered the soul and the body as two disparate and estranged quantities, as though it were a question of two "realities," two things, two parts, two pieces, or two "beings" within the human being. One imagines the soul, then, as though set down on a body in which it lives as a stranger, and which is for the soul like an envelope, or perhaps a prison. It is precisely this tendency that is contradicted by the medieval doctrine of the soul as "forma corporis," a doctrine that can be traced back to Aristotle, notwithstanding an essential transformation that has been well described by Joseph Ratzinger:

> Following Aristotle, Thomas defines the nature of the soul by means of the formula *anima forma corporis:* the soul is the "form" of the body. But in reality, this definition embodied a complete transformation of Aristoteleanism. To Aristotle, this formula meant that the soul, just like the entelechy—the formative principle of material reality in general—is tied to matter. Matter and form for him are strict correlatives. Without

"form," matter remains a mere potency, while form becomes reality only in its union with matter. If the soul is form, then it belongs to the world of bodies, marked by coming to be and passing away again. And this in turn means that the spirit, which does not belong to the world, cannot be individual or personal. Indeed, only as being neither is it immortal. Thomas' twofold affirmation that the spirit is at once something personal and also the "form" of matter would simply have been unthinkable for Aristotle.[12]

According to this way of perceiving, it is rather the soul that presents itself as an envelope of the body, the principle that confers to the latter its unity and coherence. Body and soul are two metaphysical principles within the original unity of the human being, in such a way that every activity of the human being is an "operatio totius hominis."[13]

In the contemporary context of an anthropological crisis, undertaking to speak once again of human nature and natural law is not to describe abstractly what constitutes the humanity of the human individual as a fixed code of conduct standardized by instincts and biologically determinative factors. It is to resist the dislocation of the desire and the need, of the spiritual and the physical, considering in particular that if the desire should become radically detached from its connections to the original needs that it is intended to satisfy, it will become truly deranged. In other words, affirming the existence of human nature means taking care of the animality and the corporality of the human being and maintaining a good equilibrium. But it is not so straightforward to make this meaningful in the context of the contemporary culture of the individual. Let us consider, for example, the resistance of the Church, among others, to the legislation of "new forms of parenthood" and to the implementation of new biotechnologies in the context of medically assisted procreation. That resistance takes on its full meaning only in the light of the foreseeable unrest that will accompany these developments as future generations try to comprehend what it is to be human in reference to a genealogy. The issue is to provide the equilibrium of a human environment that is truly humanizing and capable of ensuring a future for our common humanity.

A Wisdom Approach

The hermeneutic circle that I referred to above, according to which a certain number of moral qualities are required to make an adequate moral reflection, represents in our time one of the most paradoxical characteristics of Catholic doctrine concerning human nature and natural law. On the one hand, Catholic doctrine asserts that natural law is not a question of religious doctrine but rather the goal of a rational approach, in principle accessible to every upright conscience. But on the other hand, it asserts the necessity of access to the magisterium for interpreting the content of the natural law accurately: "Certainly the natural law is accessible to human reason, common to believers and nonbelievers, and it does not belong exclusively to the Church, but since Revelation takes on the requirements of the natural law, the Magisterium of the Church has been designated as its guarantor and interpreter" (§34).

In the eyes of a modern person, it is obviously a contradiction that needs to be resolved. Indeed, for the modern person, either

> natural law is a rational law—that is to say, accessible to reason alone—and therefore has no need of protection from an authoritative body; to the contrary, it should be possible, in time, to discover it through a purely rational analysis;

or

> the concept of natural law conceals a purely theological construction to which one can adhere only in faith, and so it is the assumption that it is rational that collapses.

But this is an abstract alternative; it fails to recognize that, in a very concrete way, it is often through listening to the gospel borne by the tradition of the Church that many discover the requirements of natural law. For this reason, to a certain extent, the role that the Catholic magisterium assumes in guaranteeing a correct interpretation of natural law—and, moreover, in guaranteeing the necessity of a spiritual "initiation" into moral discernment—that in the actual cultural context can no longer be considered as "that which is most greatly shared in the world."[14]

Two brief points to conclude on this issue. The International Theological Commission declares that it is the Church's desire "to share with the religions, wisdom traditions and philosophies of our time the resources of the concept of natural law." This concept is to be understood not as "a list of definitive and immutable precepts" but rather as "a source of inspiration that remains lively and energetic in the search for an objective foundation for a universal ethic" (§113). The ITC document, then, expresses the reflection of believers nourished by the gospel and the tradition of the Church. However, the fundamental assertions that it puts forward concerning the truth regarding humanity are not considered to be confessional assertions that would be true only when considered "in faith" (as when one says that one loves someone "in Christ" in order to conceal that one does not truly love the person at all). The authors of the document are convinced, to the contrary, that these assertions represent a decisive stand on human reality—a stand that is responsive to reasoned argument. It is exactly this conviction that belongs to the faith that gives expression to the concept of natural law. Hence the paradoxical status of this concept.

On the one hand, natural law presents itself as a theological concept in the sense that it is necessary for theology to express its most fundamental anthropological convictions. But, on the other hand, theology needs then to produce natural law as a truly philosophical concept, capable of mediating a reasoned debate between the ethical perspectives of heterogeneous spiritual and religious currents. In other words, this concept should be put to work inasmuch as it facilitates a rational debate that takes place independently of theological conviction. And in this sense, our document offers a basis to claim that "the concept of natural law is therefore above all philosophical, and as such, it makes possible a dialogue that, with respect for the religious convictions of all, appeals to what is universally human in every human being" (§114). Perhaps we have here a good example of what Jean-Luc Marion puts forward as the operation of a Christian philosophy:

(a) Theology deploys the discourse of charity from and about the *revelata* in the strict sense, that is, truths that only faith can reach. (b) Philosophy discusses facts, phenomena, and statements accessible to reason and its workings. (c) "Christian philosophy" (or whatever one wants to call it) finds and invents, in the natural sphere ruled by reason, phenomena and concepts that fall within the order of charity and that simple reason cannot see or discover. After having formalized them, "Christian philosophy" introduces them into philosophy and abandons them to it.[15]

From this point, the challenge for believers, philosophers and theologians alike, is not to be content with declarations of intention but to actually put the concept of "natural law" to work, not to abstractly defend its theoretic validity rather to introduce into the culture, in vivo, the discernment that it is intended to make possible.

CHAPTER 3

Personalism and the Natural Roots of Morality

Johan De Tavernier

The debate about the relevance of biology for ethics dates back to the time of Aristotle. In premodern theologies, nature and personhood have mainly been considered as two complementary notions. On the one hand, the human person was presented as a unique realization of nature; on the other, the human person fulfilled the assumptions that nature had given to him or her by virtue of his or her free will and the possibility for free choice. In other words, nature opens the possibility for free and responsible action. Since Darwin's *The Descent of Man* (1871), the question of the relevance of biology for ethics has become again highly relevant from a different angle. Christian ethicists, especially personalists, accept evolutionary insights but easily presuppose that humans are capable of transcending the biological roots of their behavior. We start as an empty sheet of paper and become what we are through socialization processes that include education and other environmental influences (nurture). Moreover, ethicists presume that the hierarchy of the *scala naturae*, presenting the species according to their unchangeable degree of perfection, not only necessitates a strong dualism between human beings and the rest of creation but also gives support to a strong anthropocentric position. Since the Swedish physician and botanist Carolus Linnaeus (1707–78), author of *Systema Naturae*, put an end to this essentialist understanding of both nature and human beings, we can reasonably ask ourselves if the contribution of "nature" to human behavioral processes is not underestimated. Is it right to present persons as contrary to nature, as is often the case in modern theological anthropologies? How do personalists react to recent scientific ideas on the rootedness of morality in dispositions that are programmed into our nature by evolution? In this chapter, we will deal with the question of whether personalism could profit from Darwinian evolutionary thoughts on human moral behavior.

Personalist Ethics: Ignoring Evolutionary Knowledge

Traditional personalist ethics accentuated in manifold ways the unique character of humans vis-à-vis nonhuman creation. Albert C. Knudson, an early twentieth-century personalist philosopher, described the debt of the personalist tradition to the ancient Greeks as consisting in "the superiority of thought to sense, the objectivity of the ideal, the speculative significance of self-activity, the shadowy and unsubstantial character of matter, various arguments for the existence of God and the immortality of the soul."[1] Significant for personalist morals is the immateriality of both the divine spirit and the rational part of the human being, a quality that stresses the unique nature of self-conscious beings or, as Augustine and Thomas Aquinas put it, the person as a unity of mental life and will. Their beliefs on the position of the human being in creation were backed by their opinions on the *scala naturae* and the idea of the *great chain of being*. The unique position of humans is further emphasized by Thomas's adoption of Boethius's well-known definition of personhood: "A person is the individual substance of a rational nature."[2] "Individual substance" means for Thomas "a complete substance, subsisting of itself, separate from all else" (*Summa* 3 q. 16, a. 12, ad 2um).

Knudson further explains that René Descartes "broke the spell which the Aristotelian distinction between matter and form has exercised over the human mind for almost two thousand years, and put in its place a radical distinction between thought and extension or mind and body, thus making the mind independent of the body and by virtue of its own unique self-identity capable of an immortal destiny."[3] In Germany, the ideas of Immanuel Kant about the creative activity of thought laid the foundation for a kind of ethical personalism, justified by his doctrine of practical reason, freedom, and immortality of the human being.

The immediate precursor of the actual personalist movement was the German philosopher Rudolf Hermann Lotze. Lotze influenced Max Scheler through one of his pupils, the Jena philosopher Rudolf Eucken.[4] For Lotze the self is a presupposition of thought and characterized by free will: without a thinker gifted with reason and intellect, no thoughts.[5] Influenced by Alexandre Marc, a Russian Jewish immigrant to Paris, who believed that the human being exists only in action ("One knows a being only in action"),[6] Emmanuel Mounier (1905–50) could describe personalism, in *Manifeste au service du personnalisme* (1936; *A Personalist Manifesto*, 1938) as a "philosophy of combat" and the leading spiritual and philosophical guide in order "to remake the Renaissance."[7] At the heart of the new personalist movement was Mounier's statement of the primacy of the person, which had to be defended against all that was antihuman: "No other person . . . no collective whole, no organism, can legitimately utilize the person as a means to its end."[8] In comparison with all other realities, the person is an "absolute," because he is "a free being that adopts, assimilates, lives and affirms values which constitute his uniqueness."[9] Mounier presents, parallel with the role of the concept "person" as the antithesis of the bourgeois individual, the concept "community" as the antithesis of modern society. In relationships with communities, human beings treat each other as persons. It starts with family life and social groups, which are prior to the state. Communities relate the world of the self with the world of other human beings, in concentric circles, and can be qualified to the degree to which they tear down or perfect human persons.

In France in the 1930s, both Mounier and Jacques Maritain defended similar ideas about the necessity of a new humanism given the crisis of the actual civilization. Maritain (1882–73), in the footsteps of his inspiring master Henri Bergson, distinguished between the individual and the person. The notion "individual" is used for the human being, animal, plant, and microbe. It contains a material component that we have in common with all others, while the notion "person" is used to mean "an individual complete substance, having an intellectual nature and master of his or her actions" and to include the spiritual.[10] It is not individuality but rather personality and its spiritual component that allows the moving out from self to others in freedom and love: *capable de donner et de se donner* ("capable of giving and self-giving"). In fact Maritain's *Humanisme intégral* (1936) could be considered his first attempt to describe the nature of a new civilization.[11] Maritain's ideas cannot be understood without knowledge of his evolution from personal involvement in and later disapproval of the reactionary

Action Française to a kind of defense of democratic pluralism in the mid-1930s, in line with Mounier's pluralist state.[12] But Maritain is more explicit on the Christian face of the new humanism, while refuting any kind of man-centered or anthropocentric humanism.[13] The German personalist movement received a great contribution when Max Scheler finished his habilitation thesis under the guidance of Rudolf Eucken in Jena. From his Kölner period from 1919 onward, Scheler became highly influential in Catholic circles, one of the reasons why Pope John Paul II has written his doctoral dissertation on Max Scheler, "Osoba I czyn" (1969; *The Acting Person*, 1979).[14] In 1923 Scheler met the Russian emigrant philosopher Nikolai Berdyaev, who in those days lived in Paris and regularly had contact with Mounier and Maritain. In Scheler's phenomenology (1874–1928), the axiological reality of values is always prior to knowing. In part 2 of the *Formalismus* (1916), Scheler introduces the notion "Person," which for him is intrinsically connected with nonformal ethics. He argues that we do not need a formal theory to illustrate the autonomy and dignity of the human person, while criticizing Kant's identification of the person with the rational. The person is more than a "logical subject of rational acts." The person is primarily an intuitional reality. The seat of value a priori is located in acts of feeling, willing, and loving, where cognition of values takes place. And so the axiological reality of values is always prior to knowing: "Man is, before he can think or will, *ens amans*."[15] His notion of "emotive a priori" expresses precisely that values can only be felt, never reasoned. Reason cannot think values. Understanding Scheler's notion of the person presupposes that one is informed of his *Aktlehre* and the question of what unites all human acts of various natures (willing, loving, feeling, judging, thinking). Scheler presents the person as the "unity-of-acts-of-different-natures."[16] The sphere of the entire person is *in* every act.

And finally there is his idea of intersubjectivity. Other persons can only be really known by way of co-execution of acts (*Mittvollzug*), co-acting, co-operation, or co-thinking—a *thinking together*. In other words, persons can be really understood only in their interrelationships.[17] From Scheler's idea that the sphere of the entire person is in every single act, the Louvain personalist Louis Janssens could conclude that the person is a complex totality, existing in a spatiotemporal universe. It is not through reason but through the particularity of the body that human beings are able to actualize their lives in particular times and spaces. Persons reveal themselves in their activities, and these activities reveal persons to themselves.[18] The polarity between acting and being, between what already is and the potentialities for becoming, describes the process of the actualization of a person: "A person is a destiny. For the person to live, then, is for him to realize his value as person."[19]

In conclusion: All personalists believe that the mind is never reducible to some material or physical substance. They present the person as the supreme principle based on arguments referring to volitional human actions, intelligence, and the human capacity for spirituality and intersubjectivity, all of which not only mediate but also support the theological conviction that only human beings have been created in the imago Dei. However, these traditional personalist accounts are now under attack because they ignore to a great extent other conditions of being a person, such as the capacity for psychological experiences such as enjoying pleasure, or the desire to avoid suffering, understood as not only intimately related to the bodily and the physical (nature) but also rooted in our long evolutionary history. The mention of "substance" is problematic, therefore, as it runs the risk of fostering a dichotomist view of the human being, omitting the historical embodiment of brain and mind and upholding the view that the emotions are only *accidentiae*. Moreover, personalist accounts of morality normally give support to a strict separation between an evolutionary "is" and a moral "ought," resulting in the idea that good and evil are exclusively theological and philosophical concepts and merely cultural phenomena (nurture). Here we touch the key problem of Christian ethics today. A concept of person that not only ignores but also obscures essential natural characteristics and considers them as nonessential (*accidentiae*) has lost its relevance for present-day discussions on morality.

Is Human Morality Innate? Darwin versus Huxley

Evolutionary biology instructs us that morality has roots in dispositions that are programmed by evolution into our nature. Darwin's evolutionary theory (*Origin of Species*, 1859) can be considered a radical paradigm shift of which all the consequences are not yet visible.[20] Providing a supernatural cause in order to explain the origins of life, including human life, is no longer needed. The young Darwin in Cambridge still believed in Paley's "argument from design,"[21] taking for granted not only the essentialist and static nature of Aristotle's *scala naturae* but also the idea that complexity could never be the outcome of chance. During his voyage (1831–36) with the *Beagle*, Darwin discovered that a complex design does not necessarily entail an intelligent designer (a God engineer as *prima causa*), because evo-

lution itself is able to account for complexity. Darwin's "dangerous idea"—
that all life can be explained through insights into the efficiency of natural
selection, as reflected in the famous dictum "Natura non facit saltum"—
works out as a *universal acid*.[22]

In *The Descent of Man* (1871), especially chapters 4 and 5, Darwin focuses on the evolutionary roots of men and their morality. Obviously a lot
of analogies between animal and human behavior could be observed. He
sees continuity between animals and humans, even in the moral domain.
Since morality is based on underlying capacities (e.g., sympathy, empathy,
sensitivity to the needs of others, understanding "do ut des"), he wonders
whether animals and human beings do not share emotions and "gut feelings" such as anger and courage, revenge and cooperation, playfulness and
seriousness, and the need to care for offspring. Like other primates, humans are pleased if they can help each other in stress and in sorrow. Both
internalize group values and are sensitive to approval and disproval of own
behavior by others. In chapter 4, "Comparison of the Mental Powers of
Man and the Lower Animals," Darwin describes how evolution gives an advantage to animals that support each other. He observes that most animals
are emotionally engaged in social relations and are concerned about the
welfare of both their offspring and companions and even prepared to offer
their lives in some conditions. Wolves help each other; dogs know empathy, fidelity, and obedience; baboons enjoy company.[23] Even altruism is not
excluded by evolution. The harshness of evolutionary processes could go
hand in hand with a kind of gentleness. On the capacity for sympathy and
empathy, for instance, he writes: "The following proposition seems to me in
a high degree probable—namely, that any animal whatever, endowed with
well-marked social instincts, the parental and filial affections being here
included, would inevitably acquire a moral sense or conscience, as soon as
its intellectual powers had become as well, or nearly as well developed, as
in man. . . . Many animals, however, certainly sympathize with each other's
distress or danger. This is the case even with birds."[24] All cooperating animals show sociality, group loyalty, and the tendency to help each other.
Humans as well as animals are touched by emotions of members of their
own sort (comparable with young parents vis-à-vis their offspring). These
emotions support human reasoning. Moral choices are built on strong
convictions and moral sentiments. They do not produce morality as such
but are rather a conditio sine qua non. Darwin not only sees continuity
between animals and human beings, however. He also observes discontinuity, such as the absence of caring for the elderly and sick among animals

and, above all, the absence of conscience in them. He recognizes that the difference in mental powers between human apes and primitive human beings is huge, but it is a question of degree, not of kind. Specific aspects of consciousness—in particular, the capacity for remembering—are present in the animal world. His conclusion seems to be solid: Human beings are the result of a continuous and gradual evolution, including moral behavior.[25] But as seen so often in evolution, the direct motivation and impulse is no longer observable. However, the expression is still there, even without direct payoffs. These inclinations are not without self-interest, because in the long run they increase our chances for survival through, for example, protection against aggression from outside the kin group.

At this particular point Thomas Huxley, "Darwin's bulldog," disagrees with Darwin. Huxley (1825–95) is a "saltationist" (from *saltare*), accepting macro mutations. On the one hand, in *Evidence as to Man's Place in Nature* (1863), Huxley shows anatomic evidence (brain, skeleton) in order to prove the congeniality between apes and humans, but on the other hand he does not seem to think of the rich diversity in life forms as the result of small, gradual steps. For instance, he accepts that there is physical impact on the nature of human condition but that humans are capable of controlling it. In his lecture *Evolution and Ethics* (1893), he compares it with the task of a gardener pulling out weeds: "Human morality is a victory over brutal evolutionary processes."[26] He is convinced that humans act competently and ethically by explicit choices based on free will, not by evolution. Social behavior seems to him entirely a matter of nurture, and morality something that differentiates humans from animals. Because of the immense difference in mental powers between the highest ape and the "lowest savage," morality is not in line with animal behavior and only humans can be moral beings. Followers of Huxley, such as George C. Williams, see morality not as "an accidental capability produced, in its boundless stupidity, by a biological process that is normally opposed to the expression of such a capability."[27] Hence, evolutionary theory triggered a debate over the roots of morality.

Nature versus Nurture? Evolutionists/Gradualists versus Saltationists

Primatologist Frans de Waal characterizes Huxley's view as the "veneer theory of morality," by which he means that human morality must be seen as "a cultural overlay, a thin veneer hiding an otherwise selfish and brutish nature."[28] Other critics of Huxley's theory are sociologist Edvard Westermarck, biologist Edward O. Wilson, and philosopher of biology Michael

Ruse.[29] They compare Huxley's theory to a piranha that suddenly decides to become vegetarian. What is at stake?

Westermarck (1862–1939) is the first scholar who defends a comprehensive view integrating both evolution and culture and both animal and human behavior. Without having knowledge of ethology, he sketches stories of retaliation involving chimpanzees, macaques, and elephants. For him, retributive emotions, be they positive (repayment, gratitude) or negative (revenge), could be considered the cornerstone of morality. Arnhart situates Westermarck in a long tradition, going back to Aristotle, which firmly believes that "'thought by itself moves nothing,' although Aristotle believes that reason can guide the desires that do move us. Desire always moves us, but thought never moves us without desire. . . . Deliberate choice [*proairesis*], according to his *Nichomachean Ethics*, therefore requires a conjunction of desire and reason into 'desiring thought' or 'thinking desire.'"[30] The idea that morality is anchored in the natural inclinations and desires has been taken over by Thomas Aquinas.

Much later, evolutionary biologists, defending the idea that human morality is innate, situate in a similar manner the roots of morality in emergent emotional, social, and cognitive capacities in order to address serious human interests. Richard Joyce mentions that the hypothesis that human morality is innate could mean that we act spontaneously in morally desirable ways because our "moral sense" relies on underlying, innate psychological mechanisms. We "naturally act in ways that are morally laudable" because "the process of evolution has designed us to be social, friendly, benevolent, fair."[31] Of course, this does not mean that humans always act this way—we could also be insensitive, violent, egoistic, etc., but that is not considered the predominant natural behavior. A slightly different interpretation is offered by sociobiologists E. O. Wilson and Michael Ruse, who see the "moral sense" as a biological adaptation.[32] Both authors say that—notwithstanding what Christian ethics has to say about metaphysics, Christian intentionality, and the "spark" of God in each person's conscience—morality serves inclusive reproductive-fitness goals and that this is as true in the cases of marriage, truth-telling, and membership in dominance hierarchies as it is in acts of compassion and cooperation.[33] Both of them believe that it is in our self-interest to uphold reciprocal fairness, to fulfill duties, to be loyal, to accept social control, and even to sacrifice ourselves. However, how does cooperation come into being in the natural condition, in the absence of a central authority? Has Hobbes not said that the natural condition is characterized by a war of all against all (*homo homini lupus*), in which there is no room for altruism, mercy, and empathy?

And can there be morality without social contract? But even in the natural environment, according to E. O. Wilson, there is a will to cooperate and there are universally shared similar moral codes (no tolerance for violence, robbery, and rape).[34] In conclusion, morality is certainly not the sole result of a cultural process, but it is rather vice versa—culture has to be interpreted as the end product of a kind of morality deeply rooted in our biology. Moral systems are motivated by "enlightened self-interest," and hence the need to manage conflicts, to guarantee personal security, and to promote social cohesion.

Could even altruistic behavior be explained from an evolutionary viewpoint? A comparison could be made with game theory. Game theory is a study of strategic decision-making. In game theory one makes a distinction between zero-sum and non-zero-sum games. In a zero-sum game, each player is willing to cooperate, because cooperation means that each person's gains will equal his net losses. But also in non-zero-sum games, one is sometimes willing to cooperate, but not at any price. Unconditional altruism will not be possible (except in the case of kin altruism)—the risk of exploitation is too high—but reciprocal altruism is possible. Authors such as Robert Trivers describe tit-for-tat strategies, in which temporary sacrifices are made and payoffs are expected later.[35] Robert Axelrod shows that cooperation could be fruitful and even the best strategy in particular circumstances (e.g., tit-for-tat strategies to avoid unnecessary conflicts by cooperating).[36] Emotions do play a major role in this because they are the lubricants, creating cooperation in the long run. Reciprocal altruism is not a cool, rational, cost-benefit analysis but an emotional commitment that makes it possible to receive moral benefit from social ties. It originates in emotions and even includes mental accounting: honor if we keep promises, guilt if we misuse someone's trust, shame if we are unmasked as cheats, sadness if someone is dishonest with us, happiness if we encounter altruism. Human apes also do know all these emotions and sentiments. Given their mental power, however, humans try to rationalize their innate morality.

In line with Darwin, de Waal sees morality as a further development of social instincts (reciprocity, fairness, community concern, conflict resolution) and emotions such as protest, shame, anger, tenderness at being touched, compassion, consolation, and fidelity, which we have in common with other primates. De Waal calls them "building blocks of morality"[37] or "proto-morality."[38] De Waal is convinced that morality originates out of a need for cooperation, a need that has an emotional basis. If profit maximization were the only motive, cooperation would not exist. Rather than only looking for advantage, both humans and animals alike are afraid of deceit and loss. Being realistic, one knows that love can alter into jealousy, envy, and revenge. In this context, conscience could be seen as a functional emotion balancing self-interest and group interests. Group interests are best served with generosity, unselfishness, and cooperation. Morality serves solidarity within the group and creates harmony and social order and we-feeling. Whoever sees morality as an evolutionary product has, for de Waal, a better, livable world in mind than do Huxley and his followers, because it is not realistic to believe in universal brotherhood.

A slightly different interpretation of the innate character of morality is possible. For Joyce, moral behavior relies on underlying, innate psychological mechanisms. Evolutionary psychology claims that human behavior is the outcome of psychological mechanisms that are adaptations although the behavior itself is not necessarily adaptive. The evolved psychological mechanisms are triggered by contextual factors that explain why the mechanisms are not always developed. Moreover, the extraordinary human brain enables humans to deal with contextual variation. The innate emotional, social, and cognitive faculties result in a kind of open-ended plasticity, shaping memory capacity, a kind of will, a capacity for understanding, and reflection. Our biological makeup provides the conditions for the rise of morality but does not dictate any concrete moral behavior.[39] The Spanish American biologist, philosopher, and theologian Francis Ayala holds that three evolved faculties make morality possible: "(i) the ability to anticipate the consequences of one's own actions; (ii) the ability to make value judgments; and (iii) the ability to choose between alternative courses of action."[40] Like Ayala, neuroscientist Antonio Damasio thinks that the emergence of the capacity for suffering and the idea of vulnerability to suffering enabled the capacity for remembering the past, explaining why humans have a special interest in morality. In *Descartes' Error*, Damasio describes, for instance, how the body's production of oxytocin supports both the emotional feelings between lovers and mothers in their caregiving for their infants.[41] In general, these innate faculties explain why we are more willing to reward those who are cooperating with us, why we are willing to treat others as they treat us, and why we are more loyal to members of our own ethnicity than to strangers. In the latter case, anthropologists refer to the principle of "primordial autochthony," explaining that we normally care more for ethnic kin than for people from an alien kin. Kin affection and altruism are universally valid but will be experienced very differently in different contexts.

Naturalism, Morality, and Normativity

A special branch of evolutionary biology is comparative neurobiology. Owing to the increasing knowledge of neurobiology, human brain phenomena lose their exclusive character. While Jacques Monod considered the transition to spoken language a coincidence, and the appearance of the neocortex a miracle, his pupil Jean-Pierre Changeux states in *L'Homme de vérité* (2004) that the difference between an animal and a human brain is rather quantitative than qualitative.[42] In *L'Homme neuronal* (1983), he mentions that everything seems to be a matter of the brain.[43] But what triggered the transition to the larger brain size in humans has still not been elucidated.[44] It is clear to him, however, that some essential, qualitative changes in the genome and the associated phenotype in the brain were sufficient to reorient evolution into something qualitatively new, the human brain.[45] Not everyone agrees with this gradualist vision. There is even less consensus about the implications of this vision for our thinking about morality. Some neurobiologists—for example, Wolf Singer—do not hesitate to conclude that *Homo sapiens* can be characterized as a metaphysical process but one without free will.[46] He cannot imagine that in a deterministic world people can be free. On the other hand, neurobiologist and Nobel laureate Gerald M. Edelman rejects the orthodox Darwinian thesis of gradual evolution by pointing to the speed at which human consciousness—still of a superior order—appeared, owing mainly to the rapid increase in brain size.[47] But as a biologist, he is convinced that consciousness is a purely biological phenomenon, resulting from complex cellular processes in our brain. For him, human consciousness stems from the unique physiology of the human brain, which consists of very many neurons operating in a network. It is estimated that the brain of a baby consists of about 100 billion cells that develop about 100 trillion connections with one another. Edelman's theory is strongly antireductionist and explains consciousness by referring to the extraordinary complex morphology of the brain. Not the old but the young brain has the most neurons, which is understandable given that neurons are the only cells in the human body that do not regenerate.

Giovanni Boniolo and Gabriele De Anna wonder what the consequences of a scientific, evolution-based interpretation of consciousness are for understanding ethics.[48] They distinguish two things: what it has to say on the level of explaining moral behavior and what the impact is on the level of the justification of ethical claims. If biological sciences have a role to play in explaining or justifying ethics, then one speaks of naturalism. But there are various forms of naturalism. They may claim to contribute to the explanation of ethics, to its justification, or to both. Weaker forms of naturalism will accept that alternatives to scientific explanations for ethics are conceivable. Defenders of stronger forms of naturalism will argue that the natural sciences can fully explain ethical behavior though not justify it. A third position is that science is able to not only explain moral behavior but also justify moral behavior. In this case, ethics does not necessarily have to be seen as a fiction or illusion; it can continue to exist as an autonomous discourse, but it will in fact be reduced to a scientific discourse in which any kind of free will is denied. So it is for Wolf Singer and brain scientist Victor Lamme, who hold that the idea of a conscious "I" is an illusion.[49] Both share the opinion that we do not control our decisions when we undertake actions, for which we therefore cannot be held responsible. For Singer, consequently, the disappearance of free will must imply the giving up of the possibility of guilt and responsibility. This is not necessarily the case, according to Lamme.[50] Incidentally, for Paul Thagard, this does not mean that we lose self-control or our individuality, rational judgment, and autonomy.[51]

The question is what we hope to explain and to justify through neurobiological and evolutionary biological insights. In other words, what is moral action? William A. Rottschaefer provides some insight into this question.[52] In his model of moral behavior, he distinguishes four levels: minimal cognitive capacities with a biological and psychological basis, a behavioral level that uses cognitively acquired moral desires, a reflective level (i.e., the understanding of moral desires and normative beliefs), and a reflective framework that helps moral agents reflect on what they do. Rottschaefer's analysis makes clear that biology can help us explain cognitive as well as emotional characteristics, necessary conditions for levels three and four. But most authors (e.g., Boniolo) choose a weak form of naturalism that could explain some characteristics of moral behavior but certainly not provide a justification for it. Michael Ruse sees a bigger impact of evolution on moral behavior. He believes that even some form of normativity can be explained by evolutionary knowledge. However, the justification of material moral norms (why norms are mandatory, what reasons there are to follow normative standards) is meta-ethical and therefore not a matter of empiricism. If the meta-ethical is also be interpreted as the consequence of evolution, then it must necessarily lead to skepticism. Unlike sociobiology, evolutionary biology cannot, Ruse believes, provide a justification for normativity, because evolution is rudderless. At the same time he believes that the justification is necessary but illusory. Ruse and Edward O. Wilson call this "a happy illusion."[53] This kind of illusion is for them not dramatic, since they believe that it will not rapidly disappear, as it is rooted in moral sentiments that are deeply settled in bodily structures. It results in a Hume-like form of moral sentimentalism that is combined with Darwinian evolutionism. Boniolo takes a similar position. With regard to the justification of moral judgments, he believes that epistemological reductionism should be accepted while existential relativism is rejected—otherwise we cannot maintain moral systems. He defends a kind of phylogenetic relativism, based on the study of evolutionary relations among groups of organisms, by concluding that the moral capacity should be considered an accidental evolutionary outcome that has been made possible by evolved mental properties.

Is there a Darwinian meta-ethics? Hyper-Darwinists believe so.[54] They support a distinct meta-ethical view that necessarily puts into question the truth of moral judgments and even suggest that moral knowledge is impossible. On the other hand, moderate Darwinists believe that evolutionary knowledge does contribute to a better understanding of some aspects of human moral behavior and may explain why people have an initial interest in the development of social systems. Finally, there is a third group of interpretations, which states that the recognition of forms of evolutionary relatedness made it possible to understand our obligations to others. Kitcher believes that natural selection has played an important role in the development of moral consciousness, and he sees morality as a fitness strategy, just like the development of limbs and senses in the past. But cultural aspects are now much stronger. He swings between two extremes: between those who believe that everything is cultural (the blank-slate hypothesis) and those who say that everything is biological (the genetic-determinism hypothesis). Kitcher raises a significant nuance. From the history of codification, starting with Hammurabi, he describes in great detail how the growing interest in legal systems can be regarded as the continuation of efforts to avoid violence among hominids.[55] But such pacification strategies lead their own life and can hardly be connected with the idea of "reproductive success."

Perception of Emotions and Inclinations within the Christian Tradition

Instead of choosing between nature and nurture as the predominant factor in human morality, it is better to accept the idea that, owing to evolutionary history, human nature manifests adaptive dispositions. The way those dispositions are expressed vary according to the circumstances in which the individual lives. One of those dispositions is the capacity to suffer and be happy. Just like sensitive mammals, people could suffer and be happy. Such empirically determinable analogies justify talking about "Tierseele." Therefore, Kant thinks, we have to respect animals—though indirectly. On the other hand, "animality" is also found in humans, as Thomas Aquinas already noted.[56] Kant also speaks of *Tiermensch* and *Tierheit in Menschen.* He relies on the fact that sentient human beings know emotions analogous to those of animals: joy, anger, love, hate, desire, sadness, aggression, hope, and fear. People are, however, able to control them through reason. In fact, Kant borrows this from Thomas Aquinas, who granted to animals even cognitive abilities, such as a degree of "prudence," although it differs in degree from that of human beings.[57] This Thomistic insight has been lost because modernity gradually evolved into a dualistic view of the matter. Man, culture, and speech were split from animal, nature, and body. In fact, Kant's sharp distinction between "is" and "ought"

> treats morality as an autonomous realm of human experience governed by its own internal logic with no reference to anything in human nature, such as natural desires or interests. He does this because he accepts the Hobbesian view of human nature. Because human beings are by nature asocial, selfish animals, they cannot live together in peace unless they conquer their natural inclinations by willing submission to moral rules devised by reason to pacify their conflicts.[58]

To the degree that the Christian tradition has embraced modernity, it has integrated a kind of nature–culture dichotomy that is now being questioned.

However, for the classic thinkers it was a mistake to think that behavior is either exclusively biological or exclusively cultural. For them, nature and culture are intimately intertwined. This explains why the original Thomistic idea that our human tendencies and emotions are better known by closely looking at other living beings is lost. Kant still refers to Thomas's idea that animals are sensitive and even have a certain decisional power, though that power is not comparable to human free will.[59] He recognizes that we share with them many natural tendencies—such as the desire to know and the desire for companionship, food, and sex—that underlie social tendencies. The good life, partly based on fairness, also implies a healthy balance in tendencies and emotions. This is by no means obvious: The classics knew that tendencies and emotions are always ambiguous. A better understanding of the natural roots of behavior is therefore critical. Kin altruism— e.g., parental love—is obviously positive but can also lead to xenophobic reactions. Understanding biological evolution will make us more alert to the innate urge to lie if we can profit from it, or to the tendency to be blind to our weaknesses, to cover up our vices and to justify prejudices. Alasdair MacIntyre came to the same conclusion in *Dependent Rational Animals: Why Human Beings Need the Virtues*. Departing from his previous works *After Virtue* and *Whose Justice? Which Rationality?* he recognizes after 1999 that he was wrong to present ethics as decoupled from biology.[60] He then acknowledges that it no longer makes sense to talk about good and evil, norms and virtues, without paying attention to the biological constitution of humans, explaining how ethics discourse is built on this.

For Jean Porter, natural inclinations and emotions are morally relevant, though they are not morally determinant. She opposes a natural-law conception whereby the normative meaning of nature is reduced to practical rationality. Moreover, she thinks that an abstract, ahistorical interpretation of the natural law does not correspond to the Christian idea that the creation itself is good. Scholasticism believed that human nature, including prerational, biological roots of behavior, is morally meaningful. Therefore it would have no problem integrating contemporary scientific knowledge.[61] Although the biological substrate of human nature is important, the person is much more than merely a biological being. Good life for persons can never be, as the Stoics claimed, "living according to nature." Porter distinguishes between natural aspects of human nature that must be suppressed and aspects that should be encouraged. The Christian tradition provides relevant criteria for this exercise.

Christian Ethics and Evolutionary Roots of Morality

Evolutionary biology suggests that exclusive cultural positions on morality (for instance, in theological anthropology, defining exclusively the human person as "imago Dei," created cocreator, steward of creation, etc.) do not deal with the whole truth about moral behavior. Easily lost in this focus is that morality is fundamentally a mixture of culture and nature. Therefore, concluding from the creation of human persons in God's image that human beings differ in kind and not just in degree from other animals seems to me no longer plausible. The imago Dei is not a disembodied notion. I prefer a starting position that takes for granted the biological nature of human beings. The embodied human being, as the imago Dei, has emerged in evolutionary history as a self-conscious being with the capacity of religious awareness and of taking up moral responsibility. An embodied belief in the imago Dei represents our disposition for the religious meaning that is embedded in our species-specific symbolic behavior. The acceptance of evolutionary accounts of morality by Christian ethics does not necessarily discredit the moral enterprise, as many still believe. The recognition of common descent does not necessarily devaluate a notion of human dignity. Scientific knowledge of the biochemistry behind maternal love does not nullify parental love. Various kinds of reciprocity, engraved in the human psyche, could explain why people around the world, although in different manners, have an interest in developing social conventions. "Christian ethics can profit by recognizing the functional value of morality without presuming that morality is only meaningful for its social functionality."[62] It is obvious that knowledge about the way natural evolution has formed our emotional, intuitional, and cognitive constitution, including a broad set of proclivities, could help us to comprehend not only human behavior but also the often limited impact of both ethical reasoning and moral judgments on concrete behavior, which include dietary changes for ethical reasons, the eradication of prejudices, the many difficulties we are struggling with while realizing distributive justice, and the attractiveness of ethnic culture for offering the experience of belonging to a community.

Moreover, Stephen J. Pope is right in confirming that the evolutionary process provided an emotional and cognitive constitution characterized by general proclivities, desires, or preferences, not a fixed moral code. Natural proclivities are always mediated through a cultural context. Pope opines that it is possible to reinterpret the belief of Thomas Aquinas that children are born "with a range of fairly indeterminate natural abilities, powers, or capacities which are gradually shaped by training, instruction, and habituation to become the adult's 'second nature,' that is, the virtues or vices that constitute character."[63] I consider it a kind of biological predisposition that has to be understood as an "open program." Any descriptive knowledge of evolutionary psychology about these natural inclinations will enrich Christian ethics to become more sensitive to morally relevant ambiguities. In the case of, for instance, kin altruism, what is a desirable and just love of parents for their offspring? What is a sound or improper ethnic nationalist feeling? And the one who teaches sexual ethics is better informed about the "relatively stronger indiscriminate male desire for sexual variety," which reflects the evolutionary answer to the need to enhancing sexual fitness amid the harsh living conditions of ancient times.[64] Knowledge of biological proclivities can also alert us to inner psychological obstacles to behaving properly, such as deception strategies and strategies to justify our biases and minimize our prejudices. At the social level, knowledge of biological proclivities explains why we sometimes are uncritically obedient and prefer conformity against protest, or why we have a desire to preserve self-esteem.[65] Having a better knowledge of the evolutionary roots of morality can, for instance, make us more critical of professional advertisers manipulating our psychological mechanisms. A better knowledge of emotions will help us recognize and avoid conditions that trigger undesirable behavior.

Understanding the evolutionary roots of morality emphasizes the need for properly coaching and tutoring evolved emotions. The moral life is in the first place a matter of constantly directing natural inclinations and emotions toward a virtuous living that benefits the good of the person. Humans are ethical beings by their biological nature. At this point we see a link with Thomas Aquinas's ideas on virtue education:

> If we take the passions as being inordinate emotions, as the Stoics did, it is evident that in this sense perfect virtue is without the passions. But if by passions we understand any movement of the sensitive appetite, it is plain that moral virtues, which are about the passions as about their proper matter, cannot be without passions. The reason for this is that otherwise it would follow that moral virtue makes the sensitive appetite altogether idle: whereas it is not the function of virtue to deprive the powers subordinate to reason of their proper activities, but to make them execute the commands of reason, by exercising their proper acts.
>
> *Summa Theologiae*, 2.1, q. 59, a. 5

Knowledge of the evolutionary roots of morality allows us to better situate the human transcendence of our evolutionary past. Human beings are not entirely free, but we "do have some room for such freedom, for willing and performing actions that may go against the apparent grain of biology and culture."[66] For sure, there is a huge difference between human and animal behavior. Loving others for their own sake, acting like a good Samaritan, is for Holmes Rolston not, contra Wilson and Ruse, of trivial importance. It is precisely through the capability for acting in ways that transcend our fitness interests that we show that the statement that "morality is nothing but adaptation" is not true. High standard Christian ethical ideals of universal solidarity and love, including love of enemies and the preferential option, or love, for the poor, the renunciation of revenge, the adoption of nonrelatives, and appeals for a disinterested regard for others, surpass the kind of morality provided by natural selection.

Conclusion

The unscientific worldview of the classics (Aristotle, Thomas Aquinas) is maybe closer to the truth than is much of modern ethics. Modern dichotomies in ethics between "is" and "ought" have to be questioned if human morality is rooted in a natural moral sense. The classic authors believed that there is no absolute gap between nature and freedom, nor between nature and nurture. Christianity should remember her own long-held tradition that morality has a natural basis, one derived from our creaturely condition. A sound Christian ethics accepts the idea that God works in and through human nature. Therefore Christian ethics may neither accept a reductionist model that equates an evolutionary basis for behavior with the essence of morality nor the spiritualist view that ignores the biological basis of morality and presents God as the only source of morality. In the Catholic tradition, the human being as person has never been presented as the counterpart of nature. And finally, the same Catholic tradition holds the idea that grace perfects nature. Therefore, Christian ethics should recognize what is best in human nature, improving at the same time what can be improved and correcting wrong inclinations.

CHAPTER 4

In God's Image and Likeness:
From Reason to Revelation
in Humans and Other Animals

Celia Deane-Drummond

One of the most heavily discussed topics in theological anthropology focuses on different interpretations of the meaning of imago Dei, humanity made in the image of God. A deeper knowledge of the common evolutionary heritage of human beings and other creatures has prompted some discussion about whether such a position of seemingly absolute human distinctiveness can still be maintained. Furthermore, mounting ecological awareness, and sensitivity to the shameless exploitation of other animals, points to the potential ethical ambiguity in maintaining a strong sense of human superiority. The divine command in Genesis to exercise human dominion has, at least in some cases, and in secularized form in practice, provided an excuse for exploitative treatment of the natural world and other creatures as resources to be used simply for human benefit.[1] While there are certainly other strands in the Christian tradition that counter this exploitative trend, the place of humans in that world remains at best ambiguous.

One way to solve this problem theologically might be to question the basis for the traditional restriction of the bearing of the divine image to *Homo sapiens*. If this restriction is lifted, then other creatures can be included in that image-bearing by a process of extension, in much the same way that other creatures are also included in the realm of, for example, justice or rights.[2] In this way other animals begin to be absorbed into the human world, and this is a common strategy for those seeking to affirm the moral status of other animals. Other animals then become part of the human, moral world rather than having only instrumental value to human beings. Particular shared capacities among humans and other animals, such as sentience for Peter Singer or in the case of Tom Regan, being subjects of a life. These are both highly influential writers, who have more often than not viewed traditional forms of Christianity as hindering this process of extension by contributing to the problem of denigrating other species.[3]

While the first approach might be tempting, the special place of other creatures in their relationship with God both within their own worlds and in communion with human subjects may become compromised, as greater attention is paid to those creatures that are most like us. A second approach, on the other hand, would be to retain the idea of human distinctiveness in the bearing of the divine image but now to interpret it in an active way that presents the particular task of humanity as recognizing a divine vocation to serve God and exist in respectful communion with other creatures. Such a theological anthropology is still prepared to restrict the theological language of divine-image-bearing to humans, but now it understands that bearing to make most sense within a communal understanding of shared creaturely being, and also in light of the particular religious vocation of humankind.

I have recently toyed with the first approach, of extending image-bearing to other creatures. I postulate its application in a qualified way by drawing on a Thomistic sense of different degrees of image-bearing in men and women, while recognizing the problematic sexism implied in such grading.[4] However, at the time I also expressed my concern that using the language of imago Dei may itself have anthropocentric overtones in that it might not allow the particular form of what reflecting divinity means in other creaturely kinds to be sufficiently recognized. In other words, if other animals are to be thought of as only weakly bearing the image of God, it still seems to put other animals on the same hierarchical scale as humans, and they are then found wanting. David Clough has argued convincingly that, while classification schemes devised by humans will inevitably lend more moral weight to some creatures than to others, unilinear scales of creaturely difference are damaging in ethical terms, and one could add that a scale of more or less image-bearing feeds into such a model.[5] The moral advantage, however, is more obvious, as other animals are included in the human world and are therefore afforded ethical treatment, as befits such a relationship.

I argue here that, rather than try to accommodate other animals to fit divine-image-bearing, it makes rather more sense to restructure the meaning of that human image-bearing so that it carries an ethical component and, further, it also makes more sense to put other animals in the category of divine likeness. Further, the common evolutionary ancestry of present-day modern humans and alloprimates does not rule out the distinctiveness of human beings, *Homo sapiens sapiens*, even if not averring the term "uniqueness." This is born out by anthropological studies on prehistory that show the relative success of *Homo sapiens* compared with other coexisting hominid species. Hence, while there are lines of continuity with other species, the distinctive aspects of human beings come to the fore once evolutionary issues are taken into account.[6] It is also hard to deny directionality in the evolutionary process, even if biologists resist the idea of teleology in the classical sense.[7] In this respect I part company with Stephen Pope's analysis in the first chapter of this volume, where he views the evolutionary trajectory of human beings as a definitive threat to the status of human beings as beings created in the image of God. Or, rather, it becomes a threat only where it is interpreted in a particular way, as a basis for interpreting that image-bearing as affirming a unique and oppressive superiority of humans over other creaturely kinds.

Thomas Aquinas through his language of divine "likeness" to describe other animals tried to capture this sense of shared creaturely being, and it may have more advantages than it seems at first sight. However, "likeness" still tends to be compared unfavorably with image-bearing and therefore may not give sufficient recognition to what we might term the particular charism of each creature. If the language of divine likeness is to carry sufficient weight, then it needs to affect how we interpret divine-image-bearing. I therefore argue that a more rigorous overhaul of the meaning of "*human* divine-image-bearing" is required. Such a reimagining of image-bearing comes, first, from closer consideration of the behavior and capacities of other animals; second, from a reexamination of traditional texts; and, third, from a discussion of the evolution of religion in human communities.

I argue in this chapter for a *performative* understanding of image-bearing that incorporates rather than rejects more traditional constitutional elements of reason and freedom, for example. However, while this points to the idea of image-bearing through particular ways of acting in the world, I am leaving to one side current debates about the evolution of morality, as this is taken up in the preceding chapter of this volume by Johan De Tavernier. Modifying human image-bearing in the manner I propose retains a sense of the distinctive capacities of each creature to follow what might be termed its own telos, including those that are distinctive for human beings. I therefore argue in favor of a radical reinterpretation of the meaning of imago Dei.

I will concentrate in this chapter on a critical reappraisal of those capacities that have been used most often to argue for a strong sense of human superiority and separation from other creatures—namely, reason and freedom, both of which are considered prerequisites for religion. While the recognition that other animals are intelligent is relatively well known, the idea that they might have something that bears at least some analogy to human freedom is not taken into account in traditional theological approaches to image-bearing. Orthodox theologian John Zizioulas, for example, characterizes freedom as the characteristic that most distinguishes humans from other creatures. For him, "whatever involves succumbing to the given, this man has in common with the animals. Whatever is free from it constitutes a sign of the presence of the human."[8] Here he means a positive understanding of human freedom as creativity that is free from succumbing to the given, rather than freedom from external constraint. Yet such positive human freedom is to be exercised correctly only in acknowledgment of God's intentions rather than simply in a libertine, unbounded sense of individual free choice.[9] Another category that he argues is exclusive to the notion of human freedom is that of the tragic, where "tragedy is the impasse created by a freedom driving towards its fulfilment and being unable to reach it."[10]

I will therefore begin with a fuller discussion of what we might mean by freedom or agency in other animals. I will next draw on a Thomistic approach to human reason as that which marks out the way that freedom is expressed in divine-image-bearing. I suggest that for Thomas human freedom presupposes that humans possess particular, distinctive cognitive capacities that are situated on a continuum between other animals and angels.[11] Thomas lived in a culture in which other animals were treated as tools to be used in an instrumental way by humans. His ethical approach did not match his ontological position with regard to other creaturely kinds. He also seemed to give a high value to revealed knowledge in humans, as in angels. But this then raises important questions about how image-bearing might be considered in the light of the emerging evolutionary understanding of religious capacities.

The Question of Animal Agency

I suggested above that, in the dominant Christian tradition characteristic of both East and West, human freedom and divine-image-bearing are intricately linked. But rather than assume that other animals cannot by definition possess any form of agency, let us consider that the presence of a capacity that approaches that in humans can give important clues about its special distinctiveness in humans. In other words, in order to clarify further the meaning of human freedom, let us ask in what specific sense other animals might be considered agents.[12] "Agency" is a broad term that designates the possibility for self-direction. The use of a term such as "free will" is unfortunate in theological terms if it implies a separate faculty from bodily existence. Philosopher Helen Steward, drawing particularly on studies of early human development, argues that many nonhuman animals need to be considered as having a basic form of agency.[13] Rather than suggest that other animals are capable of sophisticated propositional attitudes, she attempts to rule out the harsh denial that animals can be agents of any sort. She argues against those, such as Donald Davidson, who reject the idea that other animals could ever be intentional agents.[14]

Agency can be defined as the ability of an organism to move what we think of as its body; the center of a form of subjectivity; the presence of intentional states (such as trying, wanting, perceiving); an organism capable of moving its body through volition and only secondarily in response to environmental triggers.[15] In this sense, agency is a prerequisite for the possibility of freedom, understood as free choice, though animal ethologists are not known for using the language of freedom to describe animal behavior. There may be examples of simple animal movement, such as that of the paramecium, that appear to have agency but on close examination are governed by physical forces. The sheer diversity of different animal species should not be forgotten.

Steward believes that attributing agency to other animals is resisted in the academic literature because (a) of cultural and religious forms of anthropocentrism; (b) at least among natural scientists, agency might seem to imply some form of body–mind dualism; (c) parsimony dictates such resistance (i.e., only simpler explanations are acceptable); (d) an empiricist approach to the consideration of other animals distrusts any form of what is perceived as misplaced anthropocentrism—i.e., reading into animal behavior habits of human society; (e) the influence of a rationalist Kantian ethic presupposes that agency amounts to a complex form of moral judgment. Steward nevertheless argues in favor of the basic intuition that animals are capable of agency. In ignoring ethology, however, her account is disappointing, for she opens up the philosophical space for animal agency but then does little to show what evidence might be accumulating to support it. Ethologists have written significant work that questions any sharp boundary between other animals and humans, though more often than not the work is on how humans share the same emotional response as do other social animals, rather than on how animals share some cognitive functions.[16]

Steward also stops short of attributing to other animals anything like a theory of mind. Regardless of how intentionality might be mapped, it is clear that once beliefs about others or the world are present, intentionality is a capacity beyond that of internally directed responses. In this case first-order intentions are said to be present; second-order intentions are present if an agent considers the mental state of others. This can be expanded further, so that one could consider the mental state of the person thought about by the person who is close by as the third order of intention, and so on. For example, the latter is something like this—I want my children to believe that I expect them to be waiting for me at the after-school club at a certain time of day. While we may be naturally inclined to attribute second-order intentionality to other animals, careful ethological work research shows up in a more definitive way whether particular social cognition is involved or not.

Yet assuming that intentions are there in other animals may be problematic in that it fails to give them the benefit of the doubt, which popularizers of animal ethology are inclined to advocate.[17] There seems no reason not to suppose that social animals are purposive in working out which actions to take in given situations. Examples of innovation in the cultures of social animals are not all that common, but there is a good case for social learning of given traditions among many different species of social animals, such as certain bird species, roof rats, bottlenose dolphins, and chimpanzees. Such learning seems to be spread by imitation of a neighbor, though it cannot be ruled out that there may be genetic predispositions to learn in a certain way.[18] The question becomes: How far can animals actively make choices other than those governed by affective states, including emotions, instincts, and learned desires?

Harvard philosopher Christine Korsgaard argues that humans have a deeper level of intentionality that allows them to make judgments in relation to particular norms or moral principles, so that we can choose actively either to follow such purposes or not. In this scenario intentions do not simply exist in humans; rather, they are actively assessed and adopted.[19]

We need to acknowledge such distinctions. Among animals, only humans are capable of worrying about their own animality and its significance in relation to human self-identity; only humans discuss the fine points of what it means to express freedom; only humans are knowingly religious beings, and so on.

Thomas Aquinas on Rational Animals

Thomas Aquinas's interpretation of the first book of Genesis makes it clear that for him humans are created directly by God, and from this follows a superior status whereby "the highest degree of life . . . is in man."[20] Further, for Thomas the difference between human beings and other animals is sharper than that between different categories among other living things that he named as fish, birds, and land animals.[21] But all living things have what he calls a soul, and he rejects the idea that the soul is simply a vital principle, or that it is corporeal as such; rather, it is "that which actuates a body."[22] In Thomas's thought, the distinctive aspect of the human soul relates to the mind or intellect, and he presumed in this case that the body had no "intrinsic part" in the activity of understanding in humans and therefore understanding is able to subsist and can be thought of as incorporeal, even if the body is the means through which the soul of a human being comes to be incarnated.[23]

So far this portrait might imply that Thomas envisaged a clear dividing line between humans and other animals, with reason providing a high watermark. Yet there are important qualifications. He recognized, for example, that animals act not just in response to external sensations but also because of an inner judgment about what might be useful or harmful. A lamb, on seeing a wolf, will flee because it knows it is a "natural enemy," and "a bird collects straw, not because it pleases its senses, but because it needs it for building its nest."[24] Other animals' *aestimativa*, or estimative sense, can grasp intentions that are not simply sensate responses; these animals have the power of memory, with which they are able to store these up for future use.[25] It is here that the difference between humans and other animals in their reasoning powers becomes clear, since while other animals perceive intentions by the estimative sense, in humans we find an active comparison, or cogitation, which Thomas describes as "the particular reason."[26] It is the capacity of human beings to deliberate about a particular end that marks out uniquely human capacities, while other animals can aim at an end but not deliberate on it, so that the movement toward this end is unpremeditated.[27] Of course, Thomas did not have the knowledge that we now have of the relative sophistication of the cognitive acts of intelligent social animals, who do seem to have the capacity to deliberate on alternative courses of action and have at least some lower levels of intentionality.[28] For Thomas, humans have a more elaborate memory than do other animals, displaying an inner reminiscence, "a quasi-syllogistic search among memories of things past in their individuality."[29] Other animals also could show common sense and imagination. The difference yet commonality finds clear expression in his claim that

> cognition and memory reach so high in man through their similarity to and connection with abstract reason, through a kind of overflow, not through anything belonging to the sense-soul as such. So they are not new powers but the same powers, more perfect than they are in other animals.[30]

This makes it clear that the reasoning abilities of human beings are on a continuum with those of other animals, even though the particular capacity for abstraction makes human reasoning distinctive.[31] It is therefore incorrect to view Thomas's scheme as a classification system in which some animals, humans, have reasoning powers while others do not. Even Aristotle, on whom Thomas arguably relied, sought to interpret the lives of other animals by close observation of their habits and distinctive properties rather than by imposing on them a classification grid.[32]

The estimative sense in other animals relates to what Aquinas calls "the appetitive power of the soul. By this power an animal seeks after what it knows, not merely going where natural inclination leads."[33] Yet because intellectual knowledge is universal, while sense knowledge is of concrete particulars, the intellectual appetite of human beings is different from the sensitive appetite of other animals.[34] More explicitly: the intellectual appetite is able to judge something particular, in an abstract way, as having a universal quality of being good as well as to desire nonmaterial goods such as knowledge and virtue. Reasoning and understanding are related as means and ends. Reasoning is the way we arrive at knowledge that enables us to distinguish one thing from another, "so that strictly speaking we reason concerning conclusions, which become known through principles."[35] Thomas draws a parallel between the faculty of reasoning and understanding and free will, or the power to will and choose: Understanding and will are the goals to be realized through reasoning and choosing, respectively. For him the "rational appetite, termed will," is self-motivated and aims at a defined end, whereas for those lacking intelligence the tendency to act is through a "natural bent" stimulated by something outside themselves, even if he allows for some "purposive perception" in other animals.[36]

Thomas does allow that at times human beings may be driven by others or by outside forces, but in carrying out orders blindly they are acting more like nonrational creatures. Properly defined, human acts are therefore acts that come from deliberate and self-conscious willing on the part of the individual person.[37] Thomas envisaged a reasonable human will as being in command over emotional forces common to other animals; where such powers dominated, the resulting action was less than human.[38] This elevation of human reason at the expense of emotional bodily actions is well known in Thomas and Augustine and has been the subject of recent criticism.[39]

It is certainly very unfortunate to portray those characteristics that we share with other animals as somehow belittling human dignity. For Thomas, humans have the ability to exercise deliberative choice or preference as well as to detach themselves from their appetitive desires, and therefore to consent to a particular course of action.[40] This is the case even if we can claim that the irascible appetite has powers that share in a measure of reasonable activity compared with the concupiscent appetite that he portrays as a simple response to attraction.[41] Thomas envisages these various appetites in a hierarchy, so that the highest level of activity of irascible appetite comes into contact or touches the lowest rungs of reasonable activity. In this way, he is ready to admit that other animals share in the capacity for friendship or hostility, as marks of the active irascible appetite.[42] This might seem somewhat remarkable given the subsequent denigration of animal emotions in cultural history. However, in spite of this admission, Thomas still maintains that the purpose of other animals is to serve humanity. Even more remarkably, perhaps, given that he seems well aware of their capacity to suffer, he claims that other animals, even though they are innocent, are punished "by divine law," for the sole purpose of punishing the human beings who own them, who are thereby "punished by their punishment or frightened by the sharpness of their pains or instructed by the meaning of the mystery."[43] In this case human beings are punished because other animals are treated as if they were human property. It is this position with respect to the explicit ethics of the use of animals that has led to Thomas's vilification as a thinker who bears some responsibility for the negative treatment of other animals.

Notwithstanding what we might call the "graded" understanding of reasoning in other animals, in the estimative sense and appetitive powers of their souls, Thomas rejects the notion that other animals are capable of showing forth the image of God, even though he raises this as a possibility, perhaps ironically.[44] But, following Augustine, he considers the opposite scenario, that God's gift of an intelligent mind in human beings means that whatever lacks intelligence cannot bear God's image.[45] The result of this dialogue is something of a compromise between these two possibilities. While Thomas recognizes some likeness to God with respect to other creatures in that they exist and are alive, it is the human capacity for discernment and intelligence that marks out human beings as bearers of the image, even if other creatures share in God's likeness.[46] This difference reflects what, in human beings as compared to other animals, Thomas terms the greater capacity for the highest good. And it is the likeness "to the supreme wisdom in so far as they are intelligent" that makes humans as intelligent animals capable of bearing God's image as such in a way that other animals cannot.[47] Yet since wisdom, as he has defined it, is about knowledge of eternal things, it is not simply intellectual capacity but rather the intelligence of human beings as directed toward the capacity for revealed knowledge that marks out human image-bearing.

And so, while Thomas does seem to acknowledge that other animals weakly bear the image of God "in the manner of a trace," in his view only rational creatures that have an intellect or mind sufficiently bear the resemblance to God so that they can be termed bearers of the image of God, and only for this reason are such human capacities as the spiritual, the bodily or the imaginative ways of human knowing ever capable of bearing a "trace" of the image.[48] He concludes that image-bearing in the rational aspect of human nature bears the image in terms both of the uncreated Trinity and of the divine nature.[49] With respect to image-bearing in terms of the divine nature, "rational creatures seem to achieve some sort of portraiture in kind, in that they imitate God not only in his being and his living, but also in his understanding." With respect to image-bearing in terms of the uncreated Trinity, the rational creature "exhibits a word procession as regards the intelligence and a love procession as regards the will."[50] Other creatures have "a certain trace of intelligence that produced them" and "a clue that these realities may exist" when it comes to word and love, in the way that a house shows something of the mind of the architect. It is the ability of human beings to in some sense imitate God in the process of loving and willing that marks out image-bearing, and so Thomas's view of image-bearing appears to include human agency and action. A simple focus on reason as the ontological distinction between humans and other animals misses out the specifically religious and what might be termed the performative elements that are woven into Thomas's account of what it means to bear God's image.[51]

The Evolution of Religion in Homo Sapiens

If, as I have suggested above, Thomas's interpretation of human image-bearing is about the religious as much as it is about the rational capacity, then one might expect that a focus on the particular ways in which human beings have evolved would shed some light on that image-bearing. The evolutionary basis of religious belief is discussed by a number of prominent authors in the debate over science and religion.[52] Scientists do not seem to be suggesting that other animals are religious, although some ethologists do seem to permit the idea that this cannot be ruled out of court.[53] Observations by renowned primatologist Jane Goodall on chimpanzees before a waterfall suggest that they might experience feelings of wonder that is a prelude to a self-conscious religious sense.[54] Evolutionary psychologists who are also drawn to what is sometimes termed "New Atheism" are more likely to argue that the origin of human religion can be accounted for by entirely natural evolutionary mechanisms, even if they are ready to admit that science does not then test the truth of religious claims. I consider this tack to be flawed inasmuch as finding a biological basis for the capacity for religion does not amount to an explanation for religion.[55] If it is used to stress the capacity for religion, as opposed to trying to explain religion, an evolutionary account of religious experience has much to offer in the way of a deeper understanding of how the capacity for religious belief emerged in *Homo sapiens*. There are still, however, many unresolved questions to consider in charting the relationship between evolution and human nature in general as well as between evolution and religion in particular.

Biologist and theologian R. J. Berry has argued that the shift in *Homo sapiens* from nonreligious animal to religious animal was so significant that it would be more appropriate to name this a distinct species *Homo divinus*.[56] He also claims that according to the Abrahamic faith it is God who "transformed humans" at some point in their evolutionary history as *Homo sapiens*. This seems an astonishing claim, as it presupposes that the account in the book of Genesis is to be taken at face value, that God is specifically involved in the creative act of making humans in a way that is not true of other species. This sets up a divide that splits humans from their evolutionary history and makes God into a God who acts through direct supernatural intervention rather than indirectly through evolutionary processes.[57] Why is it so problematic to believe that God works in the evolution of religious capacities for the human species? While Berry resists the crude notion God's transformation of humans is like the mechanical addition of soul to body, he still seems to assume that it is a special work of God at a particular period in the history of *Homo sapiens*, at the transition from *sapiens* to *divinus*. Berry justifies this view by claiming that "we are apes, but we are more than apes and it is useful to mark this difference with a change of name."[58]

Of course the difficulty that Berry faces is that on purely historical grounds it seems that *Homo sapiens* existed as a biological species long before cultural evolution and any religious belief was clear in archeological evidence. Perhaps this is a rationale for a change in name, but it implies that *Homo sapiens* before this transformation was not really what God intended. But can we really put ourselves in the place of God and decide which individuals belonging to *Homo sapiens* are deemed worthy of the name "human"? Do we restrict this further to the subspecies *Homo sapiens sapiens*? Berry seems to be creating two subspecies of humans, *H. sapiens* and *H. divinus*, the former inferior to the latter. Of course, Berry is on safe ground in that understanding more precisely what happened in the course of the evolutionary history of *H. sapiens* is virtually impossible: All we see are hints of religious belief in the archeological record and, before that, emerging capacities for symbolism, language, and abstract metaphysical thought. The question about what precisely allowed one particular subspecies of humans to be successful over other hominids that coexisted at the time still generates heated debates among evolutionary anthropologists.

The question that confronts us here is about belief in the divine transformation of human beings and whether the distance that separates that transformation from "natural" processes in the history of *Homo sapiens* is credible in the light of evolutionary history. Or should we seek another explanatory route and use evolutionary, anthropological, and philosophical analysis, to stress the unique aspects of being human? I do agree with Berry that human beings are highly distinct, even within the lineage of hominids in early prehistory, and as self-aware religious beings they are also in this respect distinct theologically. Berry claims that the ability to bear God's image is a divine attribute rather than an evolved character, although he admits that its expression depends on our bodily nature. In light of the discussion of Thomas's position on human image-bearing, I would also agree that there is a close relationship between image-bearing and divinity, but that relationship rests on specific human capacities, for universal reason and for knowledge as revelation, that make human beings more like angels. It seems to me, however, that there is no reason why the particular capacity to receive revelation, or what might be termed the religious sense, could not also be an evolved capacity, even if in the light of faith that capacity can be thought of as one of the gifts bestowed on human beings, but a bestowal that completes natural capacity rather than being accomplished through divine intervention. In other words, the idea that image-bearing is somehow "implanted" in human nature implies an external intervention with deistic overtones that is no longer really convincing.[59]

The late Roman Catholic archbishop Józef Życiński vigorously denied that either religion or ethics could be evolved capacities, claiming that they cannot be thought of as having an evolutionary advantage. He was, of course, naive in making this claim: Even if we hold to the view that religious belief does not bring adaptive advantages, it is possible that the capacity for that belief emerged alongside other advantageous capacities—to use evolutionary jargon, it was a "spandrel." The jury is still out as to what extent religious behavior, perhaps in association with the evolution of cooperative behavior, brings what might be termed biological advantages. Życiński also accused secular writers such as Peter Singer and post-human authors such as Gregory Pence and Thomas Regan of placing humans and other animals on the same continuum in the name of anti-speciesism. Crucially, he thought that humans lose their special place and dignity when the boundary between humans and other animals is weakened, supplementing his argument with a long list of advanced characteristics, including altruism, that he believed are specific to human cultures.[60]

While it is certainly true that some sociobiologists have made exaggerated claims for the links between the origin of specific human behaviors and evolutionary psychology, and I have had reason to be highly critical of such claims, Życiński in his sharp critique of the evolutionary basis for *any* complex tasks in human communities misunderstood the specific way in which evolutionary biologists try to address these problems. For example, his belief that no animals other than humans show altruism is not well founded, unless cooperative behavior in other animals is thought to be separated sharply from altruistic tendencies in humans. While I agree that there are clear distinctions between what might be termed highly developed psychological altruism in the case of human beings and a more general cooperative behavior in other creatures, there are also lines of continuity that humans share with other highly social animals, and it is these connections that Życiński seems particularly anxious to dismiss.

I argue against the presupposition he has assumed in this case, that maintaining a sharp and dualistic divide between humans and other animals is absolutely necessary in order to give human beings a special place and dignity. Rather, human dignity should not be set over and against the special dignity of other animals in their own worlds, as if adding dignity to one detracts from that of the other, any more than giving human beings more freedom detracts from the freedom of God. I am not suggesting that there is no moral hierarchy in the relationship between human beings and other animals but rather that human beings need to consider the implications of a shared creaturely basis with other life forms, which exist along with, rather than in opposition to, our own species with its specific and distinctive characteristics. Where I would certainly agree with Życiński is in his belief that human religious life cannot be simply explained by evolutionary paradigms, but that does not mean that religion is completely disconnected from evolutionary processes. Evolutionary accounts that are biologically based are necessarily very general about tendencies toward certain behaviors and offer only a very general guide as to what can develop through learning, language, culture, religious experience, and so on. How far and to what extent specific behaviors might have evolutionary origins is a matter of intense research; however, I think it is premature to rule out the possibility that very general capacities for cooperation and, perhaps, religious belief do not have an evolutionary origin.[61]

Similarly, we might say that general capacities to reason, learn language, and express agency are evolved capacities, refined and developed subsequently through learning in a cultural and familial context. The debates surrounding the extent to which these capacities are tied to nature and to the extent to which they are tied to nurture are still unresolved, but where science attempts to exceed its reach is not so much in the claim that evolutionary processes are involved as in the claim that evolutionary accounts are sufficient to explain behavior, including religious behavior. In other words, the claims scientists make for specifically evolved capacities in humans are not always backed up by adequate empirical observations. To counter this problem, greater attention needs to be paid to the limits of scientific investigation and to the need for further research, but that does not mean, with Życiński, that evolutionary accounts have virtually nothing to say about the human condition.

However it might be conceived, the evolutionary history of religious belief shows that religion is associated with specific action and performance; it is grounded in practical wisdom of how to act well, a practical wisdom that is shared to some extent with other animals. Human image-bearing in a theological sense needs, therefore, to go beyond a straightforward and restricted discussion of ontological categories and must include an ethical dimension of what it means to act well in relation to other creatures. In practical terms, this means a refusal of the instrumental use of other animals for what might be termed superficial human needs and, at a bare minimum, a refusal to condone those agricultural practices that deny creatures the basic conditions for a flourishing life. Human beings have evolved in such a way that their lives are entangled with those of other animals, and morality grew out of close relationships between kin in a wider multispecies context. If the way we love and the way we express our freedom has to imitate God in order to express the divine image, in the way that Thomas suggested, then our concern for other creatures must be similarly universal in scope, at least in intention, even if we are inclined to care more for those creatures—such as pets or domesticated animals, for example—that play an active part in the lives of humans.

The specific ability of humans to exercise practical wisdom will curb an overly romantic approach toward other creatures, not all of which will necessarily be compatible with human flourishing.[62] But the point is to see human image-bearing in a generosity of action toward others, understanding creaturely life as gift, inspired by the gracious presence of the Holy Spirit, rather than viewing other creatures as mere products for human consumption. Human image-bearing becomes in this view not just a bare ontological or relational term but also implies building on such capacities a religious goal to be achieved, an active performance receptive to the grace of God, and a means for creating a community with other creaturely kinds, instead of a means for separation and assumption of superiority.

A detailed discussion of what this might mean in ethical terms is outside the scope of this chapter, but it is sufficient to say that ethical categories such as solidarity need to become much more broadly understood, so as to encompass not just vulnerable humans but vulnerable creatures in general. My intention in this chapter has been to stress lines both of continuity and of discontinuity from other animals, so that while the moral distinction between humans and other creatures remains, it is not used wantonly to exploit other creatures for human benefit.

Preliminary Conclusions

I have suggested here that, in order to understand theological anthropology in the context of a dominant contemporary scientific culture, it is advantageous to take its claims seriously rather than to dismissing them as inevitably weakening a theological understanding of human nature. One topic that has particularly interested me is how the boundary between the human and the nonhuman has become more porous in contemporary animal studies. Now such a shifting of this boundary as applied to the human capacity to bear the divine image raises the question whether other animals should also be regarded as displaying the divine image. I argued after some deliberation that, in the end, it makes more sense not to make this move but to see the close relationship between humans and other animals as clarifying the distinctive features of what it means to be human, rather than as obscuring all differences between them. Indeed, I have suggested that recognition of the particular telos of a species helps human beings understand how to relate to other creatures and respect their particular charism for the living community shared by humans and other creatures. Drawing on what Thomas Aquinas noted as the specific abstract reasoning capacity in humans, I suggested that the tradition is not quite as hostile to this approach as it appears to be at first sight. Indeed, Thomas ironically considers that other animals might be made in the divine image, but eventually he settles on the notion of divine likeness. As long as this view can be adapted to reflect the special and particular character of each species, the concept divine likeness may be useful as a way of affirming other species theologically. However, a far more important way of affirming them is through a revision of what it means for humans to bear the image of God in a performative sense, in which they act out divine-image-bearing in a community with God and other creatures. In humans, I suggest, religious capacity can sensibly be measured in only the human community, so that latent forms of this capacity in other creatures cannot be captured by scientific investigation and are unlikely to be able to be so captured in the future, although it is possible that capacities for more emotive or psychological prerequisites for religious belief may be found in other animals. The emergence of visible forms of religion appeared relatively late in the evolutionary history of hominids, which raises interesting questions about the biological evolution of the capacity for religious belief, questions that still subject to intense discussion among evolutionary biologists. Those who claim that evolution explains away religion or even morality have not understood the basis for religious belief, its complexity, and its rich cultural diversity. Being made in the divine image has a special place for religious capacity in humans, but divine-image-bearing is more properly understood as a call to particular actions to act responsibly toward other creaturely kinds, in accordance with a religious vocation.

PART II

Christ and the Disputed Self

CHAPTER 5

Neuroscience, Self, and Jesus Christ

Oliver Davies

Introduction: Cosmology, Anthropology, and Christ

Change in science involves a change in the way we understand materiality and the world around us. Since we ourselves are material as well as mind, what we *think*, or authoritatively hold, matter to be is significant for our own self-understanding. More than that, the introduction of the new science into our own embodied space, through new technologies, can even change our "contact" with the world: how we are in the world as self-aware creatures who are both mind and body at the same time. For anyone who doubts the potential of scientific advances to shape our humanity, it would be salutary to read more widely in the cultural thought-world of pre-Enlightenment times, or the early anthropological studies of cultures in far-flung parts of the globe.

One could understand the differences in anthropology schematically in a historical progression from premodern to modern and finally, in our own times, to a new "integrated" paradigm of the self. Like Anthony Godzieba elsewhere in this book, we consider Charles Taylor's distinction between the "porous" self of premodernity and the "buffered" self of

modernity a good point of departure. While Godzieba develops his argument using insights from the social sciences, we shall concentrate on the
new neuroscientific paradigm of the self, which is emergent within our
society but which will surely consolidate over time as more and more social
and economic practices are developed that presuppose it and are indeed
based on it.[1]

The premodern paradigm represents a "porous" self who is imagina-
tively and conceptually at home in what we might call a scriptural world or
cosmology. Characteristic is the interpenetration of mind, body, and world
in an "enchanted" universe that held all these terms together through the
createdness of all that is. All created things are united with respect to the
Creator. The boundaries between the individual mind and the "intelligible" realities of the world are unclear. The earth is full of powers and
intelligences that are no less substances than we are, though they are nonmaterial. In this world, we are deeply at home as intelligence, imagination,
and embodiment that interpenetrate the world. Here, too, the body itself
is imaged not as being over and against the world but as being itself cosmological. This is the embodiment as microcosm that we associate with
ancient religious traditions. It suggests that we are, as human beings, intrinsically part of the world that surrounds us.

We need to contrast the above, which allows for a continuity of mind
with the—"intelligible"—world (to use a word much loved by Platonists
and scholastics alike) and a continuity of the human body with the material universe, with a different model, that of Taylor's "buffered" self. This
modern paradigm reflects a Newtonian self-understanding. Here mind and
body in their unity stand out over and against the world. But mind controls
body in the sense that the body is the instrument of the mind's attempts
to bring the material world under its own control. This is the paradigm
of the technological self, or Arendt's modern *homo faber*.[2] It represents a
distanced and controlling relation between self and world.

Underlying this paradigm is the new knowledge about the world, which
Funkenstein refers to as "ergetic knowledge" by which we are able to man-
ufacture things.[3] Here mind, defining matter as forces that can be measured and thereby gaining control over materiality, finds that it is now at a
distance from the world. The human body itself takes on a highly ambiguous role since, as matter, it belongs to mind and is the instrument of mind
but, equally as matter, it is also deterministic, so that human beings have
to ask themselves whether they are—as material objects—in fact not free
at all. This places a commensurate emphasis on human subjectivity as the

secure site of our freedom. This paradigm presents a subject who is *in* the world and only remotely part *of* the world.

Our third, integrative paradigm seeks to set out the kind of self-understanding that is evolving today. It reflects the self of what we can call the "second scientific revolution" (of neuroscience, genetics, and evolutionary biology as well as physics and cosmology). Here the opposition between materiality and mind has in effect broken down. Embodiment is continuous with world. Mind is still a free domain, which is other than materiality, but this freedom is now one that is exercised within materiality and not from a point beyond it. This paradigm represents a more advanced stage of scientific understanding about ourselves, which includes the many subtle layers of the complex interpenetration of matter and mind in us. Although mind and matter are different from one another (and always resistant to the reduction of one to the other), they are now also more clearly indivisible. At the same time we now know that the material elements that constitute our bodies are all present elsewhere in the universe (so that Nicholas Humphreys can call us "soul dust").[4] What is particular about our material bodies is not its elements but the specific form they take in us—which is to say, the unparalleled complexity of material organization in us (and specifically in the brain, which supports consciousness in the first place, of course). The new scientific self-understanding prompts us to think of ourselves as being not only *in* the world, as subject, but simultaneously to think of ourselves as being also *of* the world and indeed, more correctly still, as ourselves *being* world. For contemporary science, we are indistinguishable from the universe in which we find ourselves in the basic constitution of our material form. Where we are distinct, and irreducibly so, is in the subjectivity that that materiality of unparalleled complexity supports. We are self-aware, sentient creatures, who have knowledge of our own end and of the infinity of the universe of which we are part. We are creatures capable of wonder and worship, who can feel ourselves to be addressed by God in the fullness of his creation.

Our tradition of modern theology, therefore, leaves us with a particular inheritance. This can be summarized in terms of the mind–body relation, according to which the body, as material, constitutes a domain of determinism (and so is unfree or only conditionally free), whereas the human mind, or spirit, is unconditionally free. We are as free in our interpreting, existing, experiencing, and communicating the world as we wish to be. This is a strongly dualist paradigm, which owes much to the spirit of the Idealist age, which understood our human freedom to be itself at stake in the way that we choose to read the world. Fichte's adage that everyone has his or her own philosophy (by which he meant that we are all at liberty to choose to be deterministic or free, according to whether we are Idealists or not) still has resonance for us today.

Modern theology was formed in the aftermath of the rise of a deterministic Newtonian universe, or what the Templeton Prize winner George Ellis has called the "block universe," wherein the future is already contained in the past. According to this paradigm, it makes no difference where we section the universe in terms of time, since the universe as a whole is already inexorably predetermined in every respect.[5] Within such a materialist scheme, the human mind has to take freedom to itself: It has to condition itself as free. And yet, as everyone knows, Newtonian science has long since receded in the face not least of quantum mechanics. At the same time, our understanding of material causation has developed exponentially, so that it is no longer possible to see our subjectivity as being "outside" our materiality. Developments in neuroscience, evolutionary biology, and genetics have established the material conditions of subjectivity itself. We are no longer where we once were.

These changes in theological cosmology and anthropology resonate with the developments in fundamental Christology. We cannot finally separate our beliefs about who Jesus Christ is and our beliefs about the world. This is one of the key junctures in Christian doctrine and finds its fullest expression in the New Testament doctrine of the New Creation. But the link between Christology and how we understand the world is broader even than this. Christians hold to a risen Christ: one who still lives in the integrity of his own humanity. This means that as Mediator he must continue to share our space and time. He is not absent but is rather present in a different way.[6] The premodern world understood this in terms of his "heavenly session." That the exalted Jesus was held to be present in heavenly space and time, at the very "highest point of heaven" (as Thomas Aquinas has it),[7] meant that he still lived in continuity with our own earthly life. This paradigm, in which theology and science converged (or Greek and biblical conceptions of the cosmos), is still robustly present in the early Reformers.

From the mid-sixteenth century onward, seismic changes came upon Western Christendom (on Catholic and Protestant alike) at the point where advancing scientific knowledge, which had a new and unparalleled power of description and explanation, unceremoniously displaced core Christian beliefs about the nature of the world in which we live.[8] Chief among these was simply the order of our material universe, which turned out not to be finite, circular, and transparent, like a large goldfish bowl teeming with movement and life, but was rather infinite, dark, largely empty, and expanding. In the classical "enchanted universe," the continuing life of the body of Jesus in heaven above ensured the fundamental transformability of space and time and the ultimate groundedness of matter in God and the divine energies. It ensured the potential and actual sacramentality of the material order.[9] It also ensured that the figure of Christ according to his full humanity and divinity would remain central to our understanding of the world in which we live. The dominant Pantokrator images of early Church art powerfully stated the all-encompassing presence of Christ, who, by virtue of being in heaven "above," could also be present everywhere or anywhere on earth "below" (cf. Eph. 4:10). With the dismissal of heaven, then, there was nowhere else for Christ to be, and so no point of contact between our space and time and his resurrected and exalted life.

How do we begin again, specifically in terms of Christology and anthropology? What are the key doctrinal elements that can bring about a reorientation of theological anthropology back into the material world in which, it seems, we are nevertheless at home: as complex materiality and pure subjectivity *at the same time*? How can we renew, in accessible theological ways, the twin domains of Christology and anthropology, which most directly experienced the impact of the determinism that was central to the emergence of the modern period? This becomes a key question when we consider the complexity of the doctrine of the exaltation for us today, for instance. It is in essence a simple doctrine of Christ's continuing life. But the role of cosmology in its traditional form presents to us particularly difficult problems for its reintegration into the life of the contemporary Church. We have to find less direct ways of getting at what is fundamental to this doctrine—namely, the openness of mind on the part of the theologian who needs to renounce the distancing and controlling mechanisms of the modern self in his or her engagement with the world.

What we are suggesting here is that it can be done by returning to what is one of the most fundamental questions of the Christian Church (if not the question by which it is defined). We need to learn to ask again, 'Where is Christ?' This is a question that was posed first in its fully ecclesial form with the discovery of the empty tomb. "Where is he?" was then answered in different ways in the post-resurrection narratives of encounter on the road to Emmaus and on the shore of Lake Galilee. Following the cosmology of the day, the early Church also answered the "where" question regarding the exalted Christ by reference to his place beside the Father in heaven. (In declaring that he was at the very highest point of the universe, even above the immaterial angels, Thomas Aquinas was himself answering the "where" question.) It was a question also that was of urgent concern to the Reformers, and especially to Calvin, who was already confronted with the scientific problems posed by Copernicanism.[10] But with the complete collapse of that traditional cosmology, the "where" question became redundant (even Bonhoeffer assimilates it into the question of "who" Christ is).[11]

In order to rediscover where Christ is and where we are, we shall present an exploration of the nature of the human act or, more specifically, of human acting "in the name of Christ." The anthropology of modern theology tends in fact to offer a somewhat attenuated view of human beings as historical agents of change. The location of subjectivity (in its self-understanding) as outside the material flow obscures the extent to which, as embodied human beings, we are actually within the material flow. Gathering insights from neuroscience, we shall touch on different aspects of the ethical/Christian act and show how key notions in theological anthropology appear in a new shape.[12]

The Elements of Change: Second-Person Neuroscience on Face-to-Face Cognition

If science is once again redefining our understanding of what it is to be a human embodied creature in a material world, with significant implications for future theological anthropology, then we shall have to decide where to begin. In his chapter in this book, Stephen J. Pope points to evolution as the key background to this question, in an evaluation of morality and natural law, while for Celia Deane-Drummond it is the question of our human moral and cognitive capacities as a form of evolutionary excellence, in particular in relation to other higher primates, with whom we have so much in common. For Johan De Tavernier it lies in a revived personalism; for Robyn Horner it is to be found in our Christocentric capacity for free self-giving. For Godzieba, the key point for the future lies in the potential intersection between our secular and ecclesial self-understanding in terms of our human embodied particularity and vulnerability.

All of these are valid points of departure. But if we are right to surmise that science is once again changing society (if, in Taylor's terms, a new "cosmic imaginary" is about to transform our inherited "social imaginary"), then we have to recognize that we are at a point where history itself as a dynamic process of scientific, cultural, social, and technological change is becoming visible on the surface of time in a way that demands our self-scrutiny as historical creatures. This must be a question posed within our most basic experience of being in time not individually but as a community (perhaps even "species" is not too extravagant a word here). This would mean that the background to this inquiry should be the most fundamental or "necessary" kind of history of all, even if it is not a "sufficient" one, which is surely that of our evolution. As human beings we have survived for millennia in communities that are larger than purely kinship groups. If we are the only hominid species to survive into the modern period, then this must have a good deal to do with our capacity to effect change in our own societies, allowing them to be highly adaptable to circumstances and environment, while maintaining, on balance, significant levels of social cohesion and solidarity.[13] To be human, then, is to be social, in ways that are distinct from the sociality of other higher primates, even if, as Deane-Drummond cautions us, we should not be too quick to deny the evident continuities.

It is not possible to begin with an evolutionary account of the human, which has at its center the human capacity to form resilient bonds of solidarity with those to whom we are not biologically related, without also taking into account our present scientific understanding of *how* we are capable of doing that. This introduces another field, that of human social cognition, which has recently come into prominence. All kinds of subtle things go on at a neurobiological level in face-to-face encounter (which needs to be both compared and contrasted with other higher-primate forms of social cognition).[14] These are taking place at such a level of complexity that our capacity to introduce meaningful measurement at that point is seriously disrupted. As Adam Zeman has pointed out, the human brain, with its "one hundred thousand million cells, making perhaps one hundred million million interconnections" is "the most complex system so far encountered anywhere in the universe."[15] It has recently been argued that human brains dynamically interact with each other in a way that becomes so intensive and dense that the metaphor of "dark matter" can be applied to the "event" (our term) of human social cognition.[16]

We are perhaps used to thinking of our neurobiological dimensions and our ordinary subjectivity as two quite separate zones: The physiological is the underlay, and the subjectivity sits on top. This is not right, however, since human subjectivity with all its inwardness and complexity arises or emerges from our physiology within a continuum: There is no sharp division between the two. It does not follow therefore that who we are in terms of our functionality—as reasoning, willing, and feeling beings—is confined to our subjectivity. The reality is that we already do these things at the neurobiological level (or who we are as body) prior to this activity's appearing in our consciousness (or who we are as mind). It is not at all the case, therefore, that we begin to reason, will, and feel emotions only in our consciousness; rather, the appearance of these things in our consciousness marks the point at which there are sufficient levels of activity in the brain for these biological process to enter our consciousness as our *self-aware* reasoning, willing, and feeling, with its capacity for free decision.[17]

What we need to understand here is that in human face-to-face encounter, a whole series of activities are already taking place that we tend in fact to associate solely with our higher-level subjective functioning. In our "hardwired," neurobiological self, we already dynamically interact with the second person through a set of mimetic or imitative responses that include mirroring body posture, facial expressions, and eye movement (as well, of course, as the conversational rhythms of speech). All these instinctive, biologically determined, mimetic responses simply "happen" in the face-to-face, but at the same time they are accompanied by a series of functions that we associate explicitly with our higher-level, conscious selves. In this way, we find that we engage emotionally with the other, and so make ourselves vulnerable to him or her. We also find that we are constantly monitoring the behavior of the other while also monitoring our own behavior (monitoring too what other observers might think of how we are interpreting the signs). This monitoring entails high levels of empathy (implying also the role of the imagination here). This interactive collaboration is purposeful, however, in that it is aimed at allowing us to come to a judgment about the other. Do we "get on" or not? Could we work together effectively if we had to? We are likely to feel this judgment purely as a "gut feeling" we have about the other, but it is in fact properly judgment to the degree that it combines discernment and decision through reasoning, willing, and feeling.[18]

Moreover, the judgment we come to about another person in the diagnostic interactivity of face-to-face encounter is very recognizably judgment in *complexity*. One of the many signals of its complex nature is that we are confronted with two different sources of knowledge about the other person. One involves the amygdala, with its intuitive, "nonverbal" kind of knowledge, which leaves us with a "feeling" about the other person based on our immediate encounter with him, while the other (the precuneus and posterior cingulate cortex) feeds in extraneous, secondhand, or "verbal" knowledge. These are incommensurable sources of knowledge from different areas of the brain.[19] Social judgment within the neurobiology of social cognition involves high levels of discernment and decision in highly complex contexts, even if this takes place within what we conventionally describe as our physiological "hardwiring." Our physiology is not just the organic substrate of consciousness; it is a level at which we can already recognize ourselves in the integrity of our functioning as willing, reasoning, empathizing, and feeling, and doing so already in confrontation with the complex challenges that arise from our purposeful interaction with other human beings.

The Ethical Self: Complexity and Reason

But there is, of course, more to the social self than just our hardwiring. In our higher-level subjectivity and consciousness, we are free to opt into the face-to-face of social cognition or not. We may choose to turn our backs on the other, or altogether to avoid him. We can feed in all kinds of higher-level cultural and personal strategies for managing our hardwired sociality. We do not escape our neurobiological conditioning, however, for if we find ourselves nevertheless in the face-to-face with another, our physiology will take over. We have to avoid people if we don't want that kind of engagement with them. And there are particular reasons why we may not want to engage with others (unless we already know them well, perhaps, and are relaxed in their company). New social cognition in a new face-to-face encounter always involves immense complexity, as we have seen. This is very demanding and exposes us to the risks that come from opening ourselves to another in interactive vulnerability. That nature should have made such an investment in our social cognition suggests that this must bring considerable survival benefits to *Homo sapiens*. The capacity to build new, collaborative relationships with others we do not know, or do not know well, allows us to function far more effectively as a social unit. We should consider that under normal circumstances, we are wary of complexity. Indeed, as Niklas Luhmann has it, human culture can be understood as a form of *autopoiesis*, involving extensively shared strategies for reducing or managing the complexity of the real.[20] For a big-brained hominid such as ourselves, complexity is inevitable and has to be warded off, since it exposes us to the risks of too much information, leading to incalculability and unpredictability, which may lead effectively to the disabling of our powers of judgment, which are so essential to a relatively weak, quick-witted creature.

But if the confrontation with neurobiological complexity is inevitable in our face-to-face encounters, then it is also to some degree inevitable in the higher-level life of our subject-self. After all, we bring our biology into our cultural and social forms of life. We cannot leave our own embodiment behind, since this, too, is essentially what we are. Complexity too is a feature of our close relationships, which cannot endure and flourish unless we learn to give a real place to the needs and perspective of the other when we come to decide what to do and how to live our lives. This can conflict with our instinct to reduce the complexity of the real, by filtering it through our own needs and point of view (through our own enlightened self-interest in fact). While we may be able to bring the other into this perspective of enlightened self-interest to some degree, sooner or later she will cease to fall within it and will become the center of a moral challenge for us: Can I accommodate her point of view within or beside my own? Do I so much want this relationship to flourish that I will allow the other potentially to complicate my life on an incalculable scale and even to remove the protective packaging from how I presently receive life, in all its seemingly infinite and potentially threatening complexity? This capacity to see the world through another's eyes must be closely related to the capacities for empathy and compassion that underlie our moral life.

Neuroscience can be helpful here again. In our moral decision-making, the brain is widely and diversely activated.[21] Feeling, cognition, empathy, and self-reflexivity all again come into play, and we are left again having to come to judgment about incommensurables. Everything in us wants to obviate the complexity by applying a textbook answer to our questions: We want to identify this situation as being of a specific type so that we can import a preexisting answer—textbook-wise—into it and so remove or reduce the complexity. But as we know, complexity and particularity go together, and human beings are immoderately particular. Moral situations frequently occur in clusters of complex persons, often situated with respect to each other in unstable or dynamic ways of power and powerlessness. People can be reduced to types only to a certain degree.

What we find in our situational moral decision-making, then, is exactly what we noted in the face-to-face. We are obliged to come to a decision about the other, and about ourselves in relation to the other, which means that we shall just have to come to the best decision we can, in a process of learning (which Christianity links with rich terms such as "prudence" and "wisdom"). Our ethical decisions will inevitably be to some degree personal, therefore, undertaken with an awareness of both risk and responsibility. These will be decisions that are made as a way of "choosing the other" or of choosing ourselves as being in a certain positive, empathetic, and caring relation to the other, or indeed even as a certain way of choosing that the world itself should be one in which human beings relate positively and constructively, or creatively, in this new way. The world itself becomes different according to how we manage our ethical choices. (Moral horror at Auschwitz is also the determination that this world should not be a world in which Auschwitz type events become the norm.)

We can recognize the structure of judgment that is at the heart of our ethical decision-making, as what Paul Janz has called "a finality of non-resolution."[22] This means it is a point in time where we accept that we can never know the right answer but that we must nevertheless make the best judgment we can (through patient listening to others, for instance, and openly consulting our own consciences). This is a form of "open" judgment, or judgment in vulnerability, which bears the marks of what we can think of in religious terms as self-sacrifice: It is a moment of self-giving, in responsibility and risk, for the sake of the other. It is a moment when we accept the creaturely nature of our own reasoning: that reason for us in those moments of ethical decision can be open only as *process* and not resolved or brought to an end. In our ethical "finality of non-resolution," we accept that we are deeply in life and that, in the complexity of the real, reason itself exhibits an open or even kenotic function, *for the sake of the other*, in *this* particular situation.

What we are describing here then is the following. "Second-person neuroscience" invites us to see our hardwired exposure to biological complexity as the price of being able to make an effective judgment about the other through open interaction. This judgment, in the face-to-face, is always open and *process;* and it is always personal in the sense that we ourselves are to some degree put at stake in this social cognitive process. But in the ethical act, we are seeing a similar or comparable process in the way that we accept the obligation to take seriously the perspective of the other. This too is "personal" but of course far more richly so, since the whole range of the resources of our self-awareness is available here, with its cultural, social, and personal nuances. But both states entail vulnerability, empathy, discernment, and decision, and both find a common axis in the way we reason in complexity.

The leaves open the possibility of a further conclusion. Who we are as body and who we are as mind are the same. This is the fundamental principle of the new science. To assert sameness here does not exclude difference, however. In our self-awareness we are free, while in our biological embodiment we are not. What comes into view here is the paradox of the human as "emergent" embodied consciousness, and this paradox is not without consequences. The first of these is that we have to be concerned with how this paradox is lived and resolved: How do we come into unity as both body and mind at the same time? This cannot be the same as our subjective instrumentalization of the body for purposes of pleasure, or even of well-being. This is a kind of unity of course, when the body suits or fits our intentionality seamlessly, and we are able to access the world around us without unconstraint and as we wish. But it is in fact only the semblance of a real unity in that it will fracture the moment the body fails us through weakening, ailing, and, finally, dying. Moreover, instrumentalization is a "unity" that can work only for as long as we can banish from our thoughts the certainty of death, and indeed of our own vulnerability and contingency. We can enjoy the successful instrumentalization of our body, but it is only fleeting, of the moment.

The contrast with the unity that accompanies our ethical acting is clear. This is not predicated on the successful realization of our self-centered intentionalities (however benign) but is specifically grounded in the personal acceptance of the complex reality of the other, whose own needs, or "point of view," will now disrupt our personal mechanisms for reducing complexity in life and making it manageable. Ethics understood in this sense requires a deep trust in life, sometimes seemingly against the evidence or at least in a condition of what mediators call "safe uncertainty."[23] Entering as free subject into the structure of our own hardwired neurobiology is in effect a difficult human journey into our own interdependence, vulnerability, and contingency. First and foremost, it is the embrace of our own creaturely personhood. It is not just that we have to let in complexity—the complexity of the undiluted real—but that we have to do this at the point where we also assume responsibility for coming to judgment about what to do in a complex situation. We express our creaturely personhood when we resolve to reason openly in ways that resist simple closure and reduction through self-interest (or any secondhand or textbook answer), for the sake of the other with her distinctive perspective and needs. This is to come to judgment in a way that explicitly accepts the risks of causing unwanted effects (or of finding that we have made things worse rather than better), the risks of being fallible and limited, and the risks of acting rather than not acting. In sum, the risks associated with being human.

The Religious Self: Language and the Christian Act

What we are suggesting is that new knowledge about our human social cognition offers us significant new insights into the universal properties of being human. The mind–body relation, as this comes into view in our ethical acts (where who we are as subject/mind integrates into who we are as body/matter), lies deeper than culture itself. It is a universal feature of human life, against which culture itself can be measured. The measuring of our culture against our embodiment must be in terms of the extent to which we are freely conforming with, and so allowing our subjectivity to integrate *within*, our embodied creatureliness. Another critical area here is the question of what language we use and indeed of *how* we speak. Language as conversation is itself a key factor in the face-to-face encounter. Our diagnostic capacity to evaluate each other as potential collaborator takes the form principally of language and is shown in the extent to which we can build a conversation together.

Contemporary neuroscience points to further, generally hidden dimensions of our language use in human encounter, however. Andy Clark talks of words as "material objects" that have a dual function. In the first place, they push our consciousness away from the biological flux, since language is always "amodal" in the sense that it can be transferred from one space–time context to another. In this way the development of language supports higher levels of human self-awareness and, for Clark, computational power. Here language indeed seems proximate to tool use.[24] But material words are also used to ground our "neural wet-ware."[25] The materiality of words (as sounds or shapes) fixes our fluid neural processes and allows us to know what we think. Thus words are a means that we use together in order to establish whether we can work together and *so shape this "here and now" together*. If words are genuinely like tools neurologically (i.e., if the brain thinks that words are a kind of tool—which is to say, material form that has been incorporated within the domain of our own embodiment so as to be an extension of it), then we can see their role as shaping the shared here and now of our face-to-face encounter in common and collaborative ways. We all know how deeply changed our apprehension of the world can be through certain sorts of communication with certain sorts of people. It is not just that a particular set of ideas has been transferred from one brain to another. Anyone who has heard a skilled orator speak knows that what is communicated is as much part of that shared here and now (the simple fact that "we were there") as it is of the conceptual meaning of the words used. To read Abraham Lincoln's Gettysburg Address is not the same as having been there and heard it.

It is in its use of language, in the face-to-face, that religious identity (or the "religious self") is set apart. Catholics experience the face-to-face normatively in eucharistic celebration when we celebrate and worship together, in face-to-face orientation with the officiating priest, who himself "stands in" for the person of Christ. We make direct eye contact with each other in exchanging the peace. But the language of this liturgical here and now is one that reflects the sacred, ecclesial nature of the space in which we encounter one another in the "body of Christ." Church as architectural structure is a space that is constructed, as was tabernacle and temple, through a collaboration between human beings and God. This eucharistic here and now is one that is "outside" time in the sense that it belongs to the deepest level of history, in which Christ is actively present in the fullness of his sacrificial life. This does not mean, of course, that we are not ourselves historically present at that place and time (how else can we be there?), but it does mean that this historicality of our human creatureliness is one that is taken up into Christ's own historical presence as the human being who is both "face-to-face" with us and also with the Father in heaven. However we construe the ancient cosmology of the affirmation that the living Christ "sits to the right hand of the Father in heaven" (which doesn't work for us anymore as cosmology, of course), the point is clear: In Jesus Christ our own humanity, which we share with him, is transformed in such a way that his body mediates between the way we are in the world (our own creaturely historicality) and the way he is now in the world (according to the transformation of his risen life, and the way God changes the world precisely through this transformation). In the Eucharist, the creative tension between old and new creation also becomes present for us.

Language here is at the center of things. This is not the affirmation of a eucharistic trans-signification. (If Christ is risen, then the eucharistic change must rather be an ontological one.) It is the recognition in our own eucharistic space and time that history itself—the history that we live out in our own "everydayness"—has been fundamentally changed in its utmost possibilities by the presence of the living Christ in history. The risen and exalted Christ is now "historical" in a different way. He is now, concretely, the place of divine fulfillment, where the created order is brought back to its root in him through its transformed material causation. We can think of his eucharistic presence as being the irreversible manifestation in the world of his unending Lordship, whereby we can say that he is truly in history and shares our history but now as the Lord of history. The Eucharist, then, is the place of Christ's dynamic mediation, between how he is presently in history, in his "face-to-face" with God, and his continuing sharing in our own "everyday' historical reality." This mediation or extension is the work of the Spirit and is, more intensively still, the *life* of the Spirit itself.

In our eucharistic coming together and encounter, the human face-to-face is brought back to its root in Christ, as the face-to-face between humanity and God, creature and Creator. But the transformational mechanism here is language itself. Language is that visceral, embodied, mimetic system of recognition and response, of identity and community, that builds our common here and now, through intimately interactive, empathetic, second-person engagement with one another (though always in a way that also brings the "third person" of our community into play). If words are "material objects" like tools (from a scientific perspective), with which we deploy our immediate material environment in order to build a shared human habitation that transforms the space in which we live with one another as deeply social animals, then language—Christian language, scriptural language, and especially liturgical language, as we encounter it in the Eucharist—is at the center of this.[26]

But the fact that language is so central here does not indicate a return to narrativism. It is the recognition that we cannot finally separate Christian language from the Christian act, which is the bedrock of discipleship. Christian language always calls to be internalized and to be made the fabric of our being. This internalization finds its fullest realization in the Christian act, where we act in the light of the imperatives of faith, which are linguistically and also mimetically mediated. In the midst of life and the concreteness of our own situational reality, we try to live as Christ tells us to live in scripture and tradition. But it is when we encounter him also as commissioning in history that these other forms of his speaking become properly his living voice: mandating a living response.

Modern Catholicism has always insisted on bringing the human act to the center of our self-understanding, very often against the resistance of contemporary trends. Godzieba begins his chapter in this book with a quotation from Blondel,[27] for whom the act is potentially the focal point of unity within the person and between the person and the world itself, in which we are—as Christians—called to act transformatively. In a tradition that reaches down to the contemporary period and to the work of John Paul II, we are rich in philosophies of the act. But what can we now understand about the human ethical act in the light of the new science, in a way that informs our reflections here about the divine image? What might that image be? And if we can discern it, what might its implications be for natural law, for instance, as the key point of intersection between Church and world, where we hold to the objectivity of what stands at the root of the Christian ethical life as a life of following?

The Divine Image

We inherit cultural and philosophical paradigms that presuppose a dualistic account of the self in subtle or less subtle forms. The "nonreductive physicalism" of contemporary science removes the scientific support for this position and, taking its distinctive problematic having to do with the separation of mind and matter (or, more influentially, the dominance of mind over matter), replaces that with an account of the self that presupposes the essential unity of mind and matter in us (or of who we are as matter and who we are as mind). A paradigm of unity rather than separation raises the question of integration: How can we be true—as cultural, social, and political beings—to the truth of our own condition of being both matter and mind? How can the many ways in which we think and act meaningfully conform to that truth, which is itself both structural and personal at the same time? These questions about integration—integration of the free subject-self with our own embodiment-in-encounter within the complex particularity of our own situational reality—will inevitably lead to a stronger sense of our innate human complexity. The more integrated we are within the social and biological reality of encounter, the more fully integrated we are in ourselves as body and mind, and the more particular. Particularity itself, as Godzieba and Boeve have argued, is key to our understanding of the human in both secular and religious ways.[28] It is our own "embodied particularity" and vulnerability that can be a point of intersection between a secular account of the self and a Christian one, representing a Church that is "expert in humanity" (Pope Paul VI).

We have argued that our human evolutionary predisposition to cooperation, which is manifest in our hardwired or "neurobiological self," can be identified as proto-ethical. All human beings share this given tendency to what we can think of as a limited, but nevertheless unconditional, engagement with the other, engagement as a lived and open determination of potential collaboration, involving a range of faculties. We can, of course, choose whether or not we shall engage with the other in this way, or whether we shall avert our eyes, turn our back or in some other way evade this encounter. But where we do positively choose to engage with the proximate other in this way, as we do when we enact ethical and caring motivations toward them, we find that we effectively embrace this neurobiological self, through a higher-level replication of its structure of reasoning, willing, feeling, and acting, within the complexity of our situational reality. This is a characteristic potentiality for all human beings, and we can read it as the human possibility of attaining the highest integration of mind and body through enacted love. It is a potent realization of who we are as self-aware human agents who can freely choose to become human material cause for and with the other. This has to be an important realization of our personal humanity, therefore, according to our truth as "intelligent embodiment." But with our new understanding of human social cognition, it has to be understood also as the effective acknowledgment of our material proximity or interconnectedness with the other, which further points to the experience of being human as the acknowledgment of living in a shared world. We know today that we are "in" the world as subject but that we are also "of" the world, and in some important sense can also be described as *being* world (to the degree that our emergent consciousness is "a feature of the world"). But in what sense can we say that this is Church? What actually happens that is different when our loving, integrating acts are distinctively Christian?

Three themes arise at this point. The first concerns questions of what kind of freedom and identity characterizes the Christian act. The second concerns its Christology, and the third points to issues in theory of natural law, which provides the locus classicus for discussion of moral objectivity, encompassing both secular and ecclesial perspectives.

Freedom and Identity

In the spirit of Blondel, we can argue that at every moment we are capable of deliberate movements of the body that will constitute an act. The act is constituted to the extent that we make a judgment—which is to say, exercise our free power of movement deliberately and with intention (even if this also involves instinctive, habituated responses). Where this is an ethical act that accepts the complex particularity of the situational reality in which we find ourselves and in which we seek the good of the other, it will entail judgment as a process of reasoning, willing, and feeling. This judgment does not cease with the doing of the act but evolves into judgment about ourselves and about who we are becoming through having freely acted in this way, in this particular situation. We ourselves become the object of our own judgment since we are now objectified to ourselves through the act (which could now in theory appear on YouTube), just as we are objectified to others. If we judge that we do not wish to be the person we are becoming by acting in this way, then we repent and apologize for what we have done. If we like that possible person, then we are open to doing it again.

The problem with identity formation in our ethical acts is that the meaning of the ethical act is always bound up with its particularity (since this meaning is intrinsic to the way we act in the unique complexity of particular situations). Since every complex situation is different, we cannot straightforwardly carry our ethical acting from one situation to another, which is what is implied by an "ethical identity." We can of course affirm the sense, for ourselves and others, that we are someone who acts ethically, and such an affirmation will consolidate the formation of virtuous habits. But human identity in the durability of what Paul Ricoeur calls its *idem* character is quite different from who we are in the moment of acting, or from what Ricoeur calls our *ipse* identity as agent.[29] Identity formation of a strong *idem* kind requires overt, explicit repetition above all (as we find in professional training, for instance). But how can we objectify repeated forms of ethical behavior across different situations when ethical acting will always have to embrace the complex particularity of each and every individual situation? How much easier it is to say that I am a policeman or a doctor and I do what policemen and doctors do in those situations, or to say I always take "a tough line," or that I always "go by the book." *Ipse* identity in ethical contexts does not easily come to expression as an *idem* identity, therefore, and so the heightened or augmented freedom that we can associate with the second phase of judgment in the act (where we come to judgment about ourselves as having acted in this particular way) is unlikely to find full expression in our available secular identities. Since a key element in this second phase of freedom is precisely its reflexive, self-aware character, which requires its objectification (I need to pass my professional exams and dress as a policeman before I can really have the sense that I am one), the capacity to body forth the most intensive form of our freedom through its objectification in an ethical *idem* identity will be lost. And if it is in our enacted ethical particularity that we are most radically human (in the integration of our body and mind), and if this humanity is intrinsically self-reflexive or self-aware, then something of our humanity will itself remain unrealized.

This play of freedom, moving from a freedom to judge what we shall do (*ipse*) to a freedom to judge ourselves as having done it (*idem*), allows us to read a Christian identity as being precisely an *idem* identity of the ethical act (irrespective of whether Christians actually fulfill that consistently or not—we are speaking here of logics internal to cultural systems of identity formation). In effect, Christianity embeds the ethical act within a self-regulating narrativity of the act itself (or discipleship and following), in a way that brings its intensification through the development of an *idem* identity. We are now given Christian exemplars of such ethical acting and are encouraged to have the common goal of imitating these, while our ethical identity is reinforced through a series of regularly performed practices—such as regularly attending a place of worship, publicly holding a particular set of beliefs, and undertaking forms of practical self-denial as well as community practices such as intercession and prayer. We are instructed to follow principles of discerning the rightness of moral judgments; we are trained in this rather as aesthetic taste might be cultivated through imitation and experience. We can publicly and privately opt for this identity in many cultural, differently nuanced ways. But if Christianity, and especially Catholic Christianity, offers a robustly *idem* form of identity, then it also has mechanisms for recalling that this is fundamentally one that is based on our *ipse* identity of the act or is a form of being grounded in the moment of our becoming (or "following"). Here we can begin to see the potential tension between the practical, social-action dimensions of our Christian faith and the other, more cultural or purely intellectual ways in which this faith is maintained and developed. Above all, these need to be integrated, one with the other, if an ecclesial identity is to conform to the inner logics of its own transformativity.

Christology

Much turns in our argument on this second, augmented freedom of our self-reflexivity in identity formation. This is the freedom we have to affirm who we are across the spacio-temporal gaps that separate one situation of complex particularity, in which we are called to act ethically, from another. This is a strongly shared identity that, like ethical acts themselves, is self-communicating and socially transformative. The question arises, however, as to what extent it is purely a cultural identity: just one tradition among others. The claim to be more than this is not finally distinguishable from simply being a cultural tradition that is defined in part by its own claim to universalism: an increasingly incoherent claim, in fact, in an increasingly pluralistic world.

And it is difficult to see how this claim can ever be supported if Christianity rests on certain texts and memories and on a certain narrative that sustains all manner of related practices and acts. If the Christian way of life is a saving way of life in the terms outlined above, as enabling our most radical freedom through an identity formation as ethical, meaning that we can function in a distinctively personal, highly integrated way in the very midst of life's complex reality, then it is so solely on cultural grounds.

It is at this point that we encounter most directly the effects of our own dualistic age. In the modern period, language has been viewed as being most fundamentally conceptual and the communication of concepts, or narratives. We can count on the fingers of one hand those thinkers in the modern period for whom the material nature of the sign—traditionally emphasized in world religions—has been important.[30] But we know today from a scientific perspective that language is first and foremost material form and that words are encoded as such in the human brain. This means that we have to have a different, nondualistic understanding of texts, words, and narratives. If we define the Holy Spirit as being transformative of matter, according to the *ordo salutis*, rather than being a form of transcendence that takes us away from the material, then arguably we have to consider the possibility of presence in language as such but above all in those texts and words that the Christian community has judged to be divinely inspired and that form the bedrock or matrix of the narratives by which we live. In other words, we have to extend the concept of divine presence in history, where history is defined as the flow of material causation, from apostolic succession and eucharistic real presence to other forms of Christian material culture. In a parallel way, we need to allow the possibility that the living body of Christ is mediated, through the work of the Holy Spirit, into diverse material contexts and situations, beyond the purely sacramental. There is a corollary here, however, since it is only according to his Lordship that Christ is exalted and "distributed" in this sense. What can appear to be a purely cultural extension will necessarily turn out to be also a claim concerning the authority of God and the transformative power of Christ's commissioning us into his Church in the world today.

It is in our being commissioned, more than anywhere else, that we presuppose the reality of our encounter with Christ in faith. This must finally be objective if it is to have its proper authority. Most of us would want to argue for the objectivity or reality of Christ's presence in the Eucharist, however ecclesial and cultural the Eucharist may also be. In the same way we need to learn to be more explicit theologically about how we understand the reality or ontology of Christ for us today as we encounter him in our own situational particularity, as the one who calls us into the complexity of the real.

What this may mean, furthermore, is that the "augmented" freedom we experience in the formation of our identity as Christian, and which is the deepest realization of *our creatureliness* (from a Christian point of view), emerges from the intersection of our own natural freedom and his divine freedom, or sovereign, liberating power as risen, which is communicated to us historically in the life of the Holy Spirit. We can certainly acknowledge the place of the imagination, as the images of Christ we have open immense horizons of possibility in our Christian judgments. But there must be something more than this at work. If the Christian claim is that Christ is risen, and if the Holy Spirit flows between him and us, then there must be a sense too in which we can claim that our Christian freedom is not just culturally produced but is a human-to-human effect (a "face-to-face" effect, indeed) between Christ and his Church. His risen life must touch our own lives precisely at the point where we are called into our own deepest freedom, in the complex depths of history and the real. Furthermore, the objectivity of this must be bound up with the nature of the world as now containing his risen body. This implies in the calling of faith the sense—surely always an aesthetic rather than calculative logic—that his Easter space and time intersects with our own space and time in a way that changes our experience of being human in the sense of being in the world, as part of the world, as being world, through being in him.

Natural Law

But can we move back from this strongly theological way of speaking into natural law, as a structure that can hold Church and world positively together, while observing necessary distinctions? In his discussion of the natural-law tradition, Stephen Pope draws attention to John Mahoney's sense that there must be an interplay between our "evolutionary social cognition" and our "altruism." The very recent "second-person neuroscience" presented here allows us to fill out this intuition in the quite precise terms of the structure of the "neurobiological self" as we appear to ourselves through scientific research. Can we therefore read as a form of natural law, or indeed as something consistent with a natural-law orientation, this proto-ethical structure of the self that neuroscience sees?

The answer to this has to be conditional. Since it is grounded in our human physiology as such, we can point to it as a universal structure and say that it is therefore a condition of all human life.[31] But since the key feature of the reasoning that takes place at the neurobiological level is its confrontation with complexity (in what Schilbach et al. call the "dark matter" of face-to-face cognition), we have to acknowledge the problem that the function of consciousness is overwhelmingly to reduce complexity. It does this biologically (in terms of primary perception) but also socially (in terms of social hierarchies and identifiers) and discursively (in terms of Luhmann's linguistic systems) as well as personally (through seeking our innate self-interest). We must ask therefore: If the use of our faculties of intellect and will in processes of judgment serves generally to reduce complexity, then what kind of normativity can we attribute to the obligation to embrace complexity—the complexity of the real—which seems to be innate to the ethical act?

The answer I propose here is that the normativity lies not in the ethical itself but rather in the relation between subjectivity and embodiment in us, within the continuum of mind and matter as contemporary science sees it, which underlies the ethical act. In other words, the real normativity lies in the relation between subjectivity and embodiment such that the rejection of complexity is the denial also of who we most fundamentally are as both body and mind. Alternatively, the embrace of who we are is simultaneously the *realization* of our own unity, as integration of both body and mind, or embrace of our own freedom and truth (as contingent, vulnerable, interdependent, and mortal). In this way, we could describe it also as the realization or most radical practice of our own humanity. The difference then between our "creaturely" (Christian) and "non-creaturely" (secular) humanity would lie in the nature of our integration. If Christ truly lives and is a real Christ, then for Christians who accept him in faith as the ground of their acts, integration would be not only integration of the self in the complex reality of the real world but also a further integration of who we are, or become, as creature into the world itself, as this has been taken up and transformed by the divine act in Jesus Christ. This in turn would give it an objectivity, though not one susceptible of direct verification as a datum. Its "verification" would lie in the capacity of the Christian form of life to communicate a meaning that is not just my meaning or yours but also, and more fundamentally, the meaning of the world. This would mean that Christians are differently, and more intensively, in this shared world. But as the most radical practice of our humanity, one in which our own powers of action are overtaken by a different order of power, this would also mean that this "being in the world differently" would nevertheless be recognizable by those who do not share our faith: as a transformational potential that lies within our acting in every moment, an acting that, in Godzieba's quotation from Blondel, is both a "fact" and a "necessity."

CHAPTER 6

Incarnation in the Age of the Buffered, Commodified Self

Anthony J. Godzieba

The Problem

When you catch human beings in the act of being human, what do you catch them doing, fundamentally? Maurice Blondel said that you catch them acting. They cannot not act.

> Action, in my life, is a fact, the most general and the most constant of all, the expression within me of a universal determinism; it is produced even without me. More than a fact, is it a necessity. . . . More than a necessity, action often appears to me as an obligation. . . . If I do not act out of my own movement, there is something in me or outside of me that acts without me; and what acts without me ordinarily acts against me. . . . Head, heart and hands, I must therefore give them over willingly or else they are taken from me.[1]

Despite the disproportion and conflict that occur between the infinite perfection we will and the less than fulfilled actuality we achieve, we persist in acting. For Blondel, our persistence is driven by the desire for the fullness of being, and thus by "the one thing necessary" that "keeps [my action] from falling back into nothingness,"[2] a force that *transcends* my actions but nevertheless is encountered only *within* those actions themselves: the supernatural, the mystery of God.[3] In his *Letter on Apologetics*, Blondel characterizes the correct employment of reason in apologetics as the "method of immanence" and famously describes the supernatural "as indispensable and at the same time as inaccessible for man."[4]

Charles Taylor, in *A Secular Age*, says that we catch human beings in the role of disenchanted "buffered selves" schooled by the modern "social imaginary" to disavow transcendence. His analysis of secularization describes a retreat that is the hallmark of Western culture after 1600, an "exclusive humanism" rooted in Nominalism, developed throughout early modernity, and eventually characterizing and dominating the modern secular order. Unlike the premodern "porous self" that was open to transcendent influences and forces, the buffered self is "disengaged" from any possible transcendence that lays "beyond the boundary," and rather "giv[es] its own autonomous order to its life."[5] This modern moral order infiltrates what Taylor terms the "social imaginary"—that is, "the generally shared background understandings of society, which make it possible for it to function as it does."[6] The contemporary social imaginary is a legacy of the Enlightenment, which developed a "powerful humanism" that presupposed "an eclipse/denial of transcendence which tends to make this humanism an exclusive one."[7] This social imaginary is accompanied by a "cosmic imaginary" that envisions a vast, unfathomable, disenchanted universe without a sense of God or purpose. It is "impersonal in the most forbidding sense, blind and indifferent to our fate."[8] This construal of reality is also accompanied by a shift in the conception of time, from first an eschatological and then a teleological understanding to one that makes us anxious not only by imagining the infinite stretch of time before us into the future, but especially by "the vast expanse of time which lies behind us [and] hides the process of our genesis."[9]

Finally, the American cultural critic Chris Hedges, in his book *The Empire of Illusion*, says that we catch human beings living not only commodified consumer lives but lives measured over against a celebrity culture that denigrates ordinary life and narrates "authenticity" in terms of glitzy material consumption and success.

> In the Middle Ages . . . stained glass windows and vivid paintings of religious torment and salvation controlled and influenced social behavior. Today we are ruled by icons of gross riches and physical beauty that blare and flash from television, cinema, and computer screens. . . .

We fashion our lives as closely to these lives of gratuitous consumption as we can. Only a life with status, physical attributes, and affluence is worth pursuing.[10]

While Hedges focuses on examples from contemporary American culture, his analysis can apply beyond the United States, owing to the widespread effects of globalization. According to his analysis, celebrity consumer culture creates an all-encompassing narrative where image equals reality, where attractive images generated by the entertainment industry become the dominant objects of aspiration, and where personal identity and dignity are measured by standards embodied by those who are famous because they are celebrities and who are celebrities because they are famous. This narrative sketches out a fantasy world of short-term material pleasures undergirded by narcissism, where we are urged "to generate, almost unconsciously, interior personal screenplays in the mold of Hollywood, television, and even commercials."[11] In this world, cultural participants are divided into "haves" and "have-nots." The "have-nots" are encouraged to think of themselves as possible celebrities and are offered impossible-to-fulfill aspirations that leave them permanently defeated and yet hungry for more—they become willing participants in their own degradation. "The working classes . . . are shut out of television's gated community. They have become largely invisible. They are mocked, even as they are tantalized, by the lives of excess they watch on the screen in their living rooms. Almost none of us will ever attain these lives of wealth and power. Yet we are told that if we want it badly enough, if we believe sufficiently in ourselves, we too can have everything. We are left, when we cannot adopt these impossible lifestyles as our own, with feelings of inferiority and worthlessness."[12] The result, Hedges argues, is a "cultural retreat into illusion" that is "a form of magical thinking." A celebrity culture promotes a division between the majority who chase illusions in reaction to alienation and anxiety and a small minority who critique these illusions and propose social and political alternatives to the status quo.[13]

Hedges's basic argument is not new. It has an important antecedent in Max Horkheimer's and Theodor Adorno's famous indictment of the homogenizing, vulgarizing, and manipulative character of late-capitalist Western culture.[14] It also is indebted to a tradition of critiques of capitalism represented by works such as Daniel Boorstin's *The Image: A Guide to Pseudo-Events in America* (1961), Guy Debord's *La societé du spectacle* (1967), and Neil Postman's *Amusing Ourselves to Death* (1985).[15] However, we have lingered a bit longer over his analysis because it provides a necessary repositioning of Taylor's argument.

Both authors discuss the all-important issue of the limits confronting human experience and chronicle what they estimate to be the truncated possibilities available in the contemporary West in the wake of modernity. Taylor emphasizes epistemic limits that over time have developed into social and cultural limits, and yet he finds hope in what he discerns as a widespread human yearning for a long-term fulfillment that a flattened-out secularization ultimately fails to satisfy. We must look beyond framing life as pure immanence, he argues, and see the real possibility of a spiritual ascent "beyond the boundaries."[16] On the other hand, Hedges's relentlessly downbeat portrayal of societal decay (whether one agrees with it or not) at the very least makes a reasonable case that the buffer around the "buffered self" has become narrower, tighter, offering fewer and meaner possibilities for human existence.[17] We are witnessing a truncation of possibilities that is more economic than epistemic: Consumer capitalism's ability to co-opt and colonize everything, only now more insidiously as commodified celebrity culture, denigrates ordinary life and narrates "authenticity" in terms of the twin dreams of media influence and grandiose success at material consumption. To use Vincent Miller's precise formulation, "we face a cultural infrastructure that is capable of absorbing all other cultures as 'content' to be commodified, distributed, and consumed."[18] In this context, so-called "fulfillment" is only ever short-term, if it occurs at all, and depends completely on therapeutic metaphors and consumerism's definition of "freedom" as merely the freedom to choose among attractive images. Hedges's analysis thereby provides a necessary corrective to any naive approach to the human condition—theological or otherwise—that may tend to forget capitalism's "hybridizing, transgressive, promiscuous" nature.[19]

In 2004, the Vatican's Congregation for the Doctrine of the Faith issued a "Letter . . . on the Collaboration of Men and Women in the Church and in the World," in which the very first sentence styled the Church as "expert in humanity."[20] However, in light of the "anthropological fundamentals" that Blondel, Taylor, and Hedges have identified, the Church—and more specifically Catholic theology—has proven itself rather inexpert. From a contemporary perspective, Christian theological anthropology has been good at dealing with the first constant, *action*, ever since the development of a less metaphysical and more personalist theological anthropology beginning in the decades immediately preceding the Second Vatican Council.[21] When dealing with the second constant, *secularization*, theology has been sometimes insightful but more often clumsy. When relying on a strong theology of creation and the sacramental imagination, a contemporary theological anthropology can confidently articulate and abide by the paradox that the non-divine (humanity and the world) is both theonomous and autonomous and that its autonomy is theonomously grounded, as *Gaudium et Spes* insisted: "For by the very circumstance of their having been created, all things are endowed with their own stability, truth, goodness, proper laws and order. Man must respect these as he isolates them by the appropriate methods of the individual sciences or arts."[22] But theology fumbles away its incarnational perspective when it considers the non-divine to be a godless and bankrupt "modern secular order" and treats it as the excluded other (as happens, for example, in "Neo-Augustinianism").[23] And when dealing with the third constant, *the consumer formatting and truncation of contemporary experience*, theology has been relatively ignorant or even clueless. Behind theology's back, so to speak, class and economics have become transfigured and entwined into a seemingly unstoppable hegemony.

One illustration of the power of this hegemony—consumer capitalism's ability to co-opt everything—is what it does with "difference." Over the past half-century, this concept has been the major theoretical and practical strategy for breaking down some of the monolithic prejudices that have constrained Western personal, social, and political life since the Enlightenment. As Michelle A. Gonzalez rightly notes in her chapter in this volume, "difference" is a fundamental dimension of any anthropological reflection, including the theological, especially since "we embody difference within the complexity of our identity."[24] She points us in the direction of Latino/a theologians who have productively emphasized the fundamental hybrid character of culture and how the continual embodied performance of difference helps "to dismantle dualistic constructions of race that plague identity politics" and radically undermine traditional notions of the body.[25] But the hegemony of commodified consumer culture is at work even here, functioning as the overarching grid within which we understand all of these acts of liberation. In the contemporary context, as Terry Eagleton has pointed out, there are three contested notions of "culture" jostling for space: "culture as civility, culture as identity, and culture as commercial or postmodern."[26] The first is "culture" in the nineteenth-century sense of High Culture, the all-inclusive medium of the highest aspirations and universal values of humankind. The second is culture as identity politics, "the affirmation of a specific identity—national, sexual, ethnic, regional—rather than the transcendence of it. And since these identities all see themselves as suppressed, what was once conceived of as a realm of consensus has been transformed into a terrain of conflict."[27] Lastly, there is culture as commercial, commodifying the different identities of the second type to the point of retaining fragmented differences while draining the conflict; here, the differences are sold back to their "owners" and the only overarching value is cash. Eagleton argues that today all three notions of culture uneasily coexist, but I would argue that in a globalized world it is the third, commodification, that has to power to subsume all the rest and erase difference, a danger to which Gonzalez alludes.[28]

The result of this hegemony has been that the dominant view of "person" has been reshaped to such a degree that traditional Christian notions of grace and salvation, along with the orientation toward transcendence they imply, have become literally unthinkable for many. The criterion of "authenticity" that is asserted—or rather preached—by celebrity consumer culture may eventually render, for example, the Vatican's strong emphasis on the "New Evangelization" or the attempts at evangelization through intellectual argument (e.g., the "Court of the Gentiles" initiated by Pope Benedict XVI) ineffective at best or failed curiosities at worst.[29] And the continual paranoia about "secularization," "modernity," and "liberalism" that grips certain Catholic theological reactions to the contemporary situation—an attitude rigorously pushed to the point where we can call it "the paranoid-critical method"—will not provide a productive response either. The widespread vituperative and at times "apocalyptic" Catholic critiques of modernity and its influence on contemporary life issue from a fear that modern concepts of human autonomy will necessarily morph into Pelagian or even atheist disavowals of the human dependence on God. In the end, such apocalypticism boils down to positing a univocal meaning to "modernity," one that equates modernity with the presupposition *etsi Deus non daretur*.[30] However, any claim about the bankruptcy or godforsakenness of "modernity" is not one that can be made in good faith, not only in light of the success of modern Catholic spiritual theology that took into account modern views of the self (e.g., Ignatius of Loyola, Francis de Sales, Teresa of Avila), but also in the light of recent thicker analyses of the postmedieval period that reveal not only different "modernities" but also demonstrate that belief in both transcendence and grace's presence in the world, though anguished, has never been completely extinguished, a point forcefully argued by recent developments in theological aesthetics.[31]

An Attempt at an Alternative: Incarnation Unlimited

The task of theological anthropology in the twenty-first century is to formulate an alternative narrative about God, humanity, and grace—a more convincing alternative to the default "secular" or "celebrity culture" narratives. It would be more convincing because it would be a more likely story, one that articulates the truth of human personhood and of God's relation to the person in a way that speaks to the yearnings of the human heart for true happiness, well-being, and fulfillment. In this task Blaise Pascal, of all people, helps us define our goal.

> Men despise religion. They hate it and are afraid it may be true. The cure for this is first to show that religion is not contrary to reason, but worthy of reverence and respect. Next, make it attractive, make good men wish it were true, and then show that it is. Worthy of reverence because it really understands human nature. Attractive because it prom-ises true good.[32]

The goal is the creation of an apologetic for Christian faith that is confi-dent and powerful enough to do two things: (1) show how belief in God infiltrates human experience and offers the fulfillment (the "true good") that all persons crave, and then (2) make that demonstration so attractive and pertinent to everyday life that it is almost impossible to resist.

(1) As a way of accomplishing the first major task, we can look to the type of analysis of faith and experience that the theologian Walter Kasper offers under the rubric of "natural theology." This is certainly not the natural theology defined by the standard theological reference books as "the body of knowledge about God which may be obtained by human reason alone without the aid of Revelation."[33] It is rather a more nuanced and Catholic search for "the natural 'access-point' of faith" that proposes to demon-strate "the internal reasonableness of a faith which has its substantiation in and from itself."[34] Faith and experience are joined in a hermeneutic circle: Faith is necessarily mediated by our contextually situated experience, while experience itself exhibits an always already-present transcendental faith in meaning that can be expanded by its encounter with the transcendental object of faith, the divine mystery of the God who is love (1 John 4:16).

This demonstration has two stages. The first is a transcendental-anthropological analysis of the structure of human experience, an analysis that discloses the fundamental relation of that experience to transcendence and faith. This analysis reveals five crucial aspects that, when taken to-gether, testify to human experience's intentional drive beyond any finite "closure."[35] First, experience involves both *objective and subjective elements in a dialectical relationship;* that is, the person is affected by reality and in-terprets this interaction in a meaningful way through words, images, and symbols. Next, experience is *historical, emerging over time;* it involves past memories and future hopes, both converging in the present. It is open to what is new, and is never closed or completed. Third, experience is *his-*

torical in another way: It never occurs "in general" but is always situated and inflected by historically particular horizons of understanding. Fourth, experience is always *hermeneutical,* always *interpreted experience.* "We never experience reality in itself; we always experience it as something that has a specific meaning for us; objective experience and interpretation of experience can never be completely separated."[36] Finally, experience always involves us with *what is other than us,* the crucial "non-I" element that is not a projection but that offers resistance to us and contrasts with our expectations. In sum, the convergence of these five aspects reveals experience to be both thoroughly contextual and thoroughly open beyond itself because of its inherent incompleteness; no finite experience can ever give us the certain fulfillment that we crave. "Experience becomes a way . . . into a mystery that is even greater and never to be completely plumbed."[37]

The very structure of experience, then, opens us to infinite mystery that is nothing less than the transcendental horizon of all human experience. And here, according to Kasper, we discover the religious dimension of human experience: "Religious experience is an indirect, not a direct type of experience; it is an experience which we have 'in, with and under' our other experiences. It is therefore not just one experience alongside other experiences, but rather the basic experience present in our other experiences; it is an experience that presides over and gives a pervasive tone to all other experience."[38] The indirection of religious experiences has the character of everyday "disclosure situations" that point beyond themselves to the overarching mystery, the unifying horizon of the "foreground" of our everyday experience.

This first stage, then, is a transcendental anthropological argument demonstrating the fundamental openness of historically situated human experience to all-encompassing mystery. The second stage seeks to articulate this mystery's character insofar as it is possible, highlighting the natural access-point of faith while respecting reason's limits. Kasper finds the crucial clue in modern philosophy's insistence that freedom, not substance, is the true overarching condition of reality. "Being, therefore, is act, accomplishment, happening, event. Not self-contained being but existence, or freedom that goes out of itself and fulfills itself in action, is now the starting point and horizon of thought."[39] The "melancholy of fulfillment" that permeates our experience alerts us to the unconditioned fulfillment that we fully intend but that is unavailable within the realm of human action. "Only in encounter with absolute freedom can the person reach inner peace and inner fulfillment." But we have no objective grasp of absolute freedom, only a pre-apprehension (*Vorgriff*) and "fragmentary anticipations" of its character.[40]

How, then, can we ever be fulfilled? Only in a personal way, through relationships where the "non-I" catalyst of experience has a personal character. One key to Kasper's entire argument is his insight into the meaning of "person": at the same time both a unique, irreplaceable individual and "ordered to reality in its entirety," as one "who exists only in self-actualization in response to another person and as ordered to other persons." Our fulfillment occurs "only by emptying ourselves out in love, so as to realize our own intentional infinity."[41] But this, too, seems blocked: Every relationship, no matter how intense, shares in the limits imposed by our human condition.

But while it may appear that experience is merely intentionality without fulfillment, the possibility of fulfillment exists.

> The human person can reach definitive fulfillment only if it encounters a person who is infinite not only in its intentional claims on reality but in its real being; that is, only if it encounters an absolute person. Thus a more appropriate concept of person as the always unique "there" of being leads necessarily to the concept of an absolute, a divine person. If we understand the person as an always unique realization of being, then the category of person as applied to God does not mean an objectification of God. On the contrary, the concept of person is able to express in a new way the fact that in God being subsists in a unique way, that is, that God is *ipsum esse subsistens* ["subsistent being itself," echoing Thomas Aquinas].[42]

Natural theology, then, recognizes infinite mystery as the all-pervasive ground that is present "in, with, and under" everyday experience. In addition, it can detect at least something of the fundamental character of infinite mystery and of its inherent relationship with us. Reality manifests a logic of giving that traditional metaphysics misses. The only proper language for the all-encompassing mystery is that of the personal, which necessarily implies relationality, one's openness to an other. If we use the word "God" to refer to the total meaning of reality that forms the horizon of human life and actions, then our desire for an inherently personal fulfillment can give us a pre-apprehension (*Vorgriff*) of the character of that absolute mystery: a gracious *giver* who takes the initiative to encounter us in a personal fashion and graciously grant us the free space that makes life and action possible. "Seen in the horizon of the person, the meaning of being is love. . . . To call God a person is to say that God is the subsistent being which is freedom in love."[43] But as to the authentic character of that person and the extent and specific performance of that love, however, natural theology can say no more.

This more expansive Catholic natural theology thus succeeds in depicting how experience, faith, and revelation are related in a hermeneutical circle: Human experience, desiring fulfillment, points toward revelation, which fills out and provides the true explanation of human experience, which in turn responds to revelation in faith. Faith is not defined in opposition to reason but describes a mode of life where one is personally open to absolute mystery that embraces all aspects of human activity, including rationality. And within the limits of natural theology, something else is gained: "being" is redefined. Its meaning "is therefore to be found not in substance that exists in itself, but in self-communicating love."[44] The description of experience at the natural access-point of faith thus reveals that supernatural revelation is not extrinsic to that experience but rather would be its superabundant fulfillment. Kasper's natural theology, then, is a contemporary translation of Blondel's "method of immanence" and of the paradox this method reveals: The supernatural is indispensable yet inaccessible through purely rational means. Once the transcending intentionality of human experience can be demonstrated, at this point an alternative to the "secular" and "celebrity culture" narratives can already be sketched.

(2) But this transcendental-personalist argument is not enough. The second major task—to make the alternative narrative about God, humanity, and grace relevant and attractive—demands a thicker and more detailed phenomenology of human experience. When crafting this alternative narrative, we need to take seriously Vincent Miller's distinction between ovararching strategies and the particularity of specific tactics: "In advanced capitalist societies, no religion or traditional culture maintains anything approaching a strategic control of the cultural field or, for that matter, control of the cultural formation of its own faithful. For that reason, a theological engagement with consumer culture must take place at the tactical level"—that is, at the level of particular life practices that engender local, particular resistance.[45] While not agreeing completely, I wish to point out that Lieven Boeve and I have made a similar argument about the necessity of focusing on particularity, stressing that the Incarnation, with the resulting focus on the particularity of embodiment, is the fundamental hermeneutical strategy of theology.[46]

In line with this fundamental hermeneutic, I propose that a further productive way of imagining and articulating the realities of the self and the social imaginary beyond the constraining limits of the celebrity consumerist fantasy is to think by means of the body, so that we might craft a more robust Catholic theology of embodiment. A theological anthropology and theological aesthetics built around the incarnational and sacramental imagination can be shown to offer a more likely story that acknowledges limits while pointing to what exceeds them—namely, the transcending intentionality of the human person, which is disclosed in the peak revelatory moments of creation, the Incarnation, and the Resurrection of Christ.[47]

This anthropology has both philosophical and theological aspects. Philosophically, it builds on a phenomenology of embodiment as developed by Maurice Merleau-Ponty (especially in his classic *Phenomenology of Perception*).[48] Theologically, it builds on the recognition that the Incarnation is the fundamental hermeneutical framework for Christian reflection on the experience of faith. The phenomenological analysis helps us understand embodiment as extending beyond its merely "literal" sense (i.e., the material-empirical) and revealing a core truth about the body: its intentional focus on the world as its perceptual task and its deployment toward the world in fulfillment of that task. The lived body is thus essentially "excessive"—it is active in ec-static intentional performance that, in Merleau-Ponty's words, "surges toward objects to be grasped and perceives them," embodied action with intentional meaning.[49] Theologically, it presupposes the intimate connections among creation, Incarnation, and the Resurrection of Christ. The theonomous ground of creation's autonomy is revealed both in creation's participation in divine life granted "in the beginning" by God's initiative and in humanity as it is made in God's "image and likeness" (Gen. 1:1, 26). The presence of this theonomous ground is intensified at the Incarnation (where God embraces human finitude and vulnerability to the fullest extent, except for sin [Heb. 4:15]) and, at the Resurrection of Christ, ratified as the ultimate possibility of human life. The Paschal mystery reveals an important clue about embodiment specifically and materiality more generally—their possibilities and their roles in the economy of salvation.

The grammar of resurrection is impossible without the grammar of incarnation, because resurrection is the most intense expression of the truth of incarnation. And the doctrine of the Incarnation, in one of its most fundamental meanings, is the recognition and celebration of the capacity of materiality and the particular to mediate divine presence. The Resurrection actualizes the possibilities of embodiment already disclosed in the Incarnation, which in turn has actualized the *capax divinitatis* already inherent in corporeality from creation. The incarnation of God in Christ confirms the revelatory value of this always vulnerable embodied mediation. In other words, the Incarnation is God's embrace of limitation and vulnerability from within. Christ takes on every bit of human vulnerability, and when the destiny of that vulnerability is revealed in death, Christ takes that upon himself as well. What is also revealed, however, is that this mortal destiny is not ultimate, but penultimate: embodied life's rootedness in God, ratified at creation and made even more explicit with the Incarnation, has its ultimate destiny in *theōsis*. Thus we become holy not in spite of our lives but because of our lives. The body's paradoxical status—radically particular, and yet open to universal solidarity—is both confirmed and intensified by the Incarnation. Indeed, the Incarnation reveals and performs the lived body's dialectical structure: singular, and yet open to others; finite, and yet open to infinite grace; vulnerable, and yet redeemed, not in spite of but because of its vulnerability. On God's initiative, this dialectical "and yet" structure becomes a *locus theologicus* and one crucial arena wherein the economy of salvation is performed. Indeed, the intentional "and yet" structure of embodied subjectivity and of materiality generally is our point of access to grace.[50] If the lived body's intentional arc can be seen as "excessive," as a surge "outward" and toward relationship and fulfillment, the revelation of God's gift of relationship with creation can be construed as a surge "inward" toward us and toward the world. We are thus given a share in divine life and are rooted in what the theologian Klaus Hemmerle termed a "trinitarian ontology," which defines "being" not in terms of substance but in terms of love, relationality, and communion. The "secret" of this ontology, according to Hemmerle, "is called love, self-giving. From this structure all being, all thinking, all activity opens out," impelling the believer to see everyday phenomena anew and "reread" them for signs of revelation.[51]

Thus the very center of Christian faith, belief in God as Trinity—that God is a communion of persons in love—provides a resource for an alternative narrative of the human condition. The tradition of faith affirms our own rootedness in divine love and the ec-static intentionality and relationality that flows from this. For example, the heart of the Christian tradition supports the theological anthropology and the reconstruction of public theology that Rosemary P. Carbine advocates in her essay in this volume: a move away from a "modern rationalist view of public life . . . constituted by autonomous, self-interested individuals" and toward a view that persons are constituted by relationality and are "shaped via negotiation of these relations."[52] This alternative narrative, as Carbine points out, is found not only in feminist, womanist, and *mujerista* theological anthropology but also in Vatican II's *Gaudium et Spes*, which "outlines a relational anthropology, rooted in creation in the image and likeness of a triune God."[53] What Carbine describes as the task of negotiating relations and working for the common good across multiple communities of belonging is nothing less than an incarnated practical performance of the surging intentionality that characterizes embodied personhood. Seeking the good of others and doing so based on the love that God has given us is Blondel's "action" projected on a cultural scale.

There is yet a further important point to be made. A theological anthropology that has the Incarnation as its fundamental hermeneutical strategy can lead seamlessly to a theological aesthetics. This is clearly a necessary step for a twenty-first-century theology, since it is necessarily practiced in a hyper-aestheticized postmodern (or even post-postmodern) context. Images, music, and media are everywhere—they are the common vehicles for meaning in contemporary capitalist culture, and it is theology's duty to tell a "more likely story" about them as well. That story would start with the two surging intentionalities, human faith and divine revelation, meeting at the locus of the lived body's finite particularity; its limits are the necessary precondition for the experience of transcendence. The attractiveness of the good that Pascal wishes religion to engender is first and foremost an affective response, essentially an act of intentional desire by an embodied subject. "Art" construed in the widest sense (creativity, performance, and the artifacts that result from both) can model for us the sacramental action of the finite in mediating the infinite—the "excess" that gives us access—especially when viewed primarily as a practice, as action, as performance.[54]

Now, I am not so naive as to assume that the body and art are somehow immune to being positioned and absorbed by celebrity consumer culture. Our daily experience of global consumer capitalism and of postmodern digital immediacy soon convinces us otherwise. At a deeper level, as the sociologist Bryan Turner has noted, bio-politics and bio-economics are already at work in colonizing the body: "In contemporary society, the body is in one sense disappearing; it is being converted into an information system whose genetic code can be manipulated and sold as a commercial product in the new biotech economy. In global terms, the disorders and diseases of the human body have become productive in a post-industrial economy."[55] However, the body is always more than its material-empirical basis. Our ability to imagine the body differently than as raw materials or data and to see it rather as a system of meaning ("the body") or as performativity ("embodiment")[56] is a clear and positive sign that resistance in the form of critique of such objectification is still possible, even from within our consumer capitalist context. This critique of the status quo springs from the dialectical "and yet" structure of the intentionality: our refusal to settle for less than the fulfillment of our yearnings, even if we find ourselves seduced into mistaking short-term glitz for a definitive cure for our restless hearts.

The point, of course, it to activate this critique, this "thinking otherwise." That is the task that a twenty-first-century theological anthropology must take up, along with an explanation as to how this seduction is merely temporary and surpassable rather than eternally recurring. And so an "eschatology" is necessary, a goal needed for our experience of constituting ourselves by means of our actions, as Blondel insisted. A theological anthropology based on "Incarnation unlimited" should be the first step in reclaiming our vision of the "one thing necessary"—the supernatural—and of crafting the narrative that reveals how our embodied particularity, far from being consumer "wreckage," is rather the necessary access-point of divine grace.

CHAPTER 7

The Gifted Self:
The Challenges of French Thought

Robyn Horner

Vatican II remains a powerful and enduring symbol for many because it represents, above all, the preparedness of the Church to dialogue with all that is "genuinely human." There can be few higher or more hope-filled expressions of engagement with the world than *Gaudium et Spes*. Nevertheless, in the same moment that, in this document and others, Vatican II was opening the windows of the Church to dialogue, it opened onto a modern world that was already passing—if, in fact, it had ever really been. As Lieven Boeve maintains, the correlative theology (that is, theology in dialogue with modernity) that arguably both anticipates and was one of the legacies of Vatican II actually depends on modern perspectives that were soon to be called into question.[1]

In a contemporary context, there are two ways we might consider the theological anthropology emergent from Vatican II. On the one hand, we could analyze it from the perspective of some of the currents in modern philosophical anthropology. As I have argued elsewhere, in this light we might find that *Gaudium et Spes* is not very modern at all.[2] On the other hand, maintaining with Boeve that *Gaudium et Spes* presumes a modern subject to some extent, we could ask about the fate of such optimism in the wake of contemporary critiques of such a subject.³ That is the path that we will follow here.

Such an investigation has the potential to be vast. After making a brief consideration of the ways in which we might claim that *Gaudium et Spes* reflects something of a modern outlook, we will limit our study by examining two "postmodern" accounts of subjectivity, investigating their implications for a future theological anthropology. We will limit it further by working within a single trajectory, that of Husserlian phenomenology, specifically with regard to its aftermath in France, and then only by working with a few of the paths woven through that trajectory. As an example of contemporary critique, we will draw from the work of Jacques Derrida, for no other reason than that his account of the crisis of subjectivity is both compelling and closely related to the Husserlian text. By way of response to that critique we will consider the work of Jean-Luc Marion, who proposes a new approach to phenomenology, and so a new thinking of the subject (although he will no longer refer to it as such). The importance of Marion for the current work cannot be limited to this achievement, however. While Marion develops his account of what replaces subjectivity within a phenomenological context, he also has theological interests, and these enable us to extend the phenomenological account. This means that we can consider the relationship between philosophy and theology in a new light, and that the dialogue so earnestly sought by *Gaudium et Spes* can have a new point of departure.

Gaudium et Spes *and the Modern Project*

Boeve maintains that there is something intrinsically modern about *Gaudium et Spes*, and there are two fundamental elements to his position. First, there is the argument from the point of view of method. *Gaudium et Spes* proceeds from the belief that it is possible for theology to be in dialogue with modernity. This belief is dependent on a largely undifferentiated theology of correlation, which can emerge only when theology itself adopts a fundamentally modern stance: This presumes the clear identity of each of the partners in dialogue, a modern conceptual and epistemological framework, and some kind of continuity between Christianity and modern culture. Second—in a closely related step—Boeve argues that the dialogue between Church and world in *Gaudium et Spes* is based on a shared anthropology, one that reflects an understanding of human persons "as subjects both capable of and responsible for their achievement of maturity as subjects."[4] Boeve goes on to emphasize not only the centrality but the character of this theological intersection with broader notions of humanity: "Rationality, human freedom, and social liberation were considered privileged *loci theologici* from which to recontextualize the Christian faith in a God who is salvifically involved with human beings and their histories."[5]

The possibility of a shared anthropological understanding between Church and world in *Gaudium et Spes* is reinforced when we consider the historical development of theological anthropology as a distinct area of study. In his recent major opus, *Eccentric Existence*, David H. Kelsey traces the way in which theological anthropology for centuries is typically distributed across several doctrinal loci (creation, salvation, eschatology, and revelation). His claim is that it is only in modern theology that theological anthropology develops "as a *locus* in its own right."[6] This anthropological consolidation reflects in theology a culmination of the turn to the subject in philosophy and in culture more broadly. Hence, Joseph Ratzinger will argue that the starting point of *Gaudium et Spes* is distinctive theologically because it is fundamentally anthropocentric: "It is remarkable that in contrast to the essentially theological starting-point of the early Christians ('the fearers of God') an anthropological theme now comes to the fore. Anthropocentrism, which determines the whole theological conception of the text, probably represents its most characteristic option."[7]

The irony of this development is that while texts such as *Gaudium et Spes* express a degree of confidence in the rational and self-determining nature of the human person—and find here a basis for dialogue with modernity—modern thought more generally often excludes theological discourse from the realm of the rational.[8] Elsewhere in this volume, both Oliver Davies and Anthony J. Godzieba draw from Charles Taylor's work to maintain that the modern take on being human results to a large extent not only in an emphasis on autonomy but this at the price of the possibility of any engagement with transcendence. This leaves us with an anthropological model that theologically sows the seeds of its own destruction.

Davies's analysis also draws our attention to a fundamental fracture between body and mind that is typical of the modern: "This can be summarized in terms of the mind–body relation, according to which the body, as material, constitutes a domain of determinism (and so is unfree or only conditionally free), whereas the human mind, or spirit, is unconditionally free."[9] The need to reckon with bodiliness is not something that we are able to pursue explicitly here (although there are other chapters in this collection where that is at issue, and it is clearly an aspect of postmodern critique). However, we note only that one could contemplate the continued emphasis on natural law in *Gaudium et Spes* in this light—that is, as a reflection of an essentialist, almost structuralist understanding of human being, juxtaposed with an understanding that reinforces personal autonomy and freedom. On the one hand, the emphasis on the natural-law tradition in *Gaudium et Spes* could be read against any modern tendency, as a sign of the "classical consciousness" (in its commitment to what is single, universal, and permanent) at work in the document.[10] On the other hand, an essentialist approach to natural law could be understood as a distinctly modern contribution to its development.[11]

In any case, to the extent that modern thought—now epitomized almost in caricature, perhaps, by the work of René Descartes—delivered a self-certain and autonomous (if frequently disembodied) subject, "postmodern" investigations have increasingly brought the identity, unity, and potency of that subject into question.[12] It is a truism that there is no external point from which we can consider revelation apart from its being revelation "to us." If the human is, as we might understand the (arguably) modern theologian Karl Rahner to say, the privileged place of divine self-communication, then theological anthropology evidently assumes a particular importance for theological method.[13] However, if we can no longer take for granted modern analyses of subjectivity to which it has more recently been tied, then we are forced to look anew not only at how theological anthropology might be challenged to reexpress itself in a contemporary context but also at what that might mean for the possibility of doing theology itself. Here is the heart of the difficulty for a renewed theological anthropology. It is a matter not only of recognizing the always-and-already-contextual nature of theology, and hence of the need for theological anthropology to be recontextualized (a first methodological issue, which we draw from Boeve's "theology of interruption"), but also of putting in question the very *locus theologicus* as *locus anthropos* (a second methodological issue—but this time of the first order).

The Lost Self, the Unknown Other

As Jean-Luc Nancy observes in the introduction to the landmark collection *Who Comes After the Subject?* (published in English in 1991): "The question . . . bears upon the critique or deconstruction of interiority, of self-presence, of consciousness, of mastery, of the individual or collective property of an essence."[14] One of the respondents in that volume is Derrida, and it is the broad lines of his approach to the question of the subject that we sketch here.

Writing in the 1960s, Derrida first becomes well known for his detailed analysis and critique of Husserlian phenomenology. Amongst other things, he highlights the ways in which Husserl seems to take for granted that the subject is present to itself in lived experience, along with its objects. Derrida maintains that for Husserl "self-presence must be produced in the undivided unity of a temporal present so as to have nothing to reveal to itself by the agency of signs."[15] Self-presence, in other words, must ultimately be unmediated and absolute, available entirely in the perception of the present moment. However, this is not the case:

> The presence of the perceived present can appear as such only inasmuch as it is *continuously compounded* with a nonpresence and nonperception, with primary memory and expectation (retention and protention). These nonperceptions are neither added to, nor do they *occasionally* accompany, the actually perceived now; they are essentially and indispensably involved in its possibility.[16]

The present moment is perceived as such only because of its relation with what is not present and no longer (or not yet) perceived—the past and the future. For the present to be perceived as present, then, requires constant reference to what is not present and must be re-presented. Derrida's argument is that we have to have signs in order to "present ourselves to ourselves (that is, we re-present rather than present)—non-presence and otherness are internal to presence."[17] Presentation is always representation: The self is never ultimately present to itself in any unmediated way.[18]

Interviewed many years later by Nancy in the context of *Who Comes After the Subject?* Derrida maintains that any thinking of the subject typically revolves around predicates to do with "being-present." This includes presence to self, which he goes on to describe in terms of "a certain interpretation of temporality," which is played out in all those characteristics that we frequently ascribe to the subject: "Identity to self, positionality, property, personality, ego, consciousness, will, intentionality, freedom, humanity, etc."[19] By way of contrast, his understanding that presentation is always deferred in favor of re-presentation means that self-presence is illusory. He explains: "The relation to self . . . can only be *différance*, that is to say alterity, or trace."[20] We will always be too late to grasp the self in consciousness but will find only otherness: the self *as* other, always and already divided.

If this is the case, then there will be implications in terms of each of the characteristics ascribed to the subject that I have listed above.

Derrida largely resists attempting further description of "who comes after the subject," short of using aphorisms that are meaningful only in the much larger context of his work as a whole—for example, "the proper name in exappropriation, signature, or affirmation without closure, trace, differance from self, destinerrance." However, he does observe that this "who" is nevertheless characterized by responsibility, a responsibility ("or call to response") that precedes any identification as a subject.[21] In a difficult but telling passage, he writes: "The singularity of the 'who' is not the individuality of a thing that would be identical to itself, it is not an atom. It is a singularity that dislocates or divides itself in gathering itself together to answer to the other, whose call somehow precedes its own identification with itself, for to this call I can *only* answer, have already answered."[22] That there is mention of responsibility here signals that there is an ethical dimension to Derrida's work that cannot be ignored, although its ultimate direction is debated.[23]

For Derrida, we cannot know (in the sense of being present to) the self; neither can we know the other person. The other can never be the other "as such" ("the 'who' of the other . . . could only appear absolutely *as such* by disappearing as other").[24] As soon as I claim to know the other, I have brought the other within my own horizon and done away with what makes the other *other*. Further, while the call to response or responsibility comes from an-other, it cannot be objectified or appropriated. "Something of this call of the other must remain nonreappropriable, nonsubjectivable, and in a certain way nonidentifiable, a sheer supposition, so as to remain *other*, a *singular* call to response or responsibility."[25] These conditions are writ large if we want to speak of a divine other or a divine call.[26]

Insofar as we can speak of self or other in Derrida, we can speak only of loss—of a self or other who remains fundamentally unknowable because never presentable.[27] Such a reading is devastating for a modern outlook, but no less for a theological anthropology that is dependent on the capacity of the subject to return to itself as an intending, relational, free, moral agent, even if such a return does not imply complete self-knowledge. Transcendental accounts of the subject such as we find in Rahner and Bernard Lonergan (and although modern, these accounts also draw heavily from medieval thought) depend on this presence-to-self.[28] Given that Derrida calls into question not only the prospect of the subject grounding itself by its own means but also its being grounded through recourse to what he would understand to be a transcendental signified ("God"), Derrida's work raises issues for identity, moral agency, epistemology, and relationality.

The Given Self, the Giving Other

While for Derrida, Husserl's incapacity to present the self in the "lived experience" of consciousness reinforces phenomenology's failure, for Marion it is indicative of an opportunity for phenomenology that Husserl himself missed. In Marion's understanding, the phenomenological reduction (the bracketing out of what is not directly given to consciousness) is effectively correlated to the horizon, such that the horizon will dictate what can appear.[29] Where the reduction is effected according to the horizon of objectness, for example, it will inevitably fail to deliver in lived experience those phenomena that cannot be considered objects. However, Marion argues that objectity is the most mundane of horizons, allowing that phenomena other than objects can give themselves if only we do not preclude that givenness in advance. With his reduction to the given, Marion in a sense nominates givenness as its own horizon, meaning that he attempts to allow for whatever gives itself to give itself according to its own parameters.[30] Importantly, this can include phenomena that give themselves without being present.

In crude terms, Marion's phenomenological approach can be said to depend on a disjunction between the two parts constituting intentionality—or consciousness of a phenomenon: the intention (the signification or meaning ascribed to a phenomenon) and the intuition (the phenomenon as given). Marion's major claim is that some phenomena give themselves in an excess of intuition, defying any single constituting intention: These he calls "saturated phenomena," or "paradoxes."[31] A saturated phenomenon is one in which there is an intuitive givenness for which no single act of meaning-giving (or even combination of such acts) will account. Examples of such phenomena include the self and the other person, although Marion also includes revelation in this category.

The self, in Marion's view, is actually given in the act of receiving other givens and bringing them to manifestation: It receives itself from what gives itself, and hence it is "the gifted" (*l'adonné*).[32] Marion's well-known analogies here include those of goalkeeping ("if *l'adonné* therefore receives the given, it is in receiving it with all the vigor, even the violence, of a goalkeeper blocking a shot") and electrical resistance ("the greater the resistance to the impact of the given . . . , the more the phenomenological light shows *itself*"). In showing itself in this way it does not present itself;

while it cannot be constituted in lived experience (a point with which Derrida might agree), it is for Marion, nevertheless, still positively given in responding to the other—the self given in the accusative—as to a call.[33] *Il se passe*—the gifted "happens," or "takes place" as an event.[34] What is apparent in these examples, however, is that this givenness does not yet tell us anything about the personal identity of *l'adonné*. Furthermore, Marion's account risks relegating *l'adonné* to absolute passivity; while he claims that the transcendental I has not been replaced by the empirical me, this is how he has sometimes been read.[35]

Within his framework of saturated phenomena, Marion also allows for the givenness of the other person. Moreover, initially borrowing from Lévinas and his notion of the signification of the other in an ethical injunction arising from the face, Marion seeks to specify the excessive or saturated givenness of the other as distinctly individual.[36] He attempts to do this without compromising the very alterity that must continue to characterize the other as *other*. In his early work, Marion maintains that the other's gaze crosses mine and is experienced as a weight, or a pressure—as a counter-intentionality.[37] Later he focuses on the way in which love determines personal identity.[38] Using the context of the relationship of lovers, Marion describes the way in which the other gives her- or himself to me through being felt without resistance: "Thus I see there its flesh, insofar as it is felt and feels itself feel, thus insofar as it is definitively individualized, gifted to itself, in short insofar as it is definitively *inaccessible* to my own flesh. I see there the accomplished transcendence of the other [person]."[39] The excessive givenness of the other signifies in speaking and, ultimately, in the giving of an oath or promise. For Marion, this becomes the mechanism through which the identity of the self is also established. However, there is no guarantee that an oath or a promise is truthful or enduring.[40] We thus reach the limits of phenomenological description—self and other are given and signify, but we cannot be sure that this signification is lasting. Further, each is subject to an infinite hermeneutic.[41]

Some Questions About Method

In the perspectives that have been sketched above, the transcendental "I" well known to the modern world appears to have lost its potency. It is no longer secure in its capacity to return to itself, deprived of a certain identity, and unable to be sure of its relationships, and so we have to wonder about its future. In this context, we seek to develop a new conversation with theology.

Here we must pause momentarily to reconsider some methodological questions. What is at issue in this chapter is the way in which contemporary French thought is illustrative of a failure of the modern subject, a subject that to some extent is presumed in the dialogue between Church and world at Vatican II. We recognize, along with Boeve, that this dialogue is fraught, for what has been presumed in common has already been brought into question. What we must consider here is the possibility of new dialogue, and what that might mean for each of the potential partners (if, indeed, we can presume that there are two distinct partners here—this is one of the problems to which Boeve refers).

From a theological perspective, it would be possible to retreat at this point into a kind of dogmatism that remains unaffected by the problem that has been identified. This is already an option—if couched in some ways more gently and generously than elsewhere—in *Gaudium et Spes*. The theological answers to the problem, in this sense, are already in place, since we know by means of revelation that there is a higher truth to which we are called. Our anxieties about any lack of traction with which we might be faced as subjects should have been quelled in advance. Yet this kind of approach negates the very possibility of dialogue and threatens to force theology into an isolationist mentality where potential issues, such as those to do with revelation, for example, are not thoroughly engaged. Let us underline again that asking questions about theological anthropology actually leads us to fundamental questions about theological method, and to the fact that theology is never singular or without context.

From the perspective of contemporary philosophy—and already we must acknowledge that there is no one perspective, even within the post-Husserlian trajectory and its subsets in which we are moving—to have theological answers to philosophical questions simply handed down does not satisfy prima facie the integrity of the search for understanding. If we are to offer theological responses to issues, then, in the context of dialogue, those responses must take seriously the conditions from which those issues emerge.

It is for these reasons that Marion's work is of particular interest. A major focus within his corpus is arguably the question of how theology and philosophy engage one another. In his thinking of saturated phenomena, he seeks to allow for the possibility that phenomena of revelation might become thinkable—precisely in their possibility, if not in their actuality, which he leaves as a question to be determined by theology. We place here to one side the detailed arguments about how this occurs and the problems remaining to be addressed.[42] What is crucial in the current setting is to acknowledge that in Marion's work we have a consideration of the crisis of the subject, a consideration that takes account of contemporary philosophical discussion (and so contributes to philosophy in its own right) but also allows us to bring that discussion meaningfully into a theological context. In other words, we will not have to sacrifice the integrity of the philosophical approach to the problem in order to continue the conversation theologically.

Our theological conclusions will, of course, require the supplement of faith in Christian revelation; a theological interpretation depends on a revelation that is not accessible *as revelation* to the phenomenologist. At the same time, if phenomenology is not only open to whatever gives itself but arguably also has a fundamentally hermeneutic dimension (givenness is always givenness *as*), and especially if theological method itself is phenomenological (which Marion argues), then it is possible that what is given phenomenologically can also be read theologically. [43] What is distinctive will be the hermeneutic context in which givenness has significance. Faith may operate as a supplement, then, but not in a fideistic way where it would work to overcome a patent lack of evidence.[44] Instead, the supplementary aspect of faith will be the provision of a narrative context by means of which what is given reveals itself. As Emmanuel Falque notes in a distinct but very relevant discussion: "It does not matter *where* exactly the 'there' (*Da*) of man's being-there (l''*être-là*') in phenomenology might be, as long as he views his locus or his *topos* as the most proper mode according to which the corpus of texts and the lived consciousness that is embodied in texts make him think."[45]

A Contemporary Problem and a Theological Response

While there are particular ways in which theology has shown itself to have taken on board the characterizations of the subject that are typical of modernity, we need to note, first of all, that there is plenty of room in theological tradition for a thinking of the human person who is lost in terms of identity and insecure in terms of knowledge. The failure of presence, or the gap between meaning and being—which in Derrida's analysis structurally underlies the perpetual loss of the self and the inability to know the other—acutely reflects the human experience, which has otherwise frequently been articulated in terms relating to the Fall.[46] This is especially so in *Gaudium et Spes*. While we are told, on the one hand, that human persons "can with genuine certitude attain to reality itself as knowable" (15), we are reminded, on the other, that this attainment is also impaired by sin, and that "man . . . cannot fully find himself except through a sincere gift of himself" (24). We will not revisit here the trope of fallenness or speculate on its origins but simply underscore the human experience of incessant dissipation that seems to resist the bringing of self or other into focus. The experience of dissipation is a strong theme throughout the theological corpus, not least in Augustine ("my life is a kind of distraction and dispersal," *Confessions*, 9.29), with whose work both Derrida and Marion engage in various ways.[47]

Now, in Marion's phenomenological analysis, we are brought to the point where self and other are given to one another in acts of love (which he broadens from the sexual context in which he initially develops it) and signify as individuals by means of speech—specifically in the giving of an oath or promise. However, Marion recognizes that there is no guarantee that this signification endures or is authentic. From a philosophical perspective, this is as far as we get; that we are left without means to overcome this ambiguity is just part of the human condition. Human life is tragic because there is no proof of love but only professions of love that from moment to moment we can only hope are sincere. Each "I love you" is a risk. To address that problem, Marion ultimately invokes a theological solution, suggesting that those who love make their oaths with God as their witness.[48] Only making an oath *as if* the eternal is witness can underwrite the oath's lasting signification.

This move at the end of *The Erotic Phenomenon* prepares us for Marion's extended meditation, in *Au lieu de soi*, on the way in which the self struggles to find its "place." The self cannot be claimed but only given: Repeating moments from his earlier phenomenological analyses, Marion states: "I happen as the one who *receives him- or herself* at the same time as that which I receive and in order precisely to be able to receive it—*l'adonné*."[49] He also repeats the phenomenological observation—but this time situating it in the thought of Augustine—that the identification of the self is made possible ultimately by what it loves.[50] Then he offers a thoroughly theological reading of this givenness to self and of what it means in terms of identity. According to this (Augustinian-inspired) analysis, the self is truly identified as itself only when it loves God.[51] However, a number of factors militate against this love. There is between the ego and the self a gap that is opened up by the inability to love what will make one (truly) happy.[52] This gap is exacerbated by the temporal difference (*différance*) that defines finitude (but here—in an Augustinian mode—has sinful overtones) as well as by the difference (and distance) from God that characterizes creatureliness.[53] From a Christian perspective, it is not only a question, then, of needing the love of another to give one to oneself but of needing the divine other to perform that gift of love, and in so doing to bestow an enduring and authentic identity in my response to that love.[54]

While Marion's analysis is potent, there may be a need to draw out here the christological dimensions of this transformation. Only the divine other can perform the threefold—and, indeed, trinitarian—movement of graciously enabling love of ultimate goodness, thus revealing Godself in and by means of the believer as well as of bestowing an identity that endures in love's confession. For in being enabled to love God in this way, "it is no longer I who live, but it is Christ who lives in me" (Gal. 2.20) or, as the poet Gerard Manley Hopkins declares:

> . . . the just man justices;
> Keeps grace: that keeps all his goings graces;
> Acts in God's eye what in God's eye he is—
> Christ—for Christ plays in ten thousand places,
> Lovely in limbs, and lovely in eyes not his
> To the Father through the features of men's faces.[55]

In responding to God and so becoming the place where Christ is, I show Christ who, in turn, shows the Father. I become one who shows Christ and, in that showing, become most fully myself, responding and confessing my love.

This enduring identity, nevertheless, does not imply the final delivery of a static or substantial subject (as if Christ himself could be delivered to the dimensions of the intellect or the imagination) but allows for an ongoing process whereby the self is enabled to "come into" itself more and more. This is the conclusion that Marion reaches.[56] In a situation where we may have lost (to borrow Kevin Hart's phrase) "the power to say I," the gift of God is such that we are given the opportunity to respond, each one, as "me," and that we are ultimately recognized and known as this unique one.[57]

While this does not remove the human experience of dissipation (*différance* remains for the Christian as well as the non-Christian), it marks the promise of personal integrity.[58] According to this understanding of the human condition, original sin can formally be understood in something akin to the sense Thomas Aquinas gave it—as the absence of an acceptance (to the point of outright rejection) of God's grace. Materially, it is palpable in the experience of a constant tendency toward dissipation, a tendency that is eased but not eliminated in the concupiscence that remains after baptism, for we do not yet "know" as such our graced life in all its fullness.[59] It should not, then, be surprising that we do not know who we are except that, claimed by Christ, we are given in anticipation of who we will become.

Such a christological response to the question of thinking our humanity is evidently unavailable as such from within a Derridean perspective. Nevertheless, it bears a relationship in some ways to the Derridean notions both of the impossible and the promise, ideas that are richly suggestive for theology even insofar as they do not allow for the presentation of excess or the fulfillment of hope. With the theological anthropology that has been proposed, we might no longer be able to sustain a theology of correlation of the sort arguably presumed at Vatican II (theology as continuous with contemporary thought). We may, however, be able to consider it— using Boeve's terms—as an example of a theology of interruption, where the narrative of the tradition is reexpressed through its engagement with the postmodern.[60] In this way, we find ourselves at an/other new point of departure.

PART III

Relating in a Fallen World

CHAPTER 8

Difference, Body, and Race

Michelle A. Gonzalez

The nature of humanity, our relationship with each other, and our relationship with the sacred is the starting point for reflections on theological anthropology. For centuries Christians have wrestled with defining what makes us particular in light of our humanity yet at the same time interconnected with God's creation. Musings on this subject range from abstract philosophical speculation, to dialogue with the natural sciences, to a serious consideration of the diversity and complexity of the embodied human condition. Within systematic theology, the study of what it means to be human, created in the image and likeness of God, falls under the heading of theological anthropology. This has implications for both our relationship with our Creator and our relationship with each other. Theological anthropology speaks to humanity's relationship with the divine and its interrelationship within the human community. More recently, writings also look at our interconnectedness with the cosmos and the manner in which that shapes and defines the human condition. For every generation of Christians, the significance of our humanity is reinterpreted from particular sociocultural, historical, and political contexts. There is no one unified anthropology but various anthropologies that are shaped by the diverse communities that struggle to interpret God's revelation.

Throughout the centuries speculation on the nature of our humanity has often ignored concrete, lived human life. In other words, decontextualized and abstract reflections on the nature of all humanity have dominated theological anthropologies of the past. More and more today we find critical, constructive theological voices that explore the nature of humanity in all its concrete messiness. The human as abstract essence is slowly unraveling. Instead, everyday lived religion becomes the starting point of contemporary theological anthropologies. In this chapter I offer a constructive, contemporary interpretation of theological anthropology rooted in the scholarship and insights of liberation and constructive theologians in the Americas. In my discussion I highlight three themes that are vital to understanding contemporary theological anthropologies today: difference, the body, and race. I will conclude with how these themes have implications for theological anthropology broadly understood in the contemporary context.

Classic theological anthropologies have often emphasized our spiritual relationship with the divine and downplayed its implications for our concrete existence. Otherwise put, "The main focus of theological anthropology has tended to be the supernatural orientation of humankind as beings created (in the words of Gen 1:27) 'in the image of God' (*imago Dei*). As a result of this focus, the other, more material side of existence has been overshadowed, even obscured."[1] This chapter is sympathetic to these concerns. Theological anthropology must remain firmly grounded in the contemporary situation and not fall into abstract speculation that ignores the very materiality of human life. This emphasis on the hybridity of human identity, embodiment, and race grounds this theological anthropology and challenges the discipline of theology to remain rooted in lived religious practices.

Difference

A fundamental dimension of theological anthropology is difference. The category of difference refers not only to the differences and diversity that exist between different human groups but also to the difference that challenges constructions of pure identity. Difference refers to the manner in which we are different from each other and the manner in which our identity challenges the often rigid categories in which we place human beings. We are not only different from others, but we embody difference within the complexity of our identity. Too often discussions of our identity are dominated by binary categories: black–white, male–female, rich–poor. Similarly, our identity is often reduced to one component of who we are— for example, race or gender—denying the fullness of our identity.

Within the United States perhaps no other theological school has highlighted the significance of difference for theological anthropology more than Latino/a theology has. Since the early 1970s, Latino/s theologians have elaborated a theological perspective that takes the diversity and differences of the Latino/a condition as fundamental to theological reflection. The starting point of Latino/a theology is the lived religious practices of Latino/a Christian communities throughout the United States. It is only through concrete religious practices that one can enter into theological discussions of what it means to be human. The emphasis is overwhelmingly ecclesial, while including a nod to the fact that many Latino/a religious practices exist on the border of Christian ecclesial structures and in some cases incorporate non-Christian elements within them. Latino/a theologians struggle to negotiate their strong commitment to Latino/a theological categories that speak to the lived reality of Latino/a faith, while simultaneously remaining equally committed to the traditional categories of theological discourse that have been classically articulated throughout the centuries.

Broad definitions of Latino/a theology exist, such as can be derived from the statement that "Latino/a theology has taken up the task of reflecting on the articulated faith and religious symbols and practices of Hispanics in the United States in light of their cultural, economic, and social context/ situation."[2] Fundamental to this emphasis on Latino/a religious life is the importance of culture. The category of culture unites Latino/a theologians. "The defining role of culture and the critique of cultural oppression and of universalizing claims are themes that underlie most of Latino/a theology. The preferential option for culture, if we may be allowed the expression, characterizes Latino/a theology."[3] Latino/a theologians take the complexity of Latino/a culture as the primary locus of their academic reflection.

Latino/a theologians have been discussing the importance of difference and hybridity since the early days of their existence as a scholarly community. The category of *mestizaje* has come to saturate Latino/a theology. The privileging of *mestizaje* is intimately linked to Latino/a theology's emphasis on culture. Anthropologically, *mestizaje* names the ambiguity and in-between-ness of Latino/a identity. *Mestizaje/mulatez* functions to designate the mixed reality of Latino/a peoples: The former refers to the mixture of indigenous and Spanish cultures, the latter to the mixture of indigenous and African cultures. *Mestizaje/mulatez* not only portrays the Latino/a context; these terms also reflect the epistemological standpoint from which Latino/as exist in the world as hybrid people. This mixture and ambiguity is also the hermeneutical lens through which Latino/as see the world and has ontological implications for the methodology of Latino/a theology. In embracing *mestizaje-mulatez*, Latino/as are expressing solidarity with other marginalized people of color and attempting to dismantle dualistic constructions of race that plague identity politics. The complexity of Latina religious experiences is often contextualized in terms of *mestizaje*, *mulatez*, and *nepantla*. "Nepantla" is the Nahuatl (Aztec) word for "land in the middle." It is a place where the Christian and the non-Christian co-incide and coexist in harmony. This is a fundamental theme within Latina theology, the construction of identity on the border of multiple cultures, nations, and ethnicities.

A clear emphasis on hybridity is a hallmark of Cuban American ethicist Ada María Isasi-Díaz's anthropology, particularly through her appropriation of Latina philosopher María Lugones's notion of world-traveling. For Lugones, "A 'world' has to be presently inhabited by flesh and blood people. That is why it cannot be a utopia. It may also be inhabited by some imaginary people. It may be inhabited by people who are dead or people that the inhabitants of this 'world' met in some other 'world' and now have in this 'world' in imagination."[4] Worlds are the different realities or contexts in which we live and shape our identity. One can be in more than one "world" at the same time, belong to different worlds, travel between worlds. "World-traveling," therefore, is our movement between the various contexts that we enter into or have imposed upon our lives. Building on Lugones' work Isasi-Díaz articulates "a fluid social ontology, which is based on the hybridity and diversity that are key realities/understandings we need to deal with in this twenty-first century."[5] *Mestizaje/mulatez* is the locus theologicus of Latino/a theology. This category functions ethically in Isasi-Díaz's corpus as a condemnation of racism and ethnic prejudice. A fundamental aspect of her emphasis on difference is a reconceptualization of this notion as relational. As she thoughtfully points out, difference is traditionally understood as exclusionary, as what divides. Isasi-Díaz constructs difference instead in terms of relationships, showing that differences are relative. Lastly, Isasi-Diáz's use of the category of world-traveling refers to the survival tactics appropriated by Latino/as as they coexist and travel between the Latino/a world and the dominant Anglo culture. At the core of all three of these categories is the insight that the traditional, oppositional, and static categories of identity, and therefore of human beings, that have been imposed on Latino/as do not speak to their lived realities. For Isasi-Díaz, theoretical concepts must ring true to people's daily lives or they are of little value.

This racial and cultural mixture, the sense of people living between two worlds, reflects the context from which Hispanic theology emerges. "Because we choose *mestizaje* and *mulatez* as our theological locus, we are saying that this is the structure in which we operate, from which we reach out to explain who we are and to contribute to how theology and religion are understood in this society in which we live."[6] For Isasi-Díaz, *mestizaje* and *mulatez* are both descriptors of the Latino/as' cultural condition and an explicit decision by Latino/as to embrace an identity within the dominant U.S. paradigm. This normative choice to embrace the *mestizo-mulato* condition is a manner of contesting hegemonic constructions of identity within the academy and society.

The emphasis on difference is not exclusive to Latino/a theologians. In her recent book, *Being About Borders: A Christian Anthropology of Difference*, Michelle Saracino highlights the significance of difference for contemporary theological anthropologies in our globalized world. She warns us of the dangers of erasing borders through globalization, for in that process the complexity of human difference is wiped out.[7] This is of special concern for Christians, she emphasizes, for Jesus' ministry was always at the border of culture, society, religion, and identity. Fundamental to Saracino's text is the notion that we must honor the hybridity of who we are. Echoing the Latino/a emphasis on the border, she highlights that the border marks our encounter with difference. Yet this in-between-ness is not exclusive to Latino/as.

A theological anthropology that takes the encounter with difference seriously must acknowledge the affective dimension of humanity. An affective understanding of theological anthropology does not allow emotion to be subordinate to reason and recognizes that affective responses are not always positive. Just because today we are encountering difference at exponential rates does not mean that individuals are not having negative reactions to it. Too often, we celebrate our newly globalized world without recognizing the complexity and sometimes negativity associated with this interconnectedness. As Saracino points out, "the conflation of globalization with openness to others obscures the practical reality of living with those who are different in the midst of hybrid experience."[8] Christians are called to acknowledge the interconnectedness of human life and our feelings toward it. We must avoid a sense of narcissism in these encounters, a false notion of the superiority of one group over another.

An awareness of hybridity does not have to always provoke a negative response and in fact can promote empathy. This hybridity of difference is fundamental to the Christian understanding of the Incarnation. The Incarnation reminds us of the porous nature of the border between the sacred and the profane. Jesus himself was a hybrid: man, Jew, friend, son; his hybridity is theological in its salvific import to all. Jesus is, after all, on the border of God and humanity. This awareness of difference and hybridity as constituting our humanity also opens the door to the complexity and diversity of Christian faith and life.

Latin American and Latino/a spirituality represents a vital dimension of Christianity in the Americas. Latino/as serve as bridge people between the North and the South. They open the door for U.S. Christians to global Christianity, which is overwhelmingly brown and poor. With current issues such as illegal immigration dividing the United States, Latino/as give a human face to what are often abstract political discussions. Latino/as also represent the new face of Christianity as a whole in the twenty-first century. This Christianity is increasingly Spirit-driven, symbolic, and devotional. For Latino/a Catholics, the symbolic (whether through devotion to a particular apparition of Mary or participation in a Via Crucis procession) is a privileged means to the divine and often has political implications. When Latino/as locate the sacred in the everyday, spirituality saturates every aspect of their lives. Through their spirituality, Latino/as lament their struggles and sufferings while simultaneously celebrating their full humanity as created in God's image. An emphasis on Latino/a spirituality opens doors to the growing face of global Catholicism and to the theological import of their faith lives.

Within Latin American Catholicism, devotion to folk saints, a practice that has been present in the Americas long before scholars began to study this phenomenon, is receiving increasing academic attention. What are folk saints? They are often referred to in Spanish as *santos populares* or *santos paganos*. Sometimes they are deceased persons who are believed to be miraculous and around whom have developed large cults but who have not been canonized or formally recognized as holy by the Catholic Church. The relationship between folk devotion and the institutional Catholic Church is not always clear. Policy varies wildly among parish priests and local bishops: Some are tolerant, others are not. It is significant that devotees often do not distinguish between official and folk devotions. When a priest does not support a folk saint, there is a sense of offense among the people. There is also the economics of folk-saint devotion: Who is in charge of and later inherits the shrine? Devotion to folk saints at the border of institutional Roman Catholic religiosity also reveals border populations to us. These popular saints are an expression of the lived religion of communities and often coexist with those saints canonized by official religion. Their popularity often stems from their connection to the identity and struggles of those communities that are devoted to them.

This theme is picked up in a fascinating study of devotion to Holy Death (Santissima Muerte) among transgender sex workers in Mexico and California.[9] The authors, Cymene Howe, Susanna Zaraysky, and Lois Ann Lorentzen, discover a strong devotion that the sex workers have to Holy Death, who protects the sex workers from death, a genuine threat, given the nature of their profession. Scholars dig to find the devotion's origins, about which devotees do not really care. Also, the authors discover, many who pray to Holy Death think she is a Catholic saint just like official saints. The rituals and practices surrounding Holy Death mirror Catholic practices. These alternative religious practices are not constructed as a direct disavowal of Catholicism. The growing popularity of devotion to Holy Death is found not just among sex workers but often found among those who live their lives close to death. Devotions such as that to Holy Death reveal the religious worldviews and struggles of marginalized populations within the Church, ones that may not be revealed to us if we remain within the close institutional borders of Catholicism. Difference refers not only to racial ethnic diversity but also to the diversity within theological practices.

In many ways, popular saints force us into the realm of what Latino theologian Alex Nava describes as "brown theology," which "celebrates hybridity and contradiction, cultural miscegenation and cross-cultural contamination. There is no pure identity."[10] Nava argues that we need to "forge a theological openness that is attuned to the diversity and multiplicity of any human individual and community."[11] I want to encourage us to try to think "brown" when we approach theology, not only regarding Latino/a and Latin American populations, for none of us can escape the complexity of our identity and culture. I would also argue that in order to remember the dangerous memory of Jesus' life, death, and resurrection, we need to become "browner" lest we miss those stories of suffering and hope in the margins of our Church and society. A brown theology is an embodied one, recognizing that no theological anthropology can be an abstraction.

The Body

This encounter with difference forces us to leave from our security and enter into the other's space. Bodily contact is a way of being in solidarity with the oppressed. However, touch is not always sacred, for to touch someone is an act of power. Fundamental to this emphasis on touch is the question "What does the body mean being human?" After all, suffering bodies reveal the suffering that is at the heart of Christianity. In her most recent theological anthropology, black Catholic theologian M. Shawn Copeland outlines five convictions which ground her anthropology: an understanding of the body as mediator of divine revelation; the significance of the body for shaping human existence as relational and social; an emphasis on the creativity of the triune God as revealed through differences in identity; an embodied understanding of solidarity; and the role of the Eucharist in ordering and transforming bodies. As she writes, "The body provokes theology."[12]

Basing her anthropological reflections on suffering black women's bodies, Copeland argues that "no Christian teaching has been more desecrated by slavery than the doctrine of the human person or theological anthropology."[13] Copeland's starting point of black women's bodies reminds us not only of the suffering these women endured but also that no theological reflection on the body can begin in abstraction. Hers is a eucharistic mediation on the body, for both the Eucharist and racism imply bodies. The Eucharist embodies Jesus' sacrificial gift of his life in order to bring his Father's mercy and love. Eucharistic solidarity is a countersign to violence toward bodies; we are Jesus' body, and this calls for an embodied praxis of discipleship. Jesus' suffering body also reminds us of the crucified peoples who have suffered throughout history and who do not suffer alone. It reminds us both of the sinfulness of the infliction this suffering and, as Wilhelm Guggenberger argues in his chapter in this volume, of the inherited nature of sin.

In black theology, the image of God becomes a fundamental anthropological issue, especially as it is connected to embodiment. Our bodies are marked by our history, for even Jesus' body was marked in the resurrection. Yet, too often people of color are reduced to their bodies. Black theologian Dwight Hopkins argues that the black body is defined by its inability to reason within the mind–body dualism. The black body is reduced to the erotic.[14] This can also be said of many bodies of marginalized populations globally. Therefore, a theological anthropology that emphasizes the body must be cautious not to reduce persons to their bodies.

The body is not only a site of suffering; it is also a site of celebration. To speak of the body is to speak of its adornment. Adornment of the body is a characteristic of every known human culture. When we are born we are naked only momentarily, and when we die, whether cremated or buried, we are clothed for that final passage. Whether we like it or not, clothes send messages to the world about who we are. Clothes tell the story of our lives. They have religious, political, and ritual value.

Eight years ago Linda M. Scott published *Fresh Lipstick: Redressing Fashion and Feminism.*[15] This book is important and extremely significant in light of feminist studies, for it challenges the notion that attention to one's appearance is somehow antifeminist. Scott skillfully navigates the history of appearance and how it has functioned within feminism in the United States since the suffrage movement. For every generation of feminists, it appears that fashion and appearance are always connected to the construction of women's liberation. Scott rightfully points out, however, that what is often labeled as women's liberation is actually a reflection more of class and culture than of gender.

While the manner in which we present ourselves to the world is a reflection of who we are beneath that facade, the manner in which that public persona is received is coded by culture, gender, class, politics, and religion. Similarly, the old adage "You cannot judge a book by its cover" is directly refuted by the Incarnation, which ultimately teaches us that flesh and the body matter. It would be perhaps best to say, "You cannot judge a book exclusively by its cover." In a similar vein, while the Christian message favors the view that attention to one's appearance is a sign of frivolity and ungodliness, at the core of the Christian salvation narrative is Jesus' incarnation. The created world is a reflection of God's glory, and one must celebrate it while not being overly consumed by the material and the physical. The dangers of consumption are clearly highlighted in Anthony Godzieba's chapter in this volume.

Many women, in addition to dealing with the negative stereotypes regarding attention to one's appearance, have to struggle with the sexualization of their bodies and the role clothing plays in that. After all, our clothing reveals as it conceals. We are part of a religious tradition that celebrates the Incarnation, yet through the centuries the body is presented as an impediment to our relationship with the sacred. For women, our bodies have historically been the barrier to the priesthood and, in the words of some theologians, including Augustine, our ability to authentically reflect the imago Dei as women. Whether it is reducing us to mothers or to objects of sexual and moral temptation, Christianity does not promote a healthy understanding of women's body.

Feminist theologians highlight the body as a site and expression of our relationship with God. Recovering the body is a central feminist theological task. This recovery is nuanced by an acknowledgment that, when it is the focus of theological reflection the female body is often reduced to sex. So the female body is emphasized in terms of biological reproduction and, consequently, motherhood, or the body becomes sexual temptation. Feminists, therefore, want to overcome this dualism and present female bodies as an authentic reflection of our image of God and a means of expressing our relationship with the sacred.

The ambiguity surrounding Christianity's relationship with the body is also revealed in Christianity's attitudes toward dress and fashion. Clearly Christianity and fashion have a relationship, for if they did not we would not have clerical dress. Fashion is not entirely frivolous in the Christian worldview. What do I mean by Christian fashion? There are various instances of dress as a fundamental expression of Christian identity and authority. One only has to look at clerical vestments. In some denominations certain colors have ritual significance. Throughout the world, in many of the churches where the clergy wear vestments, especially in middle-class and upper-class communities, the embroidery and craftsmanship that go into stoles and other vestments is extremely intricate. The clerical collar is a crosscultural signifier of Christian authority. Christianity is not the only religion that connects fashion with authority within its tradition. Dress matters in religious ritual.

Dress is not only a marker of religious authority. It also reveals cultural and religious identity as a whole. An example of this is found in the traditional indigenous dress, or *traje tipico*, of Mayans in Guatemala. *Traje tipico* is the most significant factor in preserving Mayan culture. This functions at the regional and national levels. *Traje* is more that just an outfit. It is identity-making clothing that represents a Mayan cultural expression. Each indigenous community or municipality in Guatemala has its own particular dress and is a way of demonstrating one's pride for one's local region. The source of town-specific *traje* is a bit of a mystery for modern scholars. The most popularly heard explanation given by Guatemalans is that the source of the different outfits, patterns, and colors can be traced to the Spanish and to a means of regionally classifying the indigenous. However, there is no evidence to support this claim. We do know today that the practice of weaving on a backstrap loom is an ancient Mayan practice that has remained unchanged for the past two thousand years. Ancient Mayan women wear the same style of shirts that are worn today, the *huipile.*

Scholars today generally acknowledge that the practice of town-specific dress was solidified by the late nineteenth century. They also recognize that the Spanish did not impose town-specific dress and that the practice of municipal *traje* most likely emerged in part as a reaction to colonialism, as a form of redefining community affiliation. Nonetheless, most Guatemalans, including indigenous, self-understand their traditional dress as a practice imposed by the Spanish that was then transformed into a subversive source of empowerment for a people who were classified as if in a science experiment. The wearing of traditional dress is a public manner of expressing pride in one's culture. It is a way of showing that one is not ashamed to be indigenous; one is not trying to assimilate into Western culture. Many Mayan women wear the *traje* of their region to self-identify with their hometowns. However, more and more Mayan women are wearing *traje* from different regions, as a sign of pan-Mayan solidarity. *Traje* is not to be confused with the weavings that are mass-produced and commercially sold to tourists. For many tourists, Guatemala is synonymous with weavings. However, those types of weavings are not worn by the indigenous. They are for the tourists.

Sadly, one sees *traje* less and less in Guatemala. Various factors play into this. The first is the cost of traditional dress. As many indigenous women repeatedly told me, the cost of thread has risen and now an entire outfit costs close to 900 questzales, about $125.00. That is one outfit, equaling more than the monthly income for a twelve-person family. The second factor is a lapse of the cultural practice of showing young indigenous girls how to weave. Instead, more and more Mayan girls are going to school and entering the workforce, sometimes out of necessity. What many might view as a huge advancement for women in fact contributes to the deterioration of traditional culture. This is not a critique of the growing educational opportunities open to young indigenous girls; I am merely stating a side effect of those new avenues. A third factor emerges directly from the second. As young Mayan women enter into the workforce or attend private schools with uniforms, they wear traditional dress less and less. Most Mayan men have all but abandoned *traje,* and one will often hear them describing the women as braver than they are for embracing this deliberate statement of Mayan culture publicly. The act of wearing indigenous dress as part of one's ritual of thanksgiving in contemporary Guatemalan culture is a manner of theologically affirming the culture and voices of indigenous people. The intersection of *traje* and ritual is also seen in the indigenous practice of dressing the saints or Mary or Jesus in *traje*.

Connecting the *traje* of Mayan women to the broader theme of women, religion, and the body, we see a strong relationship between women's clothing and religious identity. Many fascinating studies exist that look at how proscriptions on women's dress and hair across the world religions are a source both of oppression and of empowerment. Whether it is the Muslim veil, the Catholic habit, or the Indian sari, there are deep connections between women's identity, culture, holiness, and dress. Often modesty is associated with holiness in religious settings. In religious circles, the dress of men and women alike often indicates religious authority. Dress, the body, and religion go hand in hand. One cannot have an authentic theological anthropology that does not take the body seriously. Our bodies are part of our humanity. Whether it is the suffering bodies of enslaved women who remind us of the crucified Christ or the religious vestment that announces who has the most authoritative voice about that crucifixion, the body matters. Our bodies are a site of negotiation at the intersection of power and identity. It is through and in our bodies that we are religious, bodies that are coded by our gender, racial, and cultural identities.

Race

A final dimension I would like to add to this discussion is the function of race within our notions of the human. For many, the centrality of race within theological anthropology seems questionable. However, as Eleazer S. Fernandez rightfully reminds us, "Racism undergirds a certain way of construing and constructing the human. In this regard, racism is a question of anthropology, of who we are in relation to others. Racism involves our deepest beliefs about the human, beliefs that have often acquired the status of essentiality and eternality."[16] An anthropology that takes seriously how race and consequently racism have functioned within theology reveals that, in our constructions of humanity as created in the image of God, certain aspects of human existence have been privileged at the expense of others.

Black liberation theology emerged in the mid-1960s as an explosive theological movement in the United States. Nurtured by church leaders and academic theologians, black theology claims that the Christian God is a God of liberation and love. Black theologians promoted a message of self-love for African Americans, as children of God born in the image of

God. Included in this message is the denouncement of racism, which defies God's will for humanity and stands in contrast to the kingdom of God.

In his groundbreaking monograph *Race: A Theological Account*, J. Kameron Carter studies race as a theological category.[17] Fundamental to Carter's argument is the insistence that to truly understand race in contemporary intellectual discourse and society at large, a theological analysis of race is necessary. Similarly, Carter argues, one cannot understand racism without taking the centrality of religion into serious consideration. Before the publication of Carter's book, black theologians relied heavily on sociological and political constructions of race. This in turn led to a presentation of race and racism that was external to Christian thought. Race appeared as something on the outside, a lens through which to approach Christianity, one that could be swapped for the lens of gender, sexuality, culture, or class. Carter takes an entirely different approach, arguing that not only is race a theological category but that it has been since the first century. Theology, he argues, is part of the intellectual process of the construction of humanity as racialized.

Early Christians created a racialized understanding of themselves that is now fundamental to modern constructions of race. Jews became the "other," and Western Christian identity was created in contrast to that other. Jews became associated with the East, and Christian identity became synonymous with the West. Western civilization becomes identical to Christianity. The West, of course, was deemed superior, laying the groundwork for a Christian understanding of white supremacy. Carter's book first outlines the creation of this Western Christian white-supremacist category of whiteness and in the later parts of his book offers a constructive reimagination of Christian identity. This abstraction of Jesus from his historical, physical body is a key moment in making Jesus white. Reconnecting Jesus to his Jewish body deconstructs the white-supremacist notion of Christianity as synonymous with Western European culture. Carter closes his text with an appeal to contemporary Christian theology to ground itself in the world of people of color; those from the underside of modernity are the foundation of our reimagining a theological understanding of race and whiteness.

Too often discussions of race fall into the binaries of "black" and "white," particularly in the United States. Racial identity is much more complex, as the discussion on difference above highlights, than the simplistic categories we often employ. And yet attention to hybridity is not the innocent answer to challenging simple, dualistic constructs of racial identity. As thoughtfully highlighted by Manny Vazquez in his reconceptualization of *mestizaje*, constructions of hybridity can often eclipse the lives and struggles of the true subalterns of society. The danger of ladinoization is a dangerous one within the concept of *mestizaje*.[18] "Ladinoization" refers to the emphasis on mixture that often subsumes indigenous people who remain marginalized and are often further ignored when hybridity becomes the dominant discourse of racial identity. Miguel de la Torre offers a similar critique of *mulatez*, arguing that the Spanish adage that we are all coffee with milk, some more coffee, others more milk, erases the function of power in racial identity. "However, *leche* [milk] has access to employment, state services, power, wealth, and privilege, while *café* is disenfranchised."[19] In other words, emphasis on hybridity can lead us to naively ignore the complexity of racial identity and hierarchy among hybrid populations.

The process of ladinoization can turn violent. Returning to Guatemala, one finds a Mayan population that is thoroughly disenfranchised by the dominant ladino (*mestizo*) population. As indicated above, Mayans are subtly and forcefully encouraged to reject their indigenous customs, dress, and worldview in order to assimilate into Ladino culture. In this context, hybridity is an arm of oppression. In a different yet related vein, Vazquez also highlights the consumerism that can accompany *mestizaje:* "We are in a world in which hybridity has become a prime commodity, in which multinational corporations like Benetton appropriate the symbols of multiculturalism and the mixing of the races to promote a brand of cosmopolitan consumerism."[20] In other words, hybridity can be exploited. Ultimately, critiques like the one raised above do not negate the importance of highlighting difference and diversity. Hybridity is an element of the human condition. We must be aware, however, as Vazques reminds us, that "not all differences are created equal."[21]

Many theologians emphasize race and culture but in a manner in which these categories become lost in debates over identity politics. A corrective to this trend is found in Brian Bantum's provocative work examining biracial identity as theological. Bantum begins by urging U.S. minority theologians to look beyond their concrete embodiment when theologically reflecting on the body and instead to reflect on our bodies through a christological reflection on Jesus' hybridity. Racial embodiment must be recast christologically, not just socially. Jesus' redemption is not the redemption just of our bodies from oppression.[22] Bantum offers a christological anthropology based on the notion that Christ is mulatto. Jesus was human and divine; his is a personhood that emerges out of difference. "Jesus is mulatto is an ontological claim that suggests the union of flesh and Spirit is a fact of Jesus' personhood."[23] In contrast to the life of the American mulatto in the nineteenth and twentieth centuries, a life that was one of violence and tragedy, Jesus' *mulatez* reveals the transformative nature of hybridity. "Yet in Christ, the tragic mulatto's identity is not bound to our descriptions, but rather utterly confounds the claims of possibility and impossibility through his very birth," Bantum writes.[24] Christ creates a mulatto community through inviting us into a hybrid community through the Spirit. Racial identity is given theological value. Bantum's deep theological analysis reveals the manner in which concepts such as "race" and "identity" have theological value.

Concluding Comments

Using the complexity of human identity as the starting point of their theologies, liberation and constructive theologians bring forth the importance of relationships in their anthropologies. Because there are various elements that shape and color identity, one must center on the relationships that unite them and count them as the key factor that is constitutive of humanity's imago Dei. The Christian God is a God that exists in relationship. The foundation of the communal understanding of human nature is the community that is the Trinity. This understanding of the image of God in humanity mirrors the trinitarian life of relationships, and just as God relates within God's self and relates to God's creation, so do we humans have relationships among ourselves and with our Creator. In a similar manner, the God of Christian faith is a God of community, in which the three persons of the Trinity exist as one in relational community. We as humans mirror that communal nature as people who are individuals yet whose individuality can be understood only through the very communities and relationships that form our humanity. Theological anthropology must take into serious consideration, however, the ambiguous nature of humanity and the manners in which power and dominance function in communal settings. In these moments the image of the Trinity in humanity is distorted, resulting in communities that do not reflect divine relationship. Theologians, as Rosemary Carbine persuasively argues in this volume, must engage these issues at the level of public theology and not merely of internal academic discussion.

Elementary to liberation theologies is an understanding, summarized by Elizabeth A. Johnson, of the Christian God as not neutral: "When people are ground down, this violates the way God wants the world to be. In response, the living God makes a dramatic decision: to side with oppressed peoples in their struggle for life."[25] Central to constructive and liberation anthropology is the assertion that one cannot understand the human condition without reference to the divine. Because we are creatures created in the image of God, our humanity is inextricably linked to divine being. As the late Alejandro García-Rivera notes, "What is human cannot be known without reference to God, and that reference lies not with the distinctiveness of the human but with the connectedness of creation."[26] Our humanity is revealed through our relationships with the divine and with God's creation. Our humanity, however, always exists within our contextual particularity, where the diversity and the unity that are the human condition manifest themselves within our limited cultural context. Culture is the inescapable reality in which we are born, one that shapes every interpretive horizon of humanity, including our understandings of the divine. Classic theological anthropologies have often emphasized our spiritual relationship with the divine and downplayed its implications for our concrete existence. Theological anthropology must remain firmly grounded in the contemporary situation and not fall into abstract speculation that ignores the very materiality of human life. An emphasis on race, the body, and difference forces us to take contextualized human experience seriously within our theological anthropologies. Our embodied selves, with all their diversity and particularity, must be the starting point of theological reflection.

Christian understandings of the image of God are intimately linked to Jesus Christ. As God's concrete revelation within human history, as the center of Christian belief, Jesus' ministry, suffering, death, and resurrection are normative for Christian theology. Christology is an ambiguous area for feminist theologians, given the adamant use of Jesus' masculinity as a weapon to oppress women. Feminist theologians offer alternative christological visions that emphasize his ministry and message versus his masculinity. Through his incarnation and crucifixion, Jesus assumes the condition of weakness, thereby accompanying suffering people. This accompaniment tells us that the marginalized do not suffer alone; the resurrection confirms the triumph of life over dehumanization.

Contemporary theological anthropologies are aware of the manner in which the concrete human condition shapes and conditions human nature. In emphasizing race, difference, and the body, I hope to reaffirm these categories, which are often seen as obstacles to authentic Christian life. Too often difference is depicted in a negative light, as if it somehow undermines Christian unity, a unity that is there because of, not in spite of, the diversity and richness of global Christianity. The body has historically been constructed within Christianity as an impediment or obstacle to authentic

Christian spirituality. An attention to the complexity of race highlights its presence throughout the history of theological constructions within Christianity. In drawing attention to these three aspects of our humanity, power becomes fundamental to understanding human nature through a material theological anthropology that begins with the concreteness of the human condition and of the individual's lived religion.

CHAPTER 9

Public Theology: A Feminist View of Political Subjectivity and Praxis

Rosemary P. Carbine

Public theology is sometimes defined by the praxis of doing theology for the differing audiences, communities of accountability, or publics of the church, academy, and society that theologians address.[1] At other times, public theology is characterized by the method used to reach those audiences, either by making religious claims more intelligible to wider society via shared norms and practices of rational public discourse or by relying on religious institutions to shape and equip persons with virtues for participating in political discourse.[2] And, at other times, public theology is determined by the goal of integrating theology and ethics into the discursive practices of a deliberative democracy (e.g., lobbying elected officials, shaping public debate) in order to add religious perspectives to debates about pressing public-policy issues and to reach consensus about those issues.[3] Thus, public theology represents a polyvalent field of Christian thought and practice regarding the mutual interplay between religious and public life, between church and world, between the body of Christ and the body politic, or what historian Martin Marty called over thirty years ago "the *res publica*, the public order that surrounds and includes people of faith."[4]

The political or public realm or sphere in public theology is often identified with a model of deliberative democracy in which a democratic assembly of citizens collectively decide their common life via open rational
argument and debate about socially significant issues.[5] Also, the political
or public realm or sphere is often construed in an idealized way as a civil
society–based arena of equal-access rational interchange that reaches for
consensus about the common good. However, public life often fails to realize this egalitarian vision of civil society's communicative practices; instead, it operates in exclusionary ways, with roots in race, gender, class,
ethnic, religious, and other social constructions of what determines rational discourse, who counts as a political actor, and what defines the common good. With regard to its anthropology, the political or public realm
or sphere is tied to and trades on still-operative modern notions about
who constitutes and contributes to public life in ways that institutionalize
patriarchal ideals of political subjectivity and agency, sociopolitical power,
and participation.[6]

For example, religion, race, and citizenship talk in recent U.S. politics
articulates and markets a discourse and practice of "othering" that fuels
political demonization and thereby disenfranchises "others" from public
life. In the fast-paced weeks prior to the 2008 U.S. presidential election,
Democratic presidential nominee Senator Barack Obama was persistently
branded as Muslim. Being Muslim was wielded as a weapon to "other," to
reassert the dominant racial and religious marks of personhood in a post-
9/11 era and thereby to render Obama an unfit candidate for embodying a
ma(i)nly white and Christian (especially Protestant) iconic ideal of political subjectivity and agency symbolized by the White House. Moreover,
immigration issues in the U.S. illuminate an increasingly economic and
legalistic approach to personhood and citizenship. Speaking of immigrants
as "undocumented workers" reduces persons to their labor, boxes persons
into their geopolitical identities, and defines "others" in reference to predominant notions of personhood tied to legal citizenship, to hypermilita-
rized fenced borders, and to economically driven xenophobic nationalism.
Partly upheld by the U.S. Supreme Court's ruling, Arizona's law SB1070
empowers police to investigate the immigration status of those arrested
or in custody if there is "reasonable suspicion" of that status, which only
further demonstrates a rising U.S. legalist as well as nativist approach to
political subjectivity. Five other states passed similar discriminatory (verg-
ing on racial-profiling) laws—Alabama, Georgia, Indiana, South Carolina,
and Utah. Finally, the U.S. Supreme Court's ruling in *Citizens United* treats

corporations as persons, which not only lifts limits on corporate contributions to political campaigns but also further entrenches patterns of economic dominance in—as well as exclusion from—political agency and participation.

Lacking political subjectivity and agency in all these ways threatens serious theological and political consequences for our very humanity. Theologically, any denial of political participation diminishes the common good, or the totality of conditions that promote individual and communal fulfillment and flourishing. Politically marginalized and disenfranchised folk—as a result, for example, of voter disenfranchisement in the 2000 and 2004 U.S. presidential elections and voter suppression prior to the 2012 U.S. presidential election in Ohio, Florida, Pennsylvania, and Wisconsin—lack not only civil rights but also full human dignity, because human beings according to Catholic social thought are created in and for sociality and actualize that sociality by contributing to, among other things, public life.[7] Politically, public theology still rests on a modern rationalist view of public life and political subjectivity constituted by autonomous, self-interested individuals. From a modernist perspective, public life is according to feminist and public theologian Linell Cady "the collective sum of autonomous individuals whose values and goals are resolutely private" and "the receptacle that contained individual units. In a very real sense public life in this scenario was the individual writ large, the duplication on the macrocosmic level of its microcosmic atomism."[8] Public theology's modern Enlightenment heritage still privileges an affluent, androcentric Euro-American model of political subjectivity that marginalizes women as well as all "others" from public life; it in effect restricts what constitutes both public life and political actors and action. Thus, a different anthropology is needed to bolster a different account of public engagement and of political subjectivity.

To address these challenges to predominant understandings of what constitutes public theology and political subjectivity and agency, this essay calls for reshaping both political subjectivity and praxis based on the notion that public theology can be construed as the work of imagining, creating, and sustaining a public, a common life. From this perspective, public theology is called "public" not because it adds religious insights to socially significant issues (and thus avoids the accusation of functionalizing or instrumentalizing religious beliefs and practices) and not because it showcases otherwise privately held confessional claims or religious performances in public (and thereby eschews engaging in an apologetic for religion in public life). Rather, public theology is "public" mainly because of its "convocative capability," or its imperative to perform community-building work, to create an overarching, transcendent, or "ultimate public" in which we live, move, and have our being, sociopolitically speaking.[9] Practices for making that public partake in what Roger Gottlieb calls "world-making," or opening up a space to envision and begin to enact a more participatory and just vision of our common life.[10]

In keeping with this definition, in this essay I propose a constructive feminist public theology that goes beyond solely rational notions of political subjectivity and participation, and that explores alternate forms of democratic personhood and praxis connected to this community-creating work of public theology. Effective public theology, in my view, has less to do with influencing debate in a not-quite-shared community of rational discourse and more to do with fostering an array of democratic practices that aim to remake the public itself, to create a more inclusive and just common life. Before attending to examples of those practices, this essay considers which theological understanding of the person acts as leverage to better advance this view of public theology and its varied ways of building community. Exploring the insights of feminist, womanist, and *mujerista* theological anthropologies will help rethink public theology's underlying notion of political personhood, which often aligns with a modern Euro-American notion of rational humanity and its associated modes of political participation, and which falsely naturalizes or ontologizes gendered, racialized, nativist, and corporatist constructs of the human person as described above. This essay then turns to cornerstone Catholic social teachings on the Church's public role in order to supply and sharpen a theological, specifically eschatological, horizon for public theology's community-building praxis. Elaborating a constructive feminist public theology in this way ultimately points toward a political reconceptualization of the imago Dei, or a theological notion of political subjectivity and agency rooted in relationality and performativity (rather than only in rationality) in ways that beckon us to live—and live into—our full humanity in community.

Insights from Feminist Theological Anthropology: Turning from Rationality to Relationality

The current U.S. sociopolitical situation, as described above, raises fundamental questions about the meaning of human being and the shape of public life that best supports full humanity. A renewed public theology, then, depends on a renewed political anthropology, or an updated understanding of political subjectivity that goes beyond rationality. Feminist, womanist, and *mujerista* anthropologies within the Christian tradition offer some key insights into rethinking subjectivity, both theologically and politically, by turning to relationality as a common mark not only of humanity but of public life. To offset the limits of rationalist understandings of the person in public theology, we will look to feminist theological anthropology, broadly construed, which advances the transformation of self and of society via relationality. As I will argue in this section, turning from rational to relational understandings of the person offers a new understanding of "public" in "public theology." This relational turn more than broadens political action beyond rationality and more than enlarges political community beyond a dominant elite; rather, this turn reconfigures the purpose of public theology altogether. Feminist theological anthropology lends a new perspective from which to consider what constitutes our being and becoming in relation to others. A relational notion of the person better allies with and accompanies the convocative goal of public theology; creating a more inclusive and just public life in which we actively hope and cocreate with one another requires this new anthropology that trades on being and becoming more human in community.

Theological anthropology emerged as its own field of religious reflection with the modern turn to the subject and its emphasis on individuality, autonomy, and subjectivity.[11] In particular, feminist theological anthropology analyzes many tacit, often troubling implications about the account of human nature that takes shape within the context of Christian theological categories, including God, creation, sin and grace, and Christology.[12] Feminist theological understandings of the human person emphasize the equal creation of all human beings in the image and likeness of God,[13] the equal distortion of that image in men and women alike through sin,[14] and the equally longed-for transformation of that image in the person and work of Jesus Christ—but do so in light of gender, race, class, sexuality, ability, and other features of the human person that challenge any fixed ontotheological notion of human nature. For example, in the preceding chapter Michelle A. Gonzalez proposes a materialist anthropology which emphasizes lived realities of human difference, embodiment, and race rather than spiritualized or abstract notions of human nature. In these ways, feminist theological anthropology challenges and seeks to avoid any essentialist portrait of humanity—including magisterial theologies that religiously justify and reinforce patriarchal norms, roles, and relations for men and women in the Church and in society—that reduces women and men to purportedly biophysically based and in other ways fixed or determined attributes that dictate and differentiate gender and other roles.[15]

Four main theological models of the person long predominated in feminist theological anthropology: a dual-nature model; a single-nature model; a transformative model; and, finally, a multipolar model.[16] A dual-nature model, based on biological sex differences and socioculturally determined gender roles that trade on and reinscribe those differences, emphasizes women's human nature as different from but complementary to men's human nature. A single-nature model proposes a shared human nature that is expressed differently by women and men, apart from biological traits and gender roles built on those traits. A transformative model supports the full subjectivity of women and men as they participate in and transform self, Church, and society through the gospel-based ministry of Jesus for justice and peace. Finally, a multipolar model identifies a set of anthropological constants or essential human elements—including but not limited to biologically based sex differences—that are shared by women and men but shaped differently in and by different social locations.

More recent trends in feminist anthropology emphasize intersectionality[17] and performance[18] to situate persons in the midst of multiple intersecting social contexts and relations[19] that we actively and perennially navigate and negotiate in order to create an integrated sense, at least partly, of self-identity-in-community. Serene Jones urges a constructivist subjectivity that forefronts women as "bricoleurs," cobbling together identity in relation and in resistance to already given scripted social roles and settings.[20] The "nature" of women and, by implication, of all of us, is not static, fixed, or already biophysically, ontologically, or socioculturally determined; rather, women's subjectivity is continually re/created and re/constructed into a more holistic self-identity by an active agential negotiation of multiple relations and communities of belonging. As Cady explains, a constructivist anthropology "rejects the abstract, unified subject of modernism. But it does so without embracing its mirror opposite. It recognizes that identity is multiple, fluid, and shifting, but for all that, it is not fictitious, ephemeral, or limitless. . . . Identity is constituted by the subject's creative, agential negotiation of the intersecting currents and competing loyalties that run through her."[21] For Cady, our subjectivity or sense of self is continually produced; we perennially "rewrite" identity while negotiating our particular given and chosen web of relations.[22] Personhood, then, is regarded in more recent feminist theoretical and theological perspectives as a relational and a performative reality.[23]

Paralleling these trends, feminist, womanist, and *mujerista* theological anthropologies illustrated in the work of Elizabeth A. Johnson, M. Shawn Copeland, and Ada María Isasi-Díaz, respectively, place sex and gender

among many "anthropological constants" in order to offset Christian theological tendencies toward idealized patriarchal definitions of humanity.
Elizabeth Johnson proposes a complex relational matrix of human identity
that entails relations to bodies and to sexuality; to the whole earthly ecol-
ogy; to other persons; to sociopolitical, economic, and cultural institutions
and structures in different historical contexts; and to the future.[24] Also,
M. Shawn Copeland focuses on social suffering in Black women's lives at
the intersections of race, gender, and class to enumerate some shared features of human personhood: a divine creation; an incarnate spirit, marked
by race, gender, sex, sexuality, and culture; a person living in just community with others via personal responsibility and freedom; a social being that
embraces difference and interdependence; and a person struggling for the
survival, ongoing re-creation, and the future of all life.[25] Furthermore, Ada
María Isasi-Díaz reflects on the *mestizaje/mulatez*–based reality of Latina
women's lives shaped by the racial, cultural, religious, and other forms of
intermixture and intermingling of multiple communities that took place
between colonizing European peoples and indigenous Latin American
peoples in the fifteenth and sixteenth centuries and that continued in the
U.S. expansion into and annexation of what is now New Mexico, Texas,
Arizona, and California in the nineteenth century. Isasi-Díaz elaborates on
the implications of this term to place personhood in the context of extended
relations—that is, to capture a way of living at the multiple borders and
intersections of racial, cultural, religious, and other differences.[26] Highlighting the need for creativity in a relational subjectivity, Asian American
feminist theologian Rita Nakashima Brock summarizes and advances these
trends via what she terms an interstitial anthropology, which underscores
how Asian American women sculpt or fashion an integrated identity at the
interstices, or in-between connective spaces, of multiple communities of
belonging that co-constitute them, for good and for ill.[27] The relational
turn in feminist, womanist, and *mujerista* anthropologies, in sum, attends
to living in between and making meaning of multiple worlds that always
already inform and shape a person in order to achieve some semblance of
personal self-identity-in-relation.

In my view, these trends in feminist, womanist, and *mujerista* theological
anthropologies help reinvent and rethink political subjectivity and agency,
and in doing so help thematize and theologize about public theology more
effectively. As argued in the previous section, public theologies share and
act on a community-building imperative to create and sustain a public,
to generate community. Negotiating and integrating multiple communities of belonging in oneself, as these anthropologies claim, parallels and

propels the convocative or community-creating work of public theology, or the work to create and sustain a more just, participatory public. Drawing on the insights of these anthropologies, public theology refers primarily to a theology that is located or situated at the relational intersections or interstices of multiple groups and that is differentiated by its forms of community-creating praxis that knit, stitch, or weave multiple groups together into a more comprehensive, inclusive, and just social fabric of public life. More importantly, following the relational turn in feminist anthropology eschews a modern rationalist and isolationist portrait of human being, and so rejuvenates political subjectivity and agency. A relational anthropology signifies being and building up a reconciled and just body within oneself, and so better accompanies doing similar community-creating work in and for the body politic in public theology.

This turn to relationality is not exclusive to feminist theologies, broadly understood. As Wilhelm Guggenberger explains in the following chapter, relationality is a core characteristic or component of contemporary mimetic theory. On my reading, feminist theological anthropology finds better allies among moral philosophers of public life on this relational turn and its impact on political subjectivity. Hannah Arendt and Paul Ricoeur emphasized a dialogical understanding of public life, very similar to what public theologians discuss as a deliberative model of democracy. In this view of civil society, the public sphere as well as persons in it are portrayed in a social ontology, or are discursively mediated and constituted in relation. In other words, persons participate in as well as emerge from public discourse; not only our society but also our very selves are adjudicated and adjusted through democratic discourse and debate. As Arendt argues, our words and deeds in public life, or what she named in one place "the web of human relationships," both reveal and shape our identities, which are always already inherently intertwined with many contexts and groups (such as families, local/national/global communities, religious traditions, movements, organizations, and so on). For Arendt, our self-identities—which result from making interpretive sense of these multiple communities—are not solely our own but serve as shared identities.[28] Thus, our identities fundamentally put us in touch with others.

Relationality not only prominently features in public life; it also results from engaging in public life. Paul Ricoeur offers an extended philosophical study of this co-constitution of the self through narrative, highlighting its implications for an ethics of responsibility. For Ricoeur, we recreate and reconstruct our personal identities by negotiating our "entanglement" in the stories of others.[29] Making meaningful sense of our embeddedness in a web of multiple relations and stories involves recounting a self-identity that both empowers an individual and places an individual in shared relations of responsibility to others. The power of "naming" oneself, according to Ricoeur, is articulated and enacted "in the power to say, in the power to do, in the power to recognize oneself as a character in a narrative, in the power, finally, to respond" to others.[30] Womanist theology reframes these powers as "generative powers: the power of voice, the power of making do, the power of memory, the power of holding things together, and the power of generation."[31] Thus, our story is always interrelated with and retains responsibilities to the stories of others. Put in terms of public theology, recognition of oneself as a political subject or actor with the ability to engage in political discourse and praxis is intimately connected to a similar recognition of others as well as of our responsibility to them and to the common good.

Feminist theological anthropology, therefore, affirms that personhood is both given and made, and in public; a person is already situated in a set of relations, and a person's subjectivity emerges and is shaped via negotiation of these relations. Integrating this insight with the field of public theology, feminist public theology affirms that negotiating political relations is integral to personhood itself. Full humanity depends at least partly on continually unpacking and understanding our relations for their political implications. As Cady writes:

> We are, of course, not members of only one community or tradition that serves as our exclusive "point of entry" to the cultivation of a global order. We belong to a variety of social units each with its own history and agenda. . . . Not only is there no overarching coherent order within which each of these associations can be located, but the social units themselves are marked by varying degrees of tension and discord. The individual, then, is perennially involved in synthesizing the competing values and demands within these associations as well as between them. . . . It makes vividly clear that the creation of public life is a perennial task with an inescapable moral dimension to it.[32]

The relational turn in feminist anthropology and in other disciplines, therefore, locates public/political life as intrinsic rather than extrinsic to being human, as one among a variety of communities that require ongoing negotiation and synthesis—not only to achieve full humanity but to aspire to a more just common life.[33]

Feminist, womanist, and *mujerista* theological anthropology assists us in remembering the relationality of all life—a relationality that on the one hand is recognized, enacted, and remade by the exchanging of our very selves in the body politic and on the other hand fuels the remaking of that body politic itself. First, these insights from feminist anthropology play a significant role in recognizing our very being and becoming more fully human in and through relationships. Subjectivity is both claimed and crafted through relationships. As feminist theologian Jane Kopas observes, our interpretation of our relationships in many communities participates in the constitution—or, in theological terms, the incarnation—of the person.[34] Second, in keeping with a relational subjectivity that underlies feminist theological anthropology, engaging in public life involves a struggle to see, deepen, and alter for the better our existing relationships. That is to say, the re/constitution of ourselves in and through public life also heralds the remaking of public life itself, which is founded on those relationships. Re/membering our relationality in the public sphere may well serve as an important step for feminist theologians to address some of the most pressing issues in our common life today that epitomize the forgetting of such relationality, such as the growing inequalities—noted at the outset of this essay—around race, gender, class, religion, and national identity. As womanist theologian M. Shawn Copeland argues, these "body marks" within patriarchy, slavocracy, empire, and globalization disrupt and devalue our relations by reducing most of humanity to parts to be consumed and cannibalized for the pleasure and profit of the few.[35] Reconciling—or re/membering—all of our bodies takes place in the body of Christ, which effects the healing of personal bodies, the ecclesial body, and the body politic.[36]

In brief, when viewed from a feminist anthropological perspective, doing public theology means occupying a middle space between different communities in order to envision and realize a reconciled sense of self and society. Doing public theology also means inhabiting a middle space between a sometimes alienating, unjust present and a longed-for future that is more reconciled, more just. Engaging Catholic social thought on the Church's sociopolitical mission provides a rich theological vision of the person and public life against which to judge what sort of ultimate public or community we seek to create in ourselves and society.

Insights from Catholic Social Thought: Returning to Anthropology and Eschatology

In its constitution on the Church's role in the modern world, *Gaudium et Spes* (hereafter *GS*), Vatican II wrestled with sociocultural, economic, and political barriers to participating in public life (*GS*, 4, 27, 73, 75). Rooted in the Church's central mission to signify and protect the dignity of humanity (*GS*, 73, 76), *GS* articulated the Church's sociopolitical role as an advocate for human dignity and rights (*GS*, 40–42, 45),[37] especially "to enable all citizens, and not just a few privileged individuals, to exercise their rights effectively as persons" in public life (*GS*, 73). Engaging the "public order" in *GS* is characterized as central to love of God and neighbor (*GS*, 24, 27), salvation (*GS*, 43), and realizing the kingdom of God, or its vision of the good society based on love, justice, and peace (*GS*, 39, 45). Revisiting and critically reappropriating this understanding of the Church's social mission reveals theological criteria, in anthropology and eschatology, for the praxis of public theology—that is, for the vision of the public that guides such praxis from a feminist theological perspective.

With respect to anthropology, *GS* correlates a fragmented public life with a fractured humanity, marked by structural sin (*GS*, 4–6, 8, 10, 13, 37; cf. 24–25) and manifested in the institutionalization of injustice and inequality along gender, race, class, sociopolitical, religious, and inter/national lines (*GS*, 4, 8, 29). Thus, in *GS*, the renewal of society is inextricably interrelated to the renewal of the human person (*GS*, 3), and the renewal of the human person is grounded in the representative model of redeemed humanity, in Christ (*GS*, 10, 22, 24, 38, 41, 45). "Conformed to the image of the Son who is the firstborn of many brothers and sisters . . . the entire person is inwardly renewed, even to the 'redemption of the body" (Rom. 8:23)" (*GS*, 22), and, in my view, even to the redemption of the body politic.[38] *GS* outlines a relational anthropology (*GS*, 12, 23–25) grounded in creation in the image and likeness of a triune God (*GS*, 12, 19, 24, 29). In this anthropology, humans are created for sociality and for relations with God (*GS*, 19) and with others in society (*GS*, 42–43) and are called to better realize that relationality by contributing to the common good (*GS*, 26, 30), social justice (*GS*, 29), and public life (*GS*, 31). In other words, such a relational anthropology sheds light on both our increasing interdependence (*GS*, 5, 23) and our resulting complex conflicts (*GS*, 10, 25). Thus, the "communitarian character" of human life (*GS*, 32)—or the task to create community or to become more fully human in the midst of multiple communities—involves actively working for a more loving, just, and peaceful world order, modeled on the kingdom of God and motivated by Jesus' liberative preaching, healing, and eating practices (*GS*, 39).[39] This relational anthropology emphasizes our lifelong spiritual and social renewal as christologically influenced artisans, or "molders of a new humanity" (*GS*, 30; cf. 4, 29, 43, 55).[40]

With respect to eschatology, *GS*'s vision of humanity as artisans of the kingdom of God supports the convocative or the community-building work of public theology.[41] *GS* places our multiple relationships in an eschatological context of the future kingdom of God. That guiding future vision motivates the Church's mission and ministry to work for this-worldly social justice (*GS*, 21, 39, 43, 57), in personal and public life. From a theological perspective, this work depends on "incarnational solidarity,"[42] or a christic praxis that emulates the life and ministry of Jesus for the kingdom of God and its associated values of justice, love, and peace (*GS*, 32): "On this earth that Kingdom is already present in mystery. When the Lord returns it will be brought into full flower" (*GS*, 39). Such praxis anticipates and partially reflects a more just sense of self and common life that ultimately awaits a future eschatological fulfillment (*GS*, 38–40).[43]

GS, therefore, offers a theological vantage point from which to challenge political exclusion and inequality (the imago Dei) and to work to create a more inclusive, participatory, and just public life (the kingdom of God). Yet the imago Dei and the kingdom of God are both partially present but still longed-for future realities in a personally and structurally sinful world.[44] After all, claiming equal creation in the imago Dei need not subvert social inequalities in race, gender, class, sexual, or human–earthly relations. As Mary Catherine Hilkert argues, the "scandal" of the gospel is not the reign of God that Jesus envisioned, preached, and lived but that "the reign of God is discovered among and entrusted to human persons and communities despite all of our limits . . . *we have the power to enflesh the communion that is our final destiny—if only in fragmentary ways.*"[45] This renewed theological vision of political subjectivity and public life based on anthropology and eschatology carries some significant implications for political life and participation. Because political subjectivity and agency are worked out within existing sinful relations, we always actively attain to and await becoming more fully human in more just and justice-oriented relations, catching only glimpses of the kind of public life that supports such full humanity. Because realizing our creation in the image of God consists largely of a future reality, creating that kind of public life is then also largely a future reality, already begun and performed in varied forms of praxis but not yet fully realized. In the following, final section of this chapter, I consider kinds of public theology involved in the praxis of "enfleshing communion," or creating community.

Praxis for Creating Community

If the definition of public theology shifts from a narrow legalistic view of shaping public policy via rational debate to a broad humanistic goal of shaping the common good, then we need to examine the kinds of practices that support that goal and that provide a means of restoring full humanity, or political and personal dignity in community. Taking a cue from marginalized and minoritized groups, philosopher Iris Marion Young observed that these groups—though largely absent from dominant discursive political arenas—relied on alternative practices (narrative, visual and symbolic media, and protest politics) to regain meaningful political agency and participation.[46] Looking beyond rationalist notions of public life-cum–civic debate reveals a rich array of practices of public engagement to do the community-building work of public theology, what I have elsewhere called rhetorical, symbolic, and prophetic praxis.[47]

First, rhetorical practices focus on a variety of aesthetic genres that give voice to and urge solidarity with marginalized peoples often denied political subjectivity and agency. As thematized by Rebecca Chopp, one genre, testimony, holds much theological potential for reconfiguring common life, especially its tacit shared self-understanding or "narrative identity," through the gaining of public recognition and justice for multiple voices.[48] Testimony involves the telling and hearing of marginalized people's stories of suffering and hope, in order to break open a counter-public space for empathy, for solidarity, and for imagining and creating a transcendent and more flourishing future common life.[49] Thus, testimony bears both anthropological and eschatological significance: "Testimony in public discourse narrates a story, a story that allows the transcendent, the possibility of the new, to break in and open us to change and transformation."[50]

For example, narrative in the work of moral and political philosopher Hannah Arendt, feminist critical theorist María Pía Lara, sociologist and activist Marshall Ganz, and theologian Mary Doak stands as one rhetorical practice of rightful political recognition for marginalized groups and for creating community by reconfiguring public life for justice.[51] Also, testimony from African American community activists and victim-survivors of Hurricane Katrina during U.S. congressional hearings in 2005 provided a political platform from which these marginalized groups regained political access and participation, enacted political agency, and reshaped the contours and constitutive values of U.S. public discourse and life, even for a short time. In doing so, these groups leveraged their personal stories into a theo-politically informed commentary (framed by the symbol of the cross) about the means to cease social suffering and to better realize the common good by building solidarity with the stories of others.[52]

Second, symbolic practices according to Michael and Kenneth Himes, David Hollenbach, and Cady reflect on the sociopolitical significance and implications of central religious symbols[53] in order to construct a transcendent normative moral framework of shared rights and responsibilities in public life.[54] Rather than sacralize a borderline theocratic nation-state, justify a certain sociopolitical order, or demand confessional conformity to a Christian theological imaginary (and thereby disregard religious pluralism),[55] public theologies draw on or extend Christianity's organizing symbols, especially God-talk,[56] in order to craft a shared political space of moral discourse and practice about the meaning of human being and the mutual obligations of human beings to one another and to society.[57] For instance, God-talk illuminates the intrinsic worth and interdependent nature of all life[58] as derived from an inherent imago Dei–based human right to relationship and to community, which then theologically articulates and bolsters a universal human-rights agenda. Creation in the image and likeness of God signifies a religious basis (but does not rule out other bases, religious or secular) for universal human dignity, while various legal, political, and social structures assure and protect that dignity.

For example, in the U.S. Catholic bishops' pastoral letter *Economic Justice for All*, the imago Dei serves as a theo-political leverage point to trump any disregard for human rights to life, food, clothing, housing, rest, health care, education, and meaningful work, including full employment, fair wages, safe and stable working conditions, and collective action via unions.[59] In the letter, all these rights in Catholic social thought flow from God-talk, especially from the theological symbol of the human person made in the image of a relational God and made for participating in community.[60] Coincident with the twenty-fifth anniversary of the U.S. bishops' letter, the Vatican's Pontifical Council for Justice and Peace issued a note on the economy and its "great economic, social and cultural inequalities" in the wake of the Great Recession since 2007.[61] In this note, the Vatican "identified the roots of a crisis that is not only economic and financial but above all moral in nature" and stated that the solution, in part, involves a return to a "people-centered" ethics that "recognize[s] their intrinsic transcendent dignity." This ethics rests on "a keen sense of belonging to the human family which means sharing the common dignity of all human beings"; it inspires the Vatican's proposal for a new global institution to fairly regulate the world's economic markets and reforms, which calls for a "new model of a more cohesive, polyarchic international society that respects every people's identity within the multifaceted riches of a single humanity."

Third, in keeping with scriptural studies of prophetic traditions, prophetic practices "criticize" or challenge injustices in public life and simultaneously "energize" or engage in practices that both imagine and live out—or, in feminist theological words, perform—hope in more-just future alternative possibilities.[62] Prophetic practices carry theo-political significance because Christian social-justice movements resonate with a this-worldly eschatology. According to Mark Taylor, these movements mediate the present and future reality, or "enable activists to taste the world for which they work." Activism in these movements "unlock[s] an actual world-making power in social and political settings. The world that is tasted aesthetically, acted out, especially when done repeatedly, issues in the enactment of new worlds, of new patterns of social and political interaction."[63] Politically marginalized and minoritized groups mobilize public support through prophetic practices that dramatize injustice and that also attempt to partly actualize an alternative possibility to that injustice through different forms of collective action—e.g., strikes, rallies, marches, and other demonstrations. Such collective action raises public awareness about and fosters solidarity with suffering peoples, and in doing so begins to reconstruct contemporary public life in more just ways.

For example, the New Sanctuary Movement—which traces its heritage to activist Christian churches that sheltered and supported Central American civil-war refugees in the 1980s[64]—began in May 2007. The NSM raises public awareness about immigration reform through education, especially about the political and moral problems with the current U.S. immigration system demonstrated by the increased U.S. Immigration and Customs Enforcement (or ICE) raids around that time, from Boston to Los Angeles, that detained and displaced parents from their families.[65] The NSM also provides legal, financial, humanitarian, and spiritual aid to immigrant families, especially in high-profile cases of women resisting displacement from their families.[66] The NSM advocates particularly for parents with U.S.-born, and therefore citizen, children who have come to signify the 12–20 million undocumented people in the United States. Formerly headed by Rev. Alexia Salvatierra of Clergy and Laity United for Economic Justice in Los Angeles, the NSM coordinates an interfaith network of religious organizations in Los Angeles, Chicago, New York, and a growing number of other U.S. cities that work with families facing deportation, keeping them together by giving them sanctuary in participating houses of worship.[67] The NSM signifies the church, physically and symbolically, as a model of the public good founded on love, justice, and peace—too long denied to immigrants under the current U.S. legal system and global labor markets but mandated by scriptural ethics and parables about the reign of God (e.g., Lev. 19:33–34; Matt. 25:34–36, 41–43).

The NSM's prophetic praxis of giving sanctuary expresses theologically and embodies politically a Christian-inspired vision of the public good, of a more just, more emancipatory body politic. Giving sanctuary imagines and begins to enact the inbreaking of an alternative radical democratic space that honors basic human dignity and rights despite narrow legalistic and border-based nationalistic views of citizenship rights.[68]

This essay's concluding section has offered some salient examples to explore some of the theological bases or underpinnings of religio-political movements that aim to restore political subjectivity and agency in our time. Rhetorical practices that educate everyday citizens and political leaders alike about institutionalized injustices within society, symbolic practices that reinterpret a religious symbol system to redirect a sociopolitical moral imaginary, and prophetic practices that pave the way for a more just alternative sociopolitical order all embrace and enact a definition of public theology as world-making, as community-building. They emphasize different forms of political participation that reach toward a reshaped shared sense of the common good. In keeping with feminist anthropologies, these practices require and reinforce a relational and performative view of the person and public life—in which we perform the relationships that inhere in our humanity but that are always imperfectly realized in our common life. In other words, world-making parallels and influences an eschatological process of self-making, and vice versa. And, in keeping with Catholic social thought, these practices urge us toward a more just and humane life, collectively and individually. As Cady observes, public theology constitutes "a perennial struggle to reform this life in light of the eschatological goal toward which creation, it may be hoped, asymptotically moves."[69] Together, these practices contribute to a hope-filled, eschatological way of being and becoming more fully human, more fully the imago Dei, in relations of love, justice, and peace that entail a rearticulated sense of political subjectivity and praxis.

CHAPTER 10

Desire, Mimetic Theory, and Original Sin

Wilhelm Guggenberger

Today it is unusual to offer a comprehensive philosophical theory about the nature of human beings, or a theory about the origins of religion, or a theory of human culture in general. The French historian, literary critic, and philosopher René Girard (born 1923) has tried to do all of this with his mimetic theory. Though not a theologian, Girard has dealt in great detail with the biblical tradition—unusual for a secular social scientist. I will present one adoption of his theory into theological research: the "dramatic theology" that originated with the Swiss systematic theologian Raymund Schwager, S.J. (1935–2004), and is still being cultivated and developed, most notably at the University of Innsbruck, in Austria.

Dramatic theology is characterized by an understanding of salvific history as a dramatic process in which free agents interact. Through this interaction the freedom of agents is mutually influenced, negatively and positively at the same time. The crucial point concerning salvific history is that God involves himself in this history, where he acts but without nullifying human freedom. God's acting, as narrated in the biblical text, cannot be understood in isolation from human acting, as it is a reaction to human behavior. Particular words or deeds of God and of Jesus Christ have to be interpreted in the context of the unfolding drama, outside of which they will make no sense or be misunderstood. Further, revelation is given not as a bundle of true sentences sent from heaven but rather as the entirety of encounters and experiences—including human refusal, conflict, and misunderstandings, handed down in stories—in which God becomes entangled.

My aim is to demonstrate that an encounter of Christian theology with mimetic theory can be a helpful contribution to Christian anthropology and to the understanding of original sin in particular. James Alison has written of the Girardian approach that "it will be possible to make theological use of this anthropology while remaining theological."[1] This character of Girard's work undoubtedly influenced Schwager's decision to choose it as a source of inspiration and also as an interlocutor in his own work to develop a theological approach that addresses practical challenges. Although the project of dramatic theology is only one possible example of such an encounter with Girard's work, it should be noted that the long-standing dialogue and friendship between Schwager and Girard has influenced Girard's own scholarship.[2] So we are dealing here with a rare example of real interdisciplinary discourse in which both parties have been able to learn from each other.

Core Elements of Mimetic Theory

In this chapter I will summarize the three essential pillars on which Girard's theory is built, in order to discuss the approach that dramatic theology takes to the topic of sin and of sin's presence in human history.

First, I should mention that the basis of Girard's anthropology is not fieldwork or any kind of empirical investigation but the analysis particularly of literary traces of the self-perception of people shaped by Western culture. Girard finds that poetry and drama sometimes offer more in this regard than does philosophical reflection, because their approach to human nature and behavior is more intuitive and direct. Girard considers, in addition to modern Western literary works, the mythological narratives of different cultures and peoples. His assumption is that these texts contain collective memories of the civilizations in question.[4] Next, he compares mythological texts with biblical ones, developing a complex conception of similarities and differences between these two kinds of narratives, culminating in a provocative analysis.

Though Girard himself has never been much interested in theory-scaffolding, from his work we may distill three crucial elements, or pillars, of the theory of mimesis: mimetic desire, the scapegoat mechanism, and the biblical change of perspective.

MIMETIC DESIRE

The human being is a longing being. Girard assumes that human beings desire by nature. The understanding of desire as dynamism driving (at least) cultural development is related to what Henry Bergson called the "élan vital."[5] Bergson sees this élan, though present in all nature, as reaching its summit in human beings. It can be understood as the prerequisite of self-transcendence. As desiring human beings we are open to something beyond us, and we are always willing to outgrow the given situation of our present existence to reach the greater goal. "A feeling of incompleteness is part of the human condition," as Jonah Wharff observes.[6] This incompleteness should not be understood in terms of Arnold Gehlen's philosophical anthropology, which focusses on fault. According to Gehlen, the human race's naturally flawed adaptation to the natural environment motivates it to develop culture. Humans in the Girardian understanding are not more incomplete than other living beings but are aware of their incompleteness, which makes them insatiable animals.[7] Desire in this sense is a kind of longing, not a vice.

A crucial element of mimetic theory is the assumption that, even if we desire by nature, there are no predetermined contents of desire. We have to want, but we do not have to want distinct objects. How do we decide what to want? Of course, we are not talking about means of subsistence here, because human desire undoubtedly does not stop at the moment basic needs are met; otherwise, there would be neither cultural development nor social conflict. Girard distinguishes desire (*désir* or *passion*) from appetite (*appétits*).[8] "Appetites are biologically preconditioned," as Michael Kirwan puts it, "whereas desire is much more a function of culture."[9]

One of the illusions particularly of modern people is to imagine that our longings result from our free individual will and our autonomous decisions. Girard calls this illusion a romantic lie.[10] Our wants and desires are always mediated. That means we are not focused on desirable objects first. Rather, we watch other subjects, recognizing what they want to be and want to have. By this we learn—more or less unconsciously—what is worth being wanted. In mimetic theory this constellation is called triangularity, consisting of subject, object, and mediator. We are social beings even with respect to our most intimate needs and wishes, involved in a dense network of relations.

Here a bridge to Martin Buber's personalism seems apt. The opinion that an "I" needs a "You" to become an "I" is understood by Girard in a radical way. Not even in our desires are we original or autonomous beings, because we remain dependent on our relationships with others. And so personal identity in its innermost components is modeled on others. The psychiatrist Jean-Michel Oughourlian uses the term "self" to mark not individuals involved in the mimetic relationship but rather the relationship itself as an emerging reality. "This relationship with the other seems to me so close and so fundamental," he writes, "that it should not be seen as merely a relation between two individuals, two subjects, but as a reciprocal movement of back and forth, carving out in each of its poles, by its very motion, an entity that could be designated as the 'self.'"[11] This may sober individuals who like to imagine themselves as rational, autonomous, and standing above all unnoticed influences. However, Oughourlian's approach allows him to give a proper description of what existing as a social being really means: "The self is not something hidden away, sheltered, and fortified within itself, but a product of a continuous process of creation taking place at the crossroads of our encounters, within our abiding, symmetrical exchanges with those around us. It cannot be born except from these exchanges."[12]

Although that may seem quite obvious, the importance of mimesis for human life often remains underestimated, although the evidence for this in the philosophical tradition as well as in the sciences is considerable. As it is not my main task to prove the scientific capacity of mimetic theory, I will only mention two corroborating voices. Girard's conception is quite similar to the arguments we find in David Hume and Adam Smith as they tackle the question of the origins of moral norms in the eighteenth century. They saw morality as emerging through sympathy—not necessarily benevolence but rather imagining what other subjects feel. This faculty, in the long run, brings out norms of behavior and even norms of feeling through mutual observation and imitation. A community based on commonly accepted rules would not come into being without imitation that follows from observation. Recently, this philosophical construct has been affirmed by neurological research. So-called mirror neurons, which were discovered in the mid-1990s, are the biological base of mimetic behavior.[13] Mimesis is part of our human nature and a necessary precondition for compassion and real human interaction. It is the precondition of learning from others. Mimesis, or mutual imitation, appears to be the engine driving the development of human culture in its entirety.

This could easily lead to an understanding of the human being as an exclusively cooperating and community-oriented being.[14] Altruism and solidarity then would be expected, being behavior based on natural mutual sensitivity. This in fact would be too simple a description of the human condition. In David Hume's understanding, sympathy, or mutual imitation, may lead to common behavior and may shape some kind of unity among people. But this uniting is not necessarily good in an ethical sense; it has to be moral in the sense of Latin *mores*, which at most means "those things that are customary," nothing more.[15] The mimetic approach takes into account not only the possible positive outcomes of mutual observation and imitation but also the problematic ones. On the one hand, imitative behavior leads to culture and the development of norms; it enables us to learn our mother tongues effortlessly and the basic rules of behavior that are customary within a particular civilization. Mimesis is the precondition for the ability of parents, teachers, or even saints to become models for children, pupils, or disciples. This is the light and life-fostering aspect of mimesis. But, on the other hand, there is its dark and destructive aspect. If we learn what to want by imitation, we will desire the same objects our models desire.

And so the model may feel acknowledged and esteemed, but the imitator increasingly becomes a rival of the model the more his or her desire resembles the model's. Thus a kind of fatal double bind develops. The model signals "Be like me!" and at the same time "Don't compete with me for the things I have or want to have." This is similar to the phenomenon that Thomas Hobbes depicts as a turning point between contented equality and harsh conflict: "And therefore if any two men desire the same thing, which nevertheless they cannot both enjoy, they become enemies; and in the way to their end . . . endeavor to destroy or subdue one another."[16] This means that the longing for final aims or objects is likely to lead to conflict. In Hobbes's view, such conflict will issue in the war of every man against every man unless there are strong barriers to prevent it.

In summary, one can say that the mimetic nature of humans is as much a source of conflict and violence as it is of community. Recognizing this ambiguity, the German philosopher Peter Sloterdijk arrives at the paradoxical dictum that envy is one of the basic forms of altruism and empathy.[17] In a more cautious statement of the matter, we can affirm that human communities are linked together as much by envy as by altruism and empathy. This curious fact leads us to the second core element of mimetic theory.

THE SCAPEGOAT MECHANISM

The signals sent by a mimetic model are twofold, meaning that we are attracted to and at the same time repelled by our models. In this light, we have to agree with the import of Michael Kirwan's question: "If Girard is correct, and rivalrous mimetic interaction poses a constant threat to human cohesion, how do societies form in the first place?"[18] A war of every man against every man is likely to be destructive in a comprehensive way. That means its tendency to escalate to the extreme will endanger the very existence of the group or society in question.[19] Insofar as mimetic behavior is common to all people, the survival of humankind and even its current existence seem highly unlikely. What prevents human self-destruction?

Analyzing mythological texts that could offer an answer to this question, Girard discerned a pattern of collective human behavior. A human community tends to create scapegoats if it is confronted with problems that ask too much of it—crises provoked by famine, epidemic, or natural disaster but also the crisis of increasing conflict among the members of the community. Girard uses the term "scapegoat," Kirwan notes, "precisely in its everyday sense, and not with reference to the 'scapegoat' mentioned in Leviticus 16. . . . Girard is not concerned with this conscious ritual, but with the more popular meaning of 'scapegoating' as a spontaneous and unconscious mechanism, by which someone is falsely accused and victimised."[20] Violence escalating within a group can easily be trained on an individual or a small group. A person or a minority may differ from others in a special way. In a tense atmosphere of mutual distrust and fear, the smallest difference will be sufficient to trigger harsh reactions.[21] If two or three members of a group accuse an individual or a subgroup of being the source of the tension or conflict, mimesis comes into play again. The kindled aggression against this presumed perpetrator is quite contagious because the relief it offers is so attractive: Violence of all against all is transformed into violence of all against one.

What is surprising about the scapegoat mechanism is that the group is suddenly able to act unanimously, even if it was fraught with conflict just some moments before—the group minus the member or the minority that has been scapegoated. An important and astonishing element present in mythological texts relating such events is that the scapegoat characters figure as the best as well as worst of the community. As demonlike culprits, they are guilty of the most horrible crimes, but they are also credited with the salvation of the community. That is precisely the classical definition of the sacred as *fascinosum et tremendum*. Girard sees the archaic deities as posthumous deifications of the victims of collective violence.[22] In being killed by the crowd, the accused perpetrator becomes the originator of a new harmony, which is rooted in blood but perceived by the group as an unexpected gift: "All human activities therefore acquire their basic structure from the event that makes peace in the community possible in the first place," Schwager writes. "Girard sees in the scapegoat mechanism the only process that gives structure to society and religious ideas."[23] Religion in this context is understood as a preconscious means to maintain human life threatened by violence. The unconscious scapegoat mechanism was transformed into sacrificial cults. And so we can attribute essential elements of the origins of societies to the scapegoat mechanism, which entails Girard's theory that the role of religion in those origins is "primordial."[24]

The Biblical Change of Perspective

The Bible is full of scapegoat episodes. The pattern fits Jesus himself, so that it can be said that there is no considerable difference between any myth and the Judeo-Christian myth. Even though some continuity between myth and revelation must perhaps be admitted, Girard never annihilates the difference between the two traditions.[25] On the contrary, he emphasizes that the notion that the two traditions are equivalent is based on a superficial understanding of them, for it ignores the meaning that the respective narrators give to the incidents they describe.

Indisputably, the gospel tells a story of rivalry, conflict, and violence. Jesus himself is the one who becomes a surface onto which smoldering conflicts are projected. In the end the plot escalates in a kind of collective murder. Around the cross a curious unification manifests itself, as bitter enemies unite in refusing Jesus and his message. Even the apostles betray and deny their master. And so he ends up an abandoned culprit, sentenced to death because of having shattered the religious and social order of his time. In this light, Jesus could be interpreted as just another posthumously divinized scapegoat. But the decisive difference from traditional myth must not be overlooked: The biblical text does not justify the crowd and does not side with the coalition of Jesus' enemies. Jesus himself never pleads guilty to the charges brought against him. This is in contradiction to typical mythological narratives, which insinuate that the judgment of an overwhelming majority becomes so pressing that it convinces even the accused scapegoat. The biblical text, however, confirms the nullity of all accusations against Jesus.

This is not only the opinion of the authors of the gospel. Jesus' resurrection has to be understood as the Father's justification of Jesus' message and way of life, while there is no justification of the crowd's decision. We can find no justification of violence in the gospel. Schwager notes: "In the resurrection brought about by the Father it is consequently not enough to see merely a verdict for his Son and against those who opposed him. Certainly this view is correct, as Jesus' opponents are convicted as sinners. But the verdict of the heavenly Father is above all a decision for the Son who gave himself up to the death for his opponents. It is therefore, when considered more deeply, also a verdict in favor of sinners."[26] This attitude is shown in an unambiguous way in Jesus' words on the cross, "Father, forgive them, for they know not what they do" (Luke 23:34), and even more in God's reaction to the cross, a reaction not of revenge but of forgiveness. Still, God's forgiveness does not mean that he sanctions the persecution of the Son.

The story of Jesus is the story of a scapegoat. But the narration and the tradition springing from this incident reveal the scapegoat as being an innocent victim. What Jesus has done is no blasphemy at all, and his being killed does not become the model for further sacrifice or further scapegoating but rather marks the turning point toward an overcoming of bloody sacrifice in general. To get to the heart of the argument: The whole story sides steadfastly with the victim. This is just the fulfillment of what has been revealed since Israel's experience of the Exodus: God advocates for the weak.

The Understanding of Sin and Grace in a Mimetic Context

Although Girard does not explicitly use the term, our theological reading recognizes as a prominent theme the traditional doctrine of "original sin," by which humanity is flawed. Girard's theory might inspire theological anthropology as it faces the challenge to reformulate the concept of original sin in contemporary language while nevertheless retaining the concept's traditional meaning.

Traditionally, original sin has been understood as the sin of Adam, meaning that the past action of one or few persons has influenced all human history up to now. The concept of original sin entails that agents of the action did it of their own free will, that it was not an act of necessity. All this is the more difficult to comprehend as the incident in question happened in a world in which all had been created perfectly, according to the biblical text. To the contemporary mind it is difficult to imagine either perfected creation or the renunciation of it. Even more, it is difficult to accept that a wrongdoing by others in the past could have such an effect, throughout history and even today, on the ability of human beings to behave justly.

The Origin of Sin

Reflecting on the Girardian concept of mimesis, one can easily imagine how rivalry and violence can emerge from a setting that is intrinsically good. The negative dynamic gains momentum not because of a sudden corruption of human potential but because of the wrong use of that potential. Right use and wrong use are not easy to distinguish. A minimal shift may be enough to make the difference between them.

Imitation, according to Girard, includes imitation of the behavior of the model, the imitation of his or her longing, and also the imitation of the being of the model. "The third sort of imitation, which depends on the functioning of the other two (which precede it), bears on the *being* of the model—and is close to what Freud called identification: wanting to *be* who the other is."[27] This leads to the complex question about the relationship between the human being and God—specifically, about how human beings could be like God, to be the image of God, without rivaling him. Exactly the wish to become (like) God is the origin of sin, according to Genesis 3:5. Willibald Sandler argues that a crucial and fatal misunderstanding takes place when a person begins his imitation of God by trying to get the only "thing" God could not give to him. This "thing" is the state of being the creator.[28] To be a creature means to be receptive. The attempt to exist without the necessity of receiving is the attempt to imitate and even rival God. It implies that a person is trying to eliminate his existence as a creature and to become the creator of himself. The voice of distrust and even envy, represented as the serpent in the biblical text, impedes Adam and Eve in their imitation of God's dimension of givingness and leads them to emulate his metaphysical autonomy. They try to become the source of their own existence by imitating their model, a paradoxical attempt at which, of course, they could never succeed. Whoever tries to achieve such an aim will be shamed in the end. The result of such mimesis will be what Kierkegaard calls "the sickness unto death."

For Kierkegaard, this sickness is characterized by the desperation to be oneself and, at the same time, not to be oneself.[29] It is the source of psychological suffering as well as of poisoned human intercourse. As much as we try to exist in absolute self-sufficiency, we have to recognize the difference between the ideal we want to be and our actual, real being. For the most part we tend to project onto others our own flaws: He or she must be the obstacle to my fulfillment. At first this obstacle seems to be God, who seems to be withholding something from me. Later, it is my fellow creatures who appear to be the obstacles, as they claim what I feel entitled to myself. The more I strive to protect myself from others, the more my identity is isolated from alterity, and the more I will feel defective, because I will lack the richness of relation in my life. This paradox, which features an acquisitive mimetic desire, could be called the trace of original sin in our everyday lives. Our capacity to receive gratuitously is damaged by the Fall, while our capacity and—more than this—our necessity to receive endures, with the result that we will exist in permanent dissatisfaction.

Such a deeply inscribed dissatisfaction is a topic not only of individual psychology but of human relations. Girard says men will become gods in the eyes of each other because they feel deeply imperfect. The other person becomes the quasi-transcendent aim of a subject's longing.[30] But at the same time, the two persons hate each other, each being seen as the obstacle that keeps the other from becoming perfect. To require the desired being of the other, I have to replace him or her. But just at the moment I achieve that objective, I recognize my failure in becoming a self-sufficient being. As we have already seen, such rivalry causes chaos within groups. And so this destructive dynamic must be tamed if society is to survive.

In modern Western societies this cycle of shortcoming, imitation, rivalry, and disappointment can be found in economic competition, consumerism, and the play of fashion, all of which mold the "celebrity consumer culture" that Anthony J. Godzieba discusses in his chapter in this volume. New idols, new aims, and must-haves emerge in this context continually. People pursue them while fighting their competitors. But just at the moment they reach what they were longing for, they recognize that they are still only part of the crowd. What they have is not exceptional at all: The status symbol, the high standing or income, the media attention—none of this grants them a position beyond self-doubt and the experience of being challenged. The common struggle for such aims makes it increasingly difficult for a person to gain unique identity: The more people search for individuality, the more homogeneous society becomes. This frustration does not necessarily lead to bloody conflict if there are always new objects of desire, new idols, new convincing aims. And so the modern economy demands permanent growth, not only for the sake of the economy itself but also as a result of sinful structures and as a remedy for their worst consequences. The market system has become the foundation of peace in modern societies. In recent decades, however, we have been forced to recognize that, in our limited world, unlimited economic growth is not possible for all of the global population, which is still growing. So this approach to preempting conflict must be called into question even if we as yet lack better alternatives.

The Duration of Sin in History and Society

Contemporary believers wrestle with the idea that sin can be inherited. It is difficult to imagine that it can be transmitted, except perhaps through magic, which to the modern mind is implausible. And so the concept of original sin is questioned in the modern world. The understanding of sin that I have tried to describe may be helpful in understanding the social dimension of sin and also its sustainable nature. The mimetic approach helps us to understand how one sin committed once could spread to others, even to members of future generations. Moreover, it shows how deeply social structures and institutions are spoiled by a corrupted form of desire. Mimetic theory retains the doctrine of original sin in a way that takes into account the importance of social conditions. What humans adopt from some kind of milieu almost develops a second nature on individual as well as on social level. Individual behavior and social structures once shaped in a particular way seem almost impossible to be remodeled. Thus pedagogical approaches fall short to correct negative influence.

If our human nature is basically mimetic, the influence of models and of the behavior of others on our own behavior is of enormous importance. Girard using the term mechanism to describe processes of victimization and scapegoating tries to emphasize the subtle power of this influence. It is almost impossible for individuals to resist such a force. We are caught in the dynamic for the most part unconsciously, though the mechanisms do not determine us completely. We do not necessarily inherit them as part of our human nature; there is no ontology of violence or sin in Girard. Still, in practice we are nearly incapable of overcoming social structures, because different models of behavior are so scarce. This dynamic of common behavior—since Plato, referred to as the "big beast"—is enormously powerful in carrying people away. In Schwager's dramatic theology it is identified with Satan. And so original sin can be understood as a matter of the human being caught in Satan's hand, although it is important to note that this interpretation does not necessarily presuppose a personal understanding of Satan or the devil as an independent agent. The satanic reality is, in my interpretation, nothing else than the vicious cycle brought about by the social group itself.[31] Once triggered, this cycle reproduces a relatively limited social violence, and the outbreak of radical violence, violence beyond control, is thereby prevented.

Anyone who has ever experienced the might of a group acting more or less unanimously knows how difficult it is to resist joining in. "Contagion" is the term Girard uses to describe this maelstrom. Many of those who resisted Nazism in Germany and Austria, for example, were members of religious communities or of the Communist party, both of which served as strong alternative role models toward which resisters could orient themselves. But the definition of sinful structures cannot be confined simply to ideological systems. Every social structure that provides security and orientation is influenced by elements of acquisitive mimetic behavior, mutual accusation, and the necessity to domesticate them. We are exposed to and confronted with examples of such behavior from earliest childhood.

It is possible to understand original sin as a negative mimesis that fits the concept of structural sin as well. The structure of sin is at work beyond the realm of mere institutions, but institutions are influenced and corrupted by it. Even the instruments for reducing violence and injustice are infected by the fallen nature of humankind. They too are "part of the vanity of human truncated creativity, which produces evil while seeking to produce good."[32] And so we are confronted with ambivalent entities of a "katechontic" structure, institutions that prevent both chaos and the realization of real peace.[33]

As for the market economy and economic growth, to criticize or challenge them honestly is not easy, as almost everyone is involved in the market economy in one way or another. Moreover, we understand that even if this system is problematic, its dismantling could lead to dire social consequences. In considering examples of social structures, we must include in that category the legal system, including criminal jurisdiction and, in particular, the death penalty. As Girard writes, "It is not only capital punishment, the law against murder, that we should conceive as the domestication and limitation of primitive violence by means of ritual violence; it is rather all great human institutions."[34] Jesus' intervention in the attempted stoning of the woman caught in adultery (John 8:1–12) is an example of what Girard means here. According to the law, the scribes and Pharisees are correct in accusing the woman who was brought to Jesus. What Jesus demonstrates is how a widespread violence is concealed through use of the law to accuse a single offender. Had the prosecutors stoned the woman quickly, they would have been spared the recognition that they too were not without sin. The institutionalized use of the law allows a group to distinguish itself from individual lawbreakers who can easily be punished, which serves to keep the social system in balance. Peace, then, depends on the majority's disavowal of the dark reality that the peace requires the sacrifice of scapegoats. Jesus' intervention in the case of the woman about to be stoned is the revelation of original sin embedded in the unfolding of everyday events.

To deny the reality of original sin commonly means to proclaim a radical difference between ourselves and those we find guilty. In her chapter in this volume, Michelle Gonzalez rightly emphasizes difference in all its complexity. Nonetheless, it is important to keep in mind our fundamental human equality. Equality based on a biblical understanding of creation and salvation does not mean only that each of us enjoys equal dignity but that all are affected by guilt in the same way. In this context Girard examines the "issue of reciprocity,"[35] which prevents us from assuming that, in their guiltiness, some individuals or groups resemble no one else and therefore can be segregated. No neat distinction between the just ones and the unjust ones can be maintained. The attempt to do so results for the most part in a kind of tyranny exercised by the purportedly just. Reciprocity, on the other hand, entails awareness of being culprit and victim at the same time. Sinful structures are created and maintained by human beings acting freely, but they are also slaves of those structures, as John Paul II argues in his encyclical *Sollicitudo Rei Socialis* (36).

> The sum total of the negative factors working against a true awareness of the universal common good, and the need to further it, gives the impression of creating, in persons and institutions, an obstacle which is difficult to overcome. If the present situation can be attributed to difficulties of various kinds, it is not out of place to speak of "structures of sin," which, . . . are rooted in personal sin, and thus always linked to the concrete acts of individuals who introduce these structures, consolidate them and make them difficult to remove. And thus they grow stronger, spread, and become the source of other sins, and so influence people's behavior.

To overcome such structures, to interrupt the closed narratives of market, law, and other institutions, which ultimately separate people from one another, first of all demands that we distinguish between sinner and sin, as Jesus himself did repeatedly.[36] The question before us is whether the biblical message can diminish the dynamic of original sin.

OVERCOMING SIN

With reference to Bernard Lonergan, Robert Daly underscores the suggestion that overcoming sin—not only in the individual but particularly in highly oppressive structures of human communities—is a threefold project: It entails "an intellectual conversion, a moral conversion, and a religious conversion."[37]

If the pitiful condition of our human nature is that of envy, resentment, mutual accusation, and violence, it should not be surprising that we are usually unable to recognize our situation clearly and distinctly. Nikolaus Wandinger comments that "sin appears as a power ruling over humans which prevents them from seeing God correctly and from having that wrong image transformed; it necessitates them to project their own sins on other people, making them into scapegoats, persecuting and prosecuting them."[38] Even use of the term and idea of Satan can contribute to the deception with which we seek to excuse ourselves from responsibility for our own wrongdoing. So, taking the satanic reality that we ourselves have created or are maintaining by ourselves, we can regard it as a nuisance or oppression imposed on us by an external force. To make this argument in a moralistic fashion, however, would be simplistic. We are usually caught in an illusion that informs our whole life. "To be a victim of illusion is to take it for true, so it means one is unable to express it as such, as illusion," Girard notes.[39]

This leads to the conclusion that we need our eyes to be opened to overcome the negative mimetic dynamic. "An experience of demystification, if radical enough, is very close to an experience of conversion,"[40] Girard writes. For him the biblical text, particularly the gospel, shows us the truth about our tendency to take on the behavior of victimization and scapegoating.

In the end, it is the resurrection of Jesus, who has become the victim of other human beings and has been acknowledged by the Father as his beloved Son, that opens our eyes to a new reality, the reality of sin as well as the reality of grace. And so, as Daly suggests, the resurrection leads us to an intellectual conversion, enabling us to see and think of God in a different way. What is clearly shown to us, in Michael Kirwan's words, is "God's absolute non-complicity with the violence carried out by religious people in God's name."[41] The heavenly Father has nothing to do with the bloody acts of sacrificial victimization, which Girard depicts as the origin and essence of manmade religion. This means that our understanding of God has been cleansed of all the false attributes that we have ever ascribed to him, attributes that were in fact only reflections of manmade reality. The outcome of this revelatory purification process—held to be the very core of dramatic theology—is that there is no violence in God. This we have learned from the one who, representing the will of God in a perfect way in the midst of our fallen world, fell victim to violence himself. Moreover, it was because he represented God's will that he was made a victim.

We should not let our familiarity with the biblical text blind us to the unexpected nature of Jesus' actions or of the Father's reaction to Jesus' fate. As Alison writes, "It was only the complete immanence of God in our history as raising a concretely dead man from the dead that revealed the complete transcendence of God."[42] What Alison means by "transcendence" here is the radical otherness of God, who completely differs from our self-made pictures of God. God's nature is not conflicting, is not both good *and* evil, or loving *and* violent. Such a God would not be the real and really transcendent God but merely the pseudo-transcendent construct of human society. The otherness of God is such that even our expectation of being punished is disappointed. To make this knowledge known is an act of liberation from idols, an act identical with liberation from self-deceit and delusion. And given the truth of this new understanding of God, we come to a new understanding of human nature as well. We recognize that the violence our world is imbued with, and even death, are realities caused by human beings. It is not God who burdens us with them. Still, sin cannot be reduced to individual faults. We are social beings to such a degree that it is impossible for us to remain unaffected by each other. Through this understanding, we are led to the concept of original sin, unavoidably. The first step of the revelation of the gospel is to mercilessly confront us with the reality of this original sin, which means that we are confronted with the violent structure of human interaction and social institutions and their ungodly origin.

No longer can the scapegoat mechanism or any sacrifice associated with it be understood as an act of piety according to God's will. Once unmasked, the scapegoat mechanism turns null and void. At the moment that a scapegoat is recognized as the victim of a group or society (and therefore recognized as innocent), the whole scapegoat mechanism loses its stabilizing power and ceases to work adequately. The revelation of innocence has dangerous implications.

In line with the prophets of the Hebrew Bible, the revelation of the gospel questions and challenges our usual behavior and social patterns. Biblical revelation, then, can be said to be destructive to some degree, as it may lead to ambivalent, if not purely negative, results. One of them is the appearance of a so-called sacrificial Christianity, which misunderstands Jesus as the source of a new form of revenge and hate whereby the disciples of the innocent victim become persecutors of the (alleged) persecutors of the victim. Elias Canetti has called this structure "moaning religion," which can cause outbursts of violence more radical and cruel than mythological structures ever knew. Girard argues that such a sacrificial reading re-infuses God with violence and "enables one to particularize the Christian event, to diminish its universality, and to search for guilty men who would absolve humankind of guilt—the role the Jews fulfill. . . . What turns Christianity in on itself, so that it presents a hostile face to all that is not Christian, is inextricably bound up with the sacrificial reading."[43] This sacrificial reading of the gospel left its marks on Christianity throughout its history and has to be understood as a clear sign of the overwhelming power of original sin. Given the all-encompassing influence that models have on our behavior, a mere intellectual clearing up may be necessary but not sufficient for breaking the fetters of the mechanisms of rivalry, mutual accusation, and victimization.

In a further ambivalent outcome of the biblical revelation, one may understand that archaic and sacrificial forms of social order have been destroyed but refuse to confront them as Jesus did. Such a halved adoption of the gospel can lead to a calamitous increase in social conflict. Modern humanity is confronted with such an increase in quite an existential form, in Girard's view. In his book *Battling to the End: Conversations with Benôit Chantre,* he observes that "Christianity demystifies religion. Demystification, which is good in the absolute, has proven bad in the relative, for we are not prepared to shoulder its consequences. We are not Christian enough."[44] This means we can no longer accept either scapegoats, strong hierarchies, traditional means of maintaining social order, or systems of permanent war or fierce competition between various groups. All of those institutions and practices are attempts to tame violence with violence. But we are also not able to overcome our habits based in envy and rivalry, and so conflicts escalate.

At this point moral conversion will be demanded as a second step, beyond mere knowledge, which leads to criticism but little change of conduct. Jesus must be understood as the only model worthy of imitation. What we have to learn from God's self-revelation in Jesus Christ is, first, the necessity to opt for the victim. The decisive importance of this is expressed in plain words in Jesus' speech on the judgment in the Gospel of Matthew (25:31–46). Nonviolence modeled after the example of Jesus must become our basic habit, which means more than mere pacifism. It means that nothing good can be reached or maintained forcibly. This is the foundation of each successful instance of nonviolent action and resistance. Heroes of nonviolence are aware that the means and the end have to correspond. It is not possible to gain freedom or justice through the infliction of new injustice, pain, and death. But nonviolent action is, of course, a demanding agenda, which has to be built on a very sound spiritual founda-

tion. People such as Mahatma Gandhi, Abdul Ghaffar Khan, Martin Luther King Jr., and representatives of the Philippine Revolution in 1986 give
eloquent testimony to nonviolent action as more than mere strategy.

Nonviolence has had an ecclesial consequence as well, most notably in
the principle of religious freedom as formulated by the Second Vatican
Council. The message of Jesus cannot be imposed. It can only be offered.
Religious coercion in the name of the gospel message only serves to undermine it and make it appear implausible. It follows that we must recognize that it is impossible to obey the biblical God if we try to shape our
communal life by exclusion, as he himself is the advocate of the excluded.
These are undoubtedly moral demands springing from biblical revelation,
but in practice, various constraints and circumstances hinder us from realizing them. The inherited structures of behavior remain powerful as ever,
greatly impeding our ability to follow the model of Jesus in our isolation.

So we move to the third dimension of conversion: the religious dimension. The move toward it is inconceivable without grace. According to
Schwager, this grace, which is the engine of a new way of living, a new kind
of community, is given in the pneumatic experience at Pentecost.[45] That
experience transforms the innermost self of Jesus' disciples and enables
them to live together in a mode in which social barriers are overcome.
The differences between sexes, between social classes, between peoples
and races matters no longer, as they are superseded by a new, rich plurality
(Gal. 3:26–29). Schwager writes:

> What was behind this concern for unity was not merely the realiza-
> tion of a noble ethical ideal; far more crucial was that this was how
> God's plan for salvation was being fulfilled. The new gathering, which
> Jesus had begun with the message of the kingdom of God, had initially
> broken down because of people's resistance. . . . Because the crucified
> one let himself be drawn into the dark world of his adversaries, far from
> God, and there lived out his obedience to the Father, the deep god-
> less realms of the human heart themselves became the place where the
> divine spirit can from now on reach and touch people.[46]

Once again God's benevolence and generosity, which goes so far that God
is ready to descend to hell for our sake, enables us both to grasp the truth
of his revelation in a comprehensive way and to overcome the satanic powers of self-destruction. As Jesus' forgiveness empowers us to confess our
guilt and to follow the way of reconciliation, the Father's gratuitous giving reenables us to receive again and so to live without the compulsion to
acquisitive behavior—a view similar to that of Jean-Luc Marion, as Robyn

Horner explains in her chapter in this volume. The self that cannot be claimed but only given is restored by the experience of an absolutely undeserved gift. We are made conscious of the givenness of our selves by the contrast between our violent refutation of God's offer and his forgiving reaction. In the liturgical language of the Easter vigil liturgy, this is the "fortunate fall" (*felix culpa*). But to reach this new acceptance of God's grace is anything but moral performance. We are in need of an innermost experience that enables us to accept God's grace.

And so Girard's approach cannot be reduced to a program of rational enlightenment. In dramatic theology, the liberating, forgiving, and healing encounter with a real person is essential if a change in the course of human affairs is to be triggered. The gospel is full of reports of people who changed, or were converted, as a result of encounters with Jesus. But of course this practice has to be continued. The drama of salvation is not over. People who have experienced God's grace are able and obliged to bear witness to the experience so that redemption is incarnated anew in our present reality. Witnesses to the redemption are initially models not in moral perfection but rather in living in the relationship with one who offers all, who is the source of abundance, whom we do not have to compete with. I think this can be interpreted as liberation from original sin, liberation whereby we become new persons who are able to create new structures of community. "Real giving and real receiving are a mutually structuring reality," James Alison writes. "We are talking of the person who is beginning to be empowered to move from feeling that society, the others, owe *him* something, toward being able to be toward other people—to act out for them—what *they* think is owed to *them*."[47]

Turtles All The Way Down?:
Pressing Questions for Theological
Anthropology in the Twenty-First Century

David G. Kirchhoffer

An Invitation and a Warning

In this book various scholars explore the new challenges for theological anthropology. They make clear that the developments of the past fifty years
in various fields of endeavor should be seen as an invitation, if not indeed as
an urgent injunction, "to open our eyes to new ways of being human" (Julie Clague).[1] At the same time, we need to heed the postmodern warning
regarding the dangers of engaging in what Henri-Jérôme Gagey called a
"giant discourse," whereby, in our attempt to unite languages into a single
coherent understanding of the human person, we end up building a tower
of Babel—an impoverished, meaningless, and "thin" conception of the human person, lacking any sound methodological basis.

   We need, in other words, to remain epistemologically critical of all the
fields of discourse with which we engage, including the discourse of theological claims. Without this self-critical epistemological suspicion, there
would be no need to try to rethink or reinterpret theological anthropological categories in the first place. One might argue that it is precisely such a
lack of self-critical epistemological suspicion that is the root cause of many

of the problems facing theological anthropology, such as why theological anthropology cannot seem to speak a language that is meaningful and relevant to other areas of human endeavor, and why theological anthropology instead often retreats into ever more rigid reiterations of the same "old" ideas.

Yet at the same time we should also remain epistemologically suspicious of what our "open eyes" at first seem to discern. Only in so doing can we avoid sliding back into the trap of what Anthony Godzieba called the "myth of the given." Godzieba used that phrase with specific reference to the need to engage with the new discoveries being made in the biological sciences, but it is relevant to many other fields of inquiry, especially theological anthropology. Such a myth—i.e., a set of claims that the ontological assumptions or ontological conclusions of a particular field are objective facts—is dangerous for theological anthropology not because it might be true but because it might be false. If we accept such ontological assumptions or conclusions uncritically, we end up back where we started, replacing one rigid ontology with another and turning the "new" ideas into "old" ones. Consequently, we would be no closer to realizing our objective of a dynamic and plastic theological understanding of the human person for the twenty-first century. Such an objective will be achieved only when, as Michelle Gonzalez put it, we can balance the "old" and the "new," recasting the old in light of new understandings of who and what we are, and this requires ongoing epistemological vigilance.

On Relationality: Substance Metaphysics versus Turtles All the Way Down

As an interpretive lens to the challenges facing theological anthropology identified below, the anecdotal account of a scientist and an old lady discussing the nature of the universe may be helpful. The story goes something like this. A scientist/philosopher (some say it was William James; others, Bertrand Russell) has delivered a lecture on the structure of the universe with its solar systems, galaxies, and so forth. An old lady confronts him afterward and tells him that everything he said was nonsense, because, as everyone knows, the world is flat. The scientist decides to play along and asks the old lady what the world is standing on. She shakes her head at the scientist's lack of common sense and states that of course it stands on the back of an elephant.

"And what is the elephant standing on?" asks the scientist.

"On the back of a giant turtle," answers the old lady.

The scientist goes in for the kill. "And what is the turtle standing on?" he asks.

"My dear boy," answers the old lady, "it is turtles all the way down."[2]

The story is usually recounted as a humorous illustration of the metaphysical problem of infinite regress. For our purposes, however, it illustrates the fundamental challenge facing theological anthropology. In a rather ironic reversal of roles necessary for the analogy to work for us here, the scientist represents "traditional," "old" theological anthropological doctrine, and the old lady represents developments of the past fifty to sixty years, both in theology and, especially, in other disciplines. The "traditional" doctrine is still talking about what it claims to be objective, anthropocentric, theological, ontological, and moral truths—truths about creation, the fall, redemption, and the nature of the human person—accessible through revelation and reason, particularly through neoscholastic interpretations of so-called natural law. This use of the very notion of law implies a belief in a certainty and immutability of these understandings of the human person, just as the scientist using the empirical observations and the experimentally verified laws of physics is certain that his understanding of the universe is true. Even so, the scientist's laws, logic, and certainty notwithstanding, he is still confronted with the unyielding reality of the old lady and her "turtles."

The point of this analogy is not to call into question scientific cosmology but to note that many of the developments over the past fifty years not only challenge the assumptions and certainties of more traditional anthropologies but indeed threaten to swallow up the assumptions and certainties in an infinite sea of turtles.

Possibly the primary challenge to theological anthropology is that twenty-first-century theological anthropology will not be defined by who or what the human person is (the classical questions of a substance metaphysics) but by *where* in the world the person is. To engage that question is to engage the question of relationships and relationality. Whereas the tradition has usually talked about the human being *in* the world, the great realization of the latter half of the twentieth century may indeed be, as Oliver Davies pointed out, that we *are* the world. We are so fundamentally bound up in an infinite network of relationships (the turtles all the way down) that to even conceive of some sort of objective self or human essence verges on the absurd. And yet, here we are, doing exactly that.

And so, for the rest of this chapter, the "turtles all the way down" analogy functions as a lens, as it highlights the almost paradoxical challenge that faces theological anthropology: the challenge to say something mean-

ingful about what it means to be human in a world in which our situated-
ness in an infinite and ultimately ineffable sea of relationships—stretching
from the micro to the mega, from the past to the future (with a few "dura-
tions" thrown in for good measure),[3] and from the concrete to the abstract,
well beyond the boundaries of any individual human life—seems to make
the very idea of the meaningfulness of human existence meaningless.

With this lens in place, we will now "open our eyes" to explore some
important challenges for theological anthropology. These challenges all in
some way reflect this fundamental relationality, this "being world" rather
than simply being in the world. We propose no solutions to these issues
here but simply highlight them as the "turtles" that we need to take into account while remaining epistemologically critical. We will categorize them
under four headings: anthropocentrism, historicity, vulnerability, and language. We will then conclude with a short reflection on the theological
nature of this enterprise.

Anthropocentrism

As Celia Deane-Drummond pointed out, theological anthropology is traditionally very anthropocentric. It is typically about "man" and "man's"
dominion. This anthropocentrism—i.e., this thinking and speaking of the
human being as the crown of creation, and of the created world as the human being's dominion—has been met with numerous challenges. The
pressing question for theological anthropology is how to take these challenges (which we might call our turtles) into account while at the same
time preserving a viable understanding of moral agency, since the latter
is arguably necessary for a workable understanding of ethics. Without a
viable understanding of human agency, it makes little sense to talk about
human responsibility or accountability. If one cannot talk about responsibility and accountability, then the very challenges to and critiques of anthropocentrism become just meaningless changes in a random universe of
infinite relationships that are ultimately irrelevant. The challenges in question include, among others, the following.

First, a new awareness of the ecological and environmental crises caused
by human activity has raised significant questions about the validity of anthropocentric worldviews. The idea that the world is made for us and that
we can do with it as we please has been turned on its head. Human beings
are discovering that they are capable of destroying the world in which they
live, at least to the extent that human habitation will become impossible. To
put it crudely: Human beings have been defecating in their own backyard

for too long, and the stench is becoming unbearable. Theological anthropology has taken some of the flack for this, because, critics argue, it is anthropocentric and uses terminology such as "subdue" and "have dominion over" when referring to the rest of the world. This alleged arrogance and lack of self-critical epistemological reflection is blamed for the situation we find ourselves in. While one could argue that romanticizing the "harmony" or "original balance" of nature, as some so-called green movements do, be they theologically inspired eco-theologies or otherwise, is itself an inaccurate representation in the face of the science, one is nevertheless compelled to take seriously the fact that unbridled anthropocentrism— and its egoist, individualist, communist, and even speciesist variants—have ultimately pushed us to the brink of our own demise.

Anthropocentrism has met with another critique—namely, questions relating to who count as persons. Theological anthropology has long gone to great lengths to draw on philosophical as well as revelatory sources to underpin the uniqueness and superiority of the human being in relation to other beings. But new research into animal behavior—for example, de Waal's work with chimpanzees—raises the question of whether what should count as a person and a bearer of rights should be expanded to include other sentient beings. More extreme, and, indeed relentlessly logical, versions of this argument (see, for example, Peter Singer) have raised the question whether, if the latter is true, it might also be true that some human beings should not be considered persons.[4]

Anthropocentrism meets a third challenge in the rapid development of technology, and particularly of artificial intelligence, a topic that has not been dealt with in this volume. Precisely the characteristics that the philosophical basis of traditional theological anthropology has always put forward for the human being's uniqueness and special place in Creation are now being emulated in advanced computer systems. Claiming a special place for the human being on the basis that it is *the* rational animal is becoming more and more difficult. Add to that the posthumanist movement, which advocates the use of technology to enhance the human person or even make possible the immortality of individual "selves" by replacing our limited biological substrate with technological hardware while nevertheless preserving something resembling a mind, and the old "brains in vats" problem is no longer just a thought experiment.

Furthermore, the systems theory of sociologist Niklas Luhmann is representative of the kind of sociology that no longer has persons or "selves" as agents as the starting point of society. Instead, it is autopoetic systems that constitute society, and humans are nothing more than psychic systems, which distinguish, like other systems, between what is system and what is environment. Society is, in this sense, already posthuman. The process of globalization, and the recent financial crises that have rocked the world, are indicative of the insignificance of the idea of autonomous moral agents in the face of all-encompassing, self-perpetuating systems. Human beings are nothing more than the substrate or, to use Luhmann's term, the environment in which the systems evolve.[5]

Historicity

The above discussion of systems theory provides a useful segue into the next issue that theological anthropology needs to deal with in the twenty-first century: historicity and the relativity it implies. The notion of historicity has been around for some time. Nevertheless, the implications of this idea, and particularly its challenge to any claim of objective moral normativity, have yet to be adequately dealt with in theological anthropology, especially insofar as a theological anthropology informs theological ethics.

Following Wilhelm Guggenberger's chapter on mimetic theory, we could, for example, explore how social-constructionist and, we would add, social-constructivist investigations of violence and its social and personal meaning have hardly been taken into account in theological anthropology or theological ethics.[6] If we are to rethink philosophical personalism through to its theological roots, we must take relationality and its consequences seriously as theological categories. Relationality is not a one-way street from the autonomous subject to the world. Indeed, the subject is constituted in part, and perhaps even fundamentally, by the world, through dependent relationships. It is striking that Christianity, with its strongly relational idea of the Holy Trinity, should nonetheless often seem to deal so inadequately with how human beings make meaning in and through relationship.

Theological anthropology also needs to look closely at social-constructionist analyses of gender,[7] race,[8] and species.[9] The challenge of social construction for theological anthropology in relation to these three categories especially is that any response that simply tries to reinforce "old" racial, gender, and species stereotypes will be met with an "Ah well, that was to be expected," because the supposedly old constructs would be seen as supporting the meaning-making of those in power in a particular social context—in this case, the Church.

We need to foster historical awareness in theological anthropology and theological ethics.[10] Theological anthropology needs to realize that the "old" ideas were once new. Consider, for example, *Gaudium et Spes* in comparison with *Casti Connubii*. The implicit theological anthropological shifts are subtle but definite. One can debate the continuity and discontinuity of these documents, and indeed of *Humanae Vitae*, but one would be hard pressed to say that they represent no historical difference at all, or that these documents were not shaped in part by their sociopolitical contexts. This continuous reframing of paradigms, to borrow from Thomas Kuhn, is normal, even if it may not always seem desirable. Therefore, understanding and, indeed, fostering the value and the implications of historical consciousness is one way in which we can remain epistemologically self-critical in theological anthropology.

Vulnerability

It is precisely through fostering such historical consciousness that one becomes aware of the next key challenge—i.e., a new awareness of human vulnerability as a necessary theological category. Vulnerability is a correlate of the relationality discussed earlier: our being the world, our being constituted by dependent relationships. Like relationality, vulnerability is a challenge to traditional ideas of agency and responsibility grounded in an absolute conception of human persons as autonomous rational agents.

Vulnerability finds expression in various aspects of life—for example, in the experience of illness or disease. Guggenberger and Rosemary P. Carbine drew particular attention to the problem of violence. How do we adequately take into account the violence of the world, not only the willful violence of other human beings but the very fact that we live in a world where, biologists tell us, death is normal?[11] This is challenging for theological anthropology precisely because death, and indeed violent death, plays such an important role in Christian soteriological accounts. Jesus dies a violent death to conquer death and thereby free us from anxiety, slavery, and, in a sense, the ontic violence of this world. Yet a biologically inspired understanding of death—and even of violent behavior, if evolutionary psychologists are correct—is that death and violence are normal consequences of our evolved biological state, without moral import.

The previous discussion of historicity is relevant here especially insofar as historicity is applied not just to cultures but to individual lives. Again, with reference to understanding violence, there is an urgent need for theological anthropology and ethics to engage with the work being done in the areas of criminology and law, which is offering profound new understandings of violence in light of human historicity and vulnerability. The idea of violence as a response to vulnerability offers a new lens through which we can understand violent behavior as a product of dysfunctional systems, some of which may themselves be a consequence of ill-conceived theological anthropologies and the moral reasoning associated with them.[12]

Finally, offering a way to "redeem" vulnerability as a theological anthropological category, theological ethicist Johan Verstraeten pointed to the insights of spiritual writers and twentieth-century "saints" such as Mother Teresa and those whom one might call extratraditional, such as Etty Hillesum. For these writers, the darkness of the twentieth century, and specifically the horrors of abject poverty and war, which are exemplary of human vulnerability, become a vital locus theologicus. Whereas a veneer theology, which we are always in danger of perpetuating in the academy and in the Church alike, can make light of suffering and as such tends to fail dismally when confronted by absolute evil, these authors offer avenues for exploring human vulnerability as itself meaningful. Their reflections offer ways of rescuing human agency, and with it personal dignity, not from but through the experience of vulnerability. When vulnerability is taken seriously, not as something external to human existence but as a morally neutral consequence of our being in a state of dependent relationality, agency can be rescued from despair, on the one hand, and, on the other, from the sometimes paternalistic moralism implied by the dominant "autonomy" paradigm present in both theological and secular moral discourse, especially in certain representations of natural law. Our relationality means that we are in a perpetual state of encounter. Just as the encounter makes us vulnerable (to the turtles all the way down), so too does the encounter become a locus of personhood. As Robyn Horner observed, it is in this encounter, this event, which by virtue of relationality is always more that the sum of its parts, that the place of decision emerges.

Language

The final category we will highlight is that of language. This is a catchall category for a number of observations that called for theological anthropology to think and express itself differently.

Michelle Gonzalez asked—and this makes an interesting counter to the discussion of the negative side of vulnerability above—"What about the beautiful?" And it is true that theology sometimes seems to have become so concerned with countering atheist attacks founded on the rationale of the so-called hard sciences that it has lost sight of beauty and the aesthetic as theological loci, be it in academia, the Church, or indeed in public discourse. Human beings are capable not only of appreciating beauty but also of creating it. This must surely have implications for how we can articulate a theological anthropology that transcends the limitations of the often reductionist language of scientific discourse.

Theological anthropology cannot seriously engage the challenge of diversity until it learns to express itself in other languages. In this sense, artists should be seen as theology's partners. Insofar as artists are "sources of common sense," the creators and interpreters of the sense of the people, their work is both a channel for theological ideas and a stimulus for theological reflection.

This need to turn or re-turn to other modes of discourse, or to "new ways of being person" (Julie Clague), is further evidenced in Johan Verstraeten's observation regarding the rise of new forms of spirituality. As an example he cited the rise of the idea of mindfulness in the business world.[13] Business leaders, often thought to be fairly reluctant to engage in theological-sounding discourse, are beginning to talk about, for example, the value of meditation, of profound encounters with a loving presence, of being a loving presence to others, and of experiencing oneself as loved so as to be able to contribute to the good of others.

Another call for new language came from Stephen J. Pope, though his concern was not beauty and aesthetics but the discourses of cultural anthropology, cognitive neuropsychology, and evolutionary psychology. Pope implied that he believed that, between these fields and theological anthropology, consensus about the fundamental meaning of morality is possible. What this consensus will require, however, is an ability to dialogue in different languages. For example, Pope felt that a priority for theological anthropology is to develop a "trinity of creation"—that is, a trinitarian understanding of different accounts of human existence, an understanding of creation, natural law, and evolution not as mutually exclusive languages but as fundamentally interrelated and valid accounts of the same phenomenon.

Finally, Robyn Horner reiterated the need to dialogue with philosophers. If we are to develop a coherent theological anthropology for the twenty-first century, we must engage philosophical methods, as these constitute, says Horner, a condition of possibility for our theological reflection.

Of course, when engaging in these other languages, we must keep in mind the warning, indicated at the beginning of this chapter, about the dangers of the "giant discourse." In a sense, this can be understood as a foundational appeal to method. We must understand and be sure of the methods we use, aware of their advantages and their limitations, so that we neither claim too much, nor too little, in the endeavor to understand the many different ways of being human, ways that contemporary research in a variety of fields continues to reveal. As we engage in these other languages, we need to avoid the temptation that may arise to accept that it is all just turtles all the way down. If anything, what this call to speak different languages reveals, as it cautions us to remain epistemologically self-critical, is the paradoxical fact that we can affirm that the Truth exists but that the Truth is at the same time out there, always slightly beyond our reach, present in our conversations but never fully contained by them.

Concluding Reflections on the Theological Nature of This Enterprise

With the cautions concerning method in mind, and the obvious desire to engage in a variety of discourses in rethinking theological anthropology for the twenty-first century, one is compelled to ask, What makes this endeavor theological at all? We could, of course, begin deductively, from revealed doctrine, and suggest that, as people of faith, we must find ways of interpreting (or, indeed, dismissing) the turtles—i.e., the many developments concerning the human person described above—in the light of classical theological concepts such as creation, sin, grace, and redemption. But an alternative presents itself.

Any attempt to understand the human being will come up against the challenge of negotiating the inevitable tension between the universal and the particular.[14] How do we reconcile universal claims regarding who and what human beings are—their purpose, their destiny, and so on—with the unique givens and experience of particular historical persons and all the limitations that those givens and that experience imply? Herein lies a possible justification for the pursuit of a specifically theological anthropology that relies not on deductive reasoning from faith but on inductive reasoning from this apparent paradox. A contextual approach must necessarily affirm that what and who a person is will be background-dependent, meaning that each human being is unique, but, at the same time, it can affirm that this particularity is itself of universal relevance. Each human being is important, warts and all. This tendency to want to understand our particularity in universal terms can be seen as grounds for the view that our endeavor is indeed theological, because that is precisely what salvation history is all about: giving universal meaning to particular experience.

The public nature of the theological anthropological enterprise means that the areas highlighted in this chapter are among the most important priorities for theological research. If theological anthropology is to be relevant in the twenty-first century and not end up either simply as an esoteric preserve of ecclesial authorities and ivory-tower academics, or as a thin syncretic hodgepodge boiled up by popular media (see Gagey's reflection on the tower of Babel above), then we must accept the invitation to open our eyes to new ways of being human and engage the turtles, ever mindful both of the need to remain epistemologically critical and of our theological objective of making universal sense of historically situated human particularities.

NOTES

EXPLORING NEW QUESTIONS FOR THEOLOGICAL ANTHROPOLOGY
Lieven Boeve, Yves De Maeseneer, and Ellen Van Stichel

1. See International Theological Commission, *Communion and Steward-ship: Human Persons Created in the Image of God* (2004); *The Search for Universal Ethics: A New Look at Natural Law* (2009); World Council of Churches, *Christian Perspectives on Theological Anthropology* (2006).

2. This collection of essays was initiated by Anthropos, a research group based at the Faculty of Theology and Religious Studies at the Catholic University of Leuven (Belgium). Anthropos is an interdisciplinary platform of systematic theologians and theological ethicists seeking to develop a contemporary theological anthropology rooted in the Christian tradition and in dialogue with contemporary science and philosophy. See our blog *Theological Anthropology* (www.theologicalanthropology.com). Anthropos was launched in April 2011 with an international seminar entitled "Exploring Anthropos: Theological Anthropology for the 21st Century," at which early versions of this volume's contributions were presented.

3. See the bibliography of Marc Cortez, *Theological Anthropology: A Guide for the Perplexed* (London; New York: T&T Clark, 2010), 156–61; also David H. Kelsey, *Eccentric Existence: A Theological Anthropology*, 2 volumes (Louisville, Ky.: Westminster John Knox, 2009) and the review symposium devoted to this work in *Modern Theology* 27, no. 1 (2011). For an introduction to recent Catholic perspectives, see Susan A. Ross, *Anthropology: Seeking Light and Beauty* (Collegeville, Minn.: Liturgical Press, 2012).

1. THEOLOGICAL ANTHROPOLOGY, SCIENCE, AND HUMAN FLOURISHING
Stephen J. Pope

1. Thomas Aquinas, *Summa Theologiae*, 1, q. 96, a. 1, and 2.1, prologue.
2. Ibid., 1–2.91.2.
3. See Augustine, *Against Faustus*, 70; Augustine, *On Free Choice of the Will*, 1.6.15; Thomas Aquinas, *Summa Theologiae*, q. 103, a. 8, and 2.1, q. 94, a. 2.

4. Stephen J. Gould, *Wonderful Life: The Burgess Shale and the Nature of History* (New York: Norton, 1990), 291.

5. See Louis Caruana, ed., *Darwin and Catholicism: The Past and Present Dynamics of a Cultural Encounter* (London: T & T Clark, 2009).

6. *Humani Generis*, §§5, 6, 37.

7. International Theological Commission, *Communion and Stewardship* (2004), §65.

8. John Paul II, "Message to Pontifical Academy of Sciences," *Quarterly Review of Biology* 72, no. 4: 381–406.

9. *Catechism of the Catholic Church*, §337, http://www.usccb.org/beliefs-and-teachings/what-we-believe/catechism.

10. Ibid., §338.

11. Ibid., §§374–415.

12. Ibid., §390.

13. Ibid., §§1952, 1954–60, 1956.

14. Ibid., §1705.

15. *Compendium of the Catechism of the Catholic Church*, §365, http://www.vatican.va/archive/compendium_ccc/documents.

16. International Theological Commission, *Communion and Stewardship: Human Persons Created in the Image of God*, §65.

17. Ibid., §66, citing §24 of *Gaudium et Spes*.

18. International Theological Commission, *Communion and Stewardship: Human Persons Created in the Image of God*, §§62, 95.

19. Ibid., §66.

20. Ibid., §24.

21. Ibid.

22. International Theological Commission, *In Search of a Universal Ethic: A New Look at Natural Law* (2009).

23. Jack Mahoney, *The Making of Moral Theology: A Study of the Roman Catholic Tradition* (Oxford: Clarendon, 1987).

24. Jack Mahoney, *The Challenge of Human Rights* (Oxford: Blackwell, 2007).

25. Mahoney, *Making of Moral Theology*, 325.

26. Jack Mahoney, *Christianity in Evolution: An Exploration* (Washington, D.C.: Georgetown University Press, 2011).

27. Ibid., 2.

28. Ibid., 219.

29. Ibid., ch. 6.

30. John Mahoney, "Christianity in Evolution: An Exploration," Gresham College, December 1, 2011, unpublished ms.

31. Karl Rahner, "The Theological Concept of Concupiscentia," in *Theological Investigations*, vol. 1 (Baltimore: Helicon Press, 1961).

32. See Lisa Sowle Cahill, *Bioethics and the Common Good*, the 2004 Père Marquette Lecture in Theology (Milwaukee: Marquette University Press, 2004); Cahill, *Theological Bioethics: Participation, Justice, Change* (Washington, D.C.: Georgetown University Press, 2005), and "Theological Ethics, the Churches, and Global Politics," *Journal of Religious Ethics* 35, no. 3 (2007): 377–99.

33. Lisa Sowle Cahill, *Global Justice, Christology, and Christian Ethics* (New York: Cambridge University Press, 2013), p. 49.

34. Ibid., 56.

35. Ibid., 57.

36. Ibid., 58.

37. Ibid., 61.

38. Ibid., 67.

39. Ibid.

40. Ibid., 37.

41. Ibid., 44.

42. Ibid., 45.

43. Ibid., 248.

44. Lisa Sowle Cahill, "Embodying God's Image: Created, Broken, and Redeemed," in *Humanity Before God*, ed. William Schweiker (Minneapolis: Fortress, 2006), 73.

45. Cahill, *Theological Bioethics*, 8.

46. *Summa Theologiae*, 2.1, q. 94, a. 2.

47. http://www.newadvent.org/cathen/09076a.htm. For a detailed discussion of current complexities of natural law conceptions, see Henri-Jérôme Gagey, "The Concept of Natural Law in the Postmodern Context," in this volume.

48. See Cahill, *Global Justice*, 252.

49. Ibid., 256.

50. On personalism, natural law, and evolution, see Johan De Tavernier, "Personalism and the Natural Roots of Morality," in this volume.

51. *Veritatis Splendor*, 78.

52. Ibid., 80.

2. THE CONCEPT OF NATURAL LAW IN THE POSTMODERN CONTEXT
Henri-Jérôme Gagey

1. International Theological Commission, *In Search of a Universal Ethic: A New Look at the Natural Law* (2009), www.vatican.va/roman_curia. This

document stirred debate in several theological journals: *Concilium*, no. 3 (2010); *Transversalités* no. 117 (2011); *Nova et Vetera* (English edition) 9, no. 3 (2011). See also, shortly before publication, the thematic issue on natural law in *Communio* 35 (Fall 2008).

2. This chapter takes up again a talk given during a day of study organized by the Theologicum de l'Institut Catholique de Paris, September 23, 2010. It has been previously published in French in *Transversalités, revue de l'institut Catholique de Paris*, no. 117 (2011): 69–83.

3. A significant example may be found in Sylviane Agacinski, *Engagements* (Paris: Seuil, 2007) and *Corps en miettes* (Paris: Flammarion, 2009). This philosopher, who claims her main affiliation to be with the secular tradition, has taken a courageous position on controversial bioethical issues. In particular, and in terms that bring her, on this point, close to the position defended by the Catholic Church, she strongly opposed the legalization of the practice of "surrogate motherhood" or, to use a more politically correct term, "surrogate gestation." In the work of hers that I have recently read, it is interesting that each time she refers to "human nature" as a reality that requires moral discernment with respect to this issue, it is to biological nature that she alludes.

4. The ITC's declaration generally avoids the use of the term "instinct," which occurs only twice: "Searching for the moral good, the person contributes to the realization of his nature, beyond impulses of instinct or the search for a particular pleasure" (§ 40); in note 95, the term is used solely in an analogical way, as concerning "an internal instinct of grace," which refers to carrying out the commandments and not transgressing what they prohibit.

5. See Antoine Vergote, *La Psychanalyse à l'épreuve de la sublimation* (Paris: Éditions du Cerf, 1997); Julia Kristeva, *Desire in Language: A Semiotic Approach to Literature and Art* (New York: Columbia University Press, 1980); Baldine Saint-Girons, "À quoi sert la sublimation?" *Figures de la psychanalyse* 2, no. 7 (2002): 57–80.

6. Albert Jacquard, *Voici le temps du monde fini* (Paris, Seuil, 1991), 112–13.

7. "In the Christian theological tradition, the person presents two complementary aspects. On the one hand, according to Boethius's definition, as taken up by scholastic theology, the person is an 'individual substance (subsisting) of a rational nature.' This refers to the uniqueness of an ontological subject who, being of a spiritual nature, enjoys a dignity and an autonomy that is manifested in self-consciousness and in free dominion over his actions. On the other hand, the person is manifested in his or her capacity to enter into relationships: A person exercises his or her activity in the area of inter-subjectivity and of communion in love" (§ 67).

8. Thomas Aquinas, *Summa Theologiae*, q. 40, a. 2, resp.

9. See, e.g., Judith Butler, *Gender Trouble: Feminism and the Subversion of Identity* (London: Routledge, 1990); *Bodies That Matter: On the Discursive Limits of 'Sex'* (London: Routledge, 1993). For the same theme in terms that are different but no less strong, see the promoters of "posthumanism," and particularly the good introduction in Jean-Michel Besnier, *Demain les Post-humains* (Paris: Hachette Littérature, 2009); also, Katherine N. Hayles, *How We Became Posthuman: Virtual Bodies in Cybernetics, Literature, and Informatics* (Chicago: University Of Chicago Press, 1999).

10. André Gorz, *L'immatériel: Connaissance, valeur et capital* (Paris, Galilée, 2003), 105.

11. The document refers here in a note to John Paul II's *Letter to Families* (1994), §19 (www.vatican.va): "The philosopher who formulated the principle of *'Cogito, ergo sum,'* 'I think, therefore I am,' also gave the modern concept of man its distinctive dualistic character. It is typical of rationalism to make a radical contrast in man between spirit and body, between body and spirit. But man is a person in the unity of his body and his spirit. The body can never be reduced to mere matter: it is a *spiritualized body*, just as man's spirit is so closely united to the body that he can be described as *an embodied spirit.*"

12. Joseph Ratzinger and Johann Auer, *Eschatology: Death and Eternal Life*, trans. Aidan Nichols (Washington, D.C.: Catholic University of America Press, 1988), 148–49.

13. 3 *Sent.*, d. 31, q. 2, a. 4c; cf. *De Veritate* 10, 8, ad 5.

14. See Pope Benedict XVI, "Address to the Participants in the General Assembly of the Pontifical Academy for Life" (February 24, 2007, www .vatican.va): "Moral conscience, to be able to judge human conduct rightly, above all must be based on the solid foundation of truth, that is, it must be enlightened to know the true value of actions and the solid criteria for evaluation. Therefore, it must be able to distinguish good from evil, even where the social environment, pluralistic culture and superimposed interests do not help it do so. . . . Not only is the rejection of Christian tradition growing, but distrust for the capacity of reason to perceive the truth also distances us from the taste for reflection. According to some, for individual conscience to be unbiased it must free itself both from references to tradition and those based on human reason. Hence, the conscience, which as an act of reason aims at the truth of things, ceases to be light and becomes a simple screen upon which the society of the media projects the most contradictory images and impulses." It is this disconnection in relation to the requirements of a rational reflection that makes it necessary to appeal to the authority of the magisterium in order to interpret natural law, an appeal that the pope puts forward as follows: "One must be *re-educated to the desire* to know authentic

truth, to defend one's own freedom of choice in regard to mass behaviour and the lures of propaganda, *to nourish passion for moral beauty and a clear conscience*" (my italics).

15. Jean-Luc Marion, *The Visible and the Revealed* (New York: Fordham University Press, 2008), 77.

3. PERSONALISM AND THE NATURAL ROOTS OF MORALITY
Johan De Tavernier

1. Albert C. Knudson, *The Philosophy of Personalism: A Study in the Metaphysics of Religion* (New York; Cincinnati: Abingdon, 1927; reprinted New York: Kraus, 1969), 428–29.

2. "Est enim persona ut dictum est naturae rationalis individua substantia." "Individua substantia" for Aquinas means "substantia completa, per se subsistens, separata ab aliis" (*Summa Theologiae* 3, q. 16, a. 12, ad 2um).

3. Knudson, *The Philosophy of Personalism*, 430–31.

4. Eucken admitted that Lotze was undoubtedly the most important thinker of those decades although he was personally disappointed about his lectures: "His philosophy seemed to me too much a matter of learning. It had too little bearing and influence on the totality of life." Joseph McCabe, trans., *Rudolf Eucken: His Life, Work and Travels* (London: T. Fisher Unwin/Adelphi Terrace, 1921), 59.

5. Rudolf Hermann Lotze, *Outlines of Psychology. Dictated Portions of the Lectures of Hermann Lotze*, trans. and ed. George T. Ladd (Boston: Ginn & Company, 1886; reprinted Bristol: Thoemmes Press; Tokyo: Maruzen co., 1998), 148–51 (§100–2).

6. Christian Roy, "Emmanuel Mounier, Alexandre Marc et les origines du personnalisme," in *Emmanuel Mounier, actualité d'un grand témoin: Actes du Colloque international des 6–7 octobre 2000*, tome 1, ed. Guy Coq (Paris: Parole et Silence, 2003), 21: "*On ne connaît l'être qu'en tant qu'on le réalise.*"

7. Emmanuel Mounier mentions this for the first time in "Refaire la Renaissance," *Esprit* 1 (1932): 5–51.

8. Emmanuel Mounier, *A Personalist Manifesto* (translated from *Manifeste au service du personnalisme* Paris: Montaigne, 1936) (London: Longmans, Green and Company, 1938), 69.

9. Joseph Amato, *Mounier and Maritain: A French Catholic Understanding of the Modern World* (Tuscaloosa: University of Alabama Press, 1975), 130.

10. Jacques Maritain, *Trois Réformateurs: Luther, Descartes, Rousseau* (Paris: éd. Plon-Nourrit et cie., 1925), 28: "*une substance individuelle complète, de nature intellectuelle et maîtresse de ses actions.*"

11. About the Action Française, see Jacques Maritain, *Humanisme intégral. Problèmes temporels et spirituels d'une nouvelle chrétienté* (Paris: Fernand

Aubier, 1936); and Maritain, *True Humanism* (New York: Charles Scribner's Sons, 1938).

12. Jean-Yves Calvez, *Chrétiens. Penseurs du social. Maritain, Mounier, Fessard, Teilhard de Chardin, de Lubac* (Paris: Cerf, 2002), 34.

13. Maritain, *True Humanism*, 19–20.

14. Pope John Paul II, *The Acting Person [Osoba i czyn]*, (1969) trans. Andrzej Potocki (1969; Dordrecht; Boston: D. Reidel, 1979).

15. Max Scheler, *Schriften aus dem Nachlass* (Bern: Francke Verlag, 1957), 356.

16. Max Scheler, *Der Formalismus in der Ethik und die materiale Wertethik: Neuer Versuch der Grundlegung eines ethischen Personalismus*, Gesammelte Werke, Band 2 (Bern: Francke Verlag), 328: "Person ist die konkrete, selbst wesenhafte Seinseinheit von Akten verschiedenartigen Wesens." For an English translation of this work, see *Formalism in Ethics and Non-Formal Ethics of Values: A New Attempt toward the Foundation of an Ethical Personalism*, trans. Manfred S. Frings and Roger L. Funk (Evanston, Ill.: Northwestern University Press, 1973).

17. Max Scheler, *Schriften aus dem Nachlass* (Bern: Francke Verlag, 1957), 186.

18. Louis Janssens, *Personne et société: Théories actuelles et essai doctrinal*, Dissertationes ad gradum magistri in Facultate Theologica vel in Facultate Iuris Canonici consequendum conscriptae, series 2, volume 32 (Gembloux: Duculot, 1939), 207.

19. Ibid., 3.

20. Charles Darwin, *On the Origin of Species by Means of Natural Selection, or the Preservation of Favoured Races in the Struggle for Life* (London: John Murray, 1859), http://www.darwin-online.org.uk.

21. William Paley, *Natural Theology or: Evidences of the Existence and Attributes of the Deity. Collected from the Appearances of Nature* (London: Wilks and Taylor, 1802).

22. Charles Darwin, *The Descent of Man, and Selection in Relation to Sex* (London: John Murray, 1871), chapter 6 (e.g. 190), http://www.darwin-online.org.uk.

23. Ibid., 77.

24. Ibid., chap. 4.

25. Ibid., 71–72; 78: "Besides love and sympathy, animals exhibit other qualities which in us would be called moral; and I agree with Agassiz that dogs possess something very like a conscience."

26. Thomas Henry Huxley, *Evolution and Ethics*, ed. Michael Ruse (Princeton: Princeton University Press, 2009), 81: "Social progress means a checking of the cosmic process at every step and the substitution for it of

another, which may be called the ethical process; the end of which is not the survival of those who may happen to be the fittest, in respect of the whole of the conditions which obtain, but of those who are ethically the best."

27. George C. Williams, "Reply to comments on Huxley's Evolution and Ethics in Sociobiological Perspective," *Zygon* 23 (1988): 437–38.

28. Frans De Waal, "Morally Evolved: Primate Social Instincts, Human Morality, and the Rise and Fall of 'Veneer theory,'" in *Primates and Philosophers: How Morality Evolved*, ed. Stephen Macedo and Josiah Ober (Princeton: Princeton University Press, 2006), 6.

29. Cf. Edvard Westermarck, *The Origin and Development of Moral Ideas*, 2 vols. (London: Macmillan, 1906).

30. Larry Arnhart, "The New Darwinian Naturalism in Political Theory," *Zygon* 33 (1998): 372.

31. Richard Joyce, *The Evolution of Morality* (Cambridge: MIT Press, 2007), 3.

32. Michael Ruse and Edward O. Wilson, "The Evolution of Morality," *New Scientist* 1478 (1985): 108–28; 124: "Ethics is an illusion put in place by natural selection to make us good cooperators."

33. Edward O. Wilson, *On Human Nature* (Cambridge: Harvard University Press, 2004), 155.

34. Edward O. Wilson, *Sociobiology: The New Synthesis* (Cambridge: Harvard University Press, 1975), 562.

35. Robert L. Trivers, "The Evolution of Reciprocal Altruism," *Quarterly Review of Biology* 46 (1971): 35–57.

36. Robert Axelrod, *The Evolution of Cooperation* (New York: Basic Books, 1984), 54.

37. Jessica C. Flack & Frans De Waal, "'Any Animal Whatever': Darwinian Building Blocks of Morality in Monkeys and Apes," *Journal of Consciousness Studies* 7 (2000): 1–29.

38. Frans De Waal, *The Age of Empathy* (New York: Souvenir Press, 2009).

39. Francis J. Ayala, "The Biological Roots of Morality," in *Issues in Evolutionary Ethics*, ed. Paul Thompson (Albany: State University of New York Press, 1995), 302.

40. Ibid., 297.

41. Antonio Damasio, *Descartes' Error. Emotion, Reason, and the Human Brain* (New York: Avon Books, 1994), 191.

42. Jacques Monod, *Le hazard et la nécessité: Essai sur la philosophie naturelle de la biologie moderne* (Paris: Seuil, 1970), 174.

43. Jean-Pierre Changeux, *L'Homme neuronal* (Paris: Hachette, 1983), 87.

44. Jean-Pierre Changeux, *L'Homme de vérité* (Paris: Odile Jacob, 2004), 247.

45. Ibid., 294.
46. Wolf Singer, *Der Beobachter im Gehirn: Essays zur Hirnforschung* (Frankfurt-am-Main, 2002), 175.
47. Gerald M. Edelman, *Bright Air, Brilliant Fire: On the Matter of the Mind* (London: Basic Books, 1992), 17.
48. Giovanni Boniola and Gabriele De Anna, introduction to *Evolutionary Ethics and Contemporary Biology*, ed. Giovanni Boniola and Gabriele De Anna (Cambridge: Cambridge University Press, 2006), 2.
49. Jan Verplaetse, *Zonder vrije wil: Een filosofisch essay over verantwoordelijkheid* (Amsterdam: Nieuwezijds, 2011), 14.
50. Ibid., 17–20.
51. Paul Thagard, *The Brain and the Meaning of Life* (Princeton: Princeton University Press, 2010), 138.
52. William A. Rottschaeffer, *The Biology and Psychology of Moral Agency* (Cambridge: Cambridge University Press, 1998).
53. Michael Ruse and Edward O. Wilson, "*The Evolution of Morality*," *New Scientist* 1478 (1985): 108–28; Michael Ruse, "Is Darwinian Metaethics Possible?" in *Evolutionary Ethics and Contemporary Biology*, ed. Giovanni Boniolo and Gabriele De Anna (Cambridge: Cambridge University Press, 2006), 21.
54. Philip Kitcher, "Between Fragile Altruism and Morality: Evolution and the Emergence of Normative Guidance," in *Evolutionary Ethics and Contemporary Biology*, ed. Giovani Boniolo and Gabriele De Anna (Cambridge: Cambridge University Press, 2006), 159–77.
55. Ibid., pp. 175–76. Cf. Philip Kitcher, *Vaulting Ambition: Sociobiology and the Quest for Human Nature* (Cambridge: MIT Press, 1985).
56. Thomas Aquinas, *Summa Theologiae*, 1a2ae, q. 40, a. 3, "Whether hope is in dumb animals." See also his comments at 1a2ae, q. 46, a. 4. Cf. Charles Darwin, *The Expression of the Emotions in Man and Animals* (London: John Murray, 1872), http://www.darwin-online.org.uk.
57. Cf. Celia Deane-Drummond, "The Ethics of Nature," *New Dimensions to Religious Ethics* (Oxford: Blackwell, 2004), 83n106.
58. Arnhart, "The New Darwinian Naturalism in Political Theology," 374.
59. Heike Baranzke, *Würde der Kreatur? Die Idee der Würde im Horizont der Bioethik* (Würzburg: Königshausen und Neumann Verlag, 2002), 171, 191.
60. Alasdair MacIntyre, *Dependent Rational Animals: Why Human Beings Need the Virtues* (Chicago: Open Court, 1999), x: "I now judge that I was in error in supposing an ethics independent of biology to be possible."
61. Jean Porter, *Nature as Reason: A Thomistic Theory of the Natural Law* (Grand Rapids, Mich.: Eerdmans, 2005), 51.

62. Stephen Pope, *Human Evolution and Christian Ethics* (Cambridge: Cambridge University Press, 2007), 259.

63. Ibid., 260. Cf. Thomas Aquinas, *Summa Theologiae*, 1–2, q. 49–54.

64. Pope, *Human Evolution and Christian Ethics*, 261.

65. Damasio, *Descartes' Error*, 191.

66. Ibid., 177; Pope, *Human Evolution and Christian Ethics*, 263.

4. IN GOD'S IMAGE AND LIKENESS: FROM REASON TO REVELATION
IN HUMANS AND OTHER ANIMALS
Celia Deane-Drummond

I am grateful to Phillip Sloan and Charles Camosy for helpful comments on a subsequent draft. This chapter also draws on Celia Deane-Drummond, *Human Nature, Evolution and Other Animals* (Grand Rapids, Mich.: Eerdmans, 2014), forthcoming.

1. The strong rebuttal to Lynn White, following his notorious article in *Science* (1967), where he blamed of Christianity for causing the ecological crisis, may be understandable, but it is hard for Christianity to avoid at least some culpability in the way that human beings in the Christian tradition are held up as exercising lordship over other animals. See Lynn White, "The Historic Roots of Our Ecologic Crisis," *Science* 155, no. 3767 (1967): 1203–7.

2. Theologians who have argued against the exclusive use of image-bearing to support human domination of the natural world include, for example, Ruth Page, who has discussed ambiguities in usage of *imago Dei* in Ruth Page, "The Human Genome and the Image of God," in *Brave New World: Theology, Ethics and the Human Genome*, ed. Celia Deane-Drummond (London: SCM Press, 2003), 68–86, and David Cunningham, who is similarly critical of the use of the term "imago Dei" and "image-bearing." He argues for greater consideration of the term "flesh" as a way of affirming human relationships with other animals, in David Cunningham, "The Way of All Flesh: Rethinking the Imago Dei," in *Creaturely Theology: On God, Humans, and Other Animals*, ed. Celia Deane-Drummond and David Clough (London: SCM Press, 2009), 100–20.

3. These accusations against and blaming of Christianity bear some resemblance to the sharp critique—launched by launched by Lynn White a decade earlier, in 1967—of Christian belief as contributing to the ecological crisis. The difference is that while Christian theologians have criticized White's interpretation of history, in the case of animal rights, theologians such as Andrew Linzey, writing from the perspective of animal-rights advocates, tend to agree with Singer and to castigate Thomas Aquinas in particular as being particularly culpable. See Andrew Linzey, *Animal Theology* (London: SCM Press, 1994). More recently, among scholars who are not yet

convinced that traditional theological accounts have to be abandoned there has emerged a more nuanced response to this problem. See, for example, John Berkman, "Towards a Thomistic Theology of Animality," in *Creaturely Theology*, ed. Celia Deane-Drummond and David Clough, 21–40. For a detailed engagement with Peter Singer from a Roman Catholic perspective, see Charles C. Camosy, *Peter Singer and Christian Ethics: Beyond Polarisation* (Cambridge: Cambridge University Press, 2012). Peter Singer is not strictly an animal-rights activist, as his argument for minimizing suffering is based on a utilitarian approach and a shared sentience. For his most influential work, see Peter Singer, *Animal Liberation*, 2nd ed. (London: Pimlico, 1995). Tom Regan is more proactive, promoting what he has termed animal rights on the basis of shared psychological capacities: Tom Regan, *The Case for Animal Rights*, 2nd ed. (Berkeley: University of California Press, 2004).

4. Celia Deane-Drummond, "Are Animals Moral? Taking Soundings through Vice, Virtue, Conscience and *Imago De*," in *Creaturely Theology*, ed. Celia Deane-Drummond and David Clough, 190–210.

5. David Clough, "Putting Animals in Their Place: On the Theological Classification of Animals," in *Animals as Religious Subjects: Transdisciplinary Perspectives*, ed. Celia Deane-Drummond, Rebecca Artinian-Kaiser, and David Clough (London: T & T Clark/Bloomsbury, 2013), 209–24.

6. See, for example, Agustin Fuentes, "Cooperation, Conflict, and Niche Construction in the Genus *Homo*," in *War, Peace, and Human Nature: The Convergence of Cultural and Evolutionary Views*, ed. Douglas P. Fry (Oxford: Oxford University Press, 2013), 78–94. I take up this point in far more detail in Deane-Drummond, *Human Nature, Evolution, and Other Animals*.

7. See, for example, debates in Simon Conway Morris, ed., *The Deep Structure of Biology: Is Convergence Sufficiently Ubiquitous to Give a Directional Signal?* (Conshohocken: Templeton Foundation Press, 2008).

8. John Zizioulas, "Preserving God's Creation," lecture 3, *King's Theological Review* 13, no. 1 (1990):1–6. He suggests that consideration of what is found in God and not in creation "forces us to seek the *imago Dei* in freedom" (2). The aspiration for absolute freedom can never be attained, because humans are finite creatures. For Zizoulas this aspiration is fulfilled by humanity's taking up its role to be priests of creation. I have also discussed the meaning of theological freedom in the work of Hans Urs von Balthasar in the light of current discussion of the capacities of other primates; see Celia Deane-Drummond, "Degrees of 'Freedom': Humans as Primates in Dialogue with Hans Urs von Balthasar," in *From Animality to Transhumanism*, ed. Charlie Blake et al. (London: Continuum, 2012), 180–200.

9. He draws on Gregory of Nyssa's claim that "imago Dei" means "man's freedom to be master of himself." Zizioulas, "Preserving God's Creation," 2.

10. Zizioulas, "Preserving God's Creation," 2.

11. There is insufficient space here to discuss in any detail Thomas Aquinas's treatment of angels, but that he situates human beings on a scale with them is significant in terms of how he understands image-bearing. Thomas situates humanity between angels and other animals, naming angels as those created beings who grasp truth and understanding without having to undertake the process of reasoning. This direct grasp of the truth is more akin to what might be termed "graced" knowledge from revelation. Human rationality aims at the truth in a way that is impossible for other animals but that is known more perfectly by angels, so that "angelic power of knowledge is not in a different general category from the rational power of knowledge, but compares with it as the finished to the unfinished." *Summa Theologiae*, vol. 11, *Man*, 1a, q. 75–83 trans. Timothy Suttor (1970) (Cambridge: Cambridge University Press, 2006), 1a, q. 79.8. All references to the *Summa* in this chapter are to the Blackfriars translation of the Latin text, reprinted by Cambridge University Press, 2006.

12. This way of treating the subject of freedom compared is different from most other approaches used in the science and religion literature, which have on the whole either have, as an aspect (the so called free-process or free-will defense) of debates on theodicy, concentrated on trying to find a general capacity for freedom as an integral aspect of the physical universe or have argued for the place of human—and scientific—freedom in the light of accounts of genetic determinism. Both accounts bypass consideration of other animals. See, for example, Ted Peters, *Playing God: Genetic Determinism and Human Freedom* (New York: Routledge, 1997); John Polkinghorne, *Science and Providence* (London: SPCK, 1989); Thomas Tracy, "Evolution, Divine Action, and the Problem of Evil," in *Evolutionary and Molecular Biology: Scientific Perspectives on Divine Action*, ed. Robert John Russell et al. (Vatican City: Vatican Observatory/Berkeley: Centre for Theology and the Natural Sciences, 1998), 511–30.

13. Helen Steward, "Animal Agency," *Inquiry* 52, no. 3 (2009): 217–31.

14. He bases his argument on the assumption that other animals do not have language. See Donald Davidson, *Subjective, Intersubjective, Objective* (Oxford: Oxford University Press, 2001).

15. This helpful definition is taken from Steward, "Animal Agency," 226.

16. See, for example, Frans de Waal, *Good Natured: The Origins of Right and Wrong in Humans and Other Animals* (Cambridge: Harvard University Press, 1996); *Chimpanzee Politics* (Baltimore: John Hopkins University Press, 1997); *The Age of Empathy* (London: Souvenir Press, 2009); *The Bonobo and the Atheist: In Search of Humanism among the Primates* (New York: Norton, 2013); Marc Bekoff, *Animal Passions and Beastly Virtues: Reflections on Redecorating*

Nature (Philadelphia: Temple University Press, 2006); *The Emotional Lives of Animals* (Novato: New World Library, 2007); Marc Bekoff and Jessica Pierce, *Wild Justice: The Moral Lives of Animals* (Chicago: University of Chicago Press, 2009); Virginia Morell, *Animal Wise: The Thoughts and Emotions of Our Fellow Creatures* (New York: Crown , 2013).

17. One such example is Jonathan Balcombe, *Second Nature: The Inner Lives of Animals* (New York: Palgrave/Macmillan, 2010).

18. Bennett G. Galef, "Culture in Animals?" in *The Question of Animal Culture*, ed. Kevin N. Laland and Bennett G. Galef (Cambridge: Harvard University Press, 2009), 222–46. The author admits that any concrete link between the evolution of animal traditions and the emergence of human cultures has yet to be proven.

19. Christine Korsegaard, "Morality and the Distinctiveness of Human Action," in *Primates and Philosophers*, ed. Frans de Waal (Princeton: Princeton University Press), 110–12.

20. Thomas Aquinas, *Summa Theologiae*, vol. 10, 1a, q. 65–74. *Cosmogony*, trans. William Wallace (1967) (Cambridge: Cambridge University Press, 2006), 1a q. 72. He interprets "beast" in the Genesis text as referring to wild animals, and oxen and cattle to stand for domesticated animals, while "creeping things" are snakes or other reptiles, with quadrupeds to cover other types, such as deer or goats. He also seems to allow for some change within this process by acknowledging the possibility of new species appearing as long as these were drawn from latent "active powers." How far this is an incipient evolutionary theory is a mute point, but at least this qualifies the negative stance toward the "chain of being" cosmology that is often subject to criticism by those among animal-rights activists who are hostile to his position.

21. *Summa Theologiae*, vol. 10, 1a, q. 74.1

22. *Summa Theologiae*, vol. 11, *Man*, trans. Timothy Suttor (1970), 1a, q. 75–83 (Cambridge: Cambridge University Press, 2006), 1a, q. 75.1.

23. *Summa Theologiae*, vol. 11, 1a, q. 75.2. See also, for example, *Summa Theologiae*, vol. 13, *Man Made to God's Image*, 1a, q. 90–102 trans. Edmund Hill (1963) (Cambridge: Cambridge University Press, 2006), 1a, q. 90.2, where Thomas speaks of the creation of the rational soul as a direct act of God's creative activity. He also rejects the idea that the rational soul could be the work of angelic forces, since only God can create a soul directly, *Summa Theologiae*, vol. 13, 1a, q. 90.3.

24. *Summa Theologiae*, vol. 11, 1a, q. 78.4.

25. While in the Blackfriars translation of the *Summa* the term "instinct" is translated for *aestimativa*, my own preference for is "estimative sense," since "instinct" in contemporary usage is too loaded with meaning.

26. Thomas, following the science of his time, and drawing on Avicenna, attributed this form of reasoning about particular things to "the middle of the head." *Summa Theologiae*, vol. 11, 1a, q. 78.4.

27. *Summa Theologiae*, vol. 17, *Psychology of Human Acts*, 1a2ae, q. 6–17, trans. Thomas Gilby (1969) (Cambridge: Cambridge University Press, 2006), 1a2ae, q. 6.2.

28. There are heated debates on how far and to what extent animals can perceive the thought processes in other animals—that is, to what extent they have a theory of mind. Observation of other animals does not prove convincingly what they might be thinking, though clearest evidence seems to come from quail behavior rather than from that of our closest living primate relatives. See Clive D. L. Wynne, *Animal Cognition: The Mental Lives of Animals* (Basingstoke: Palgrave MacMillan, 2001), 9–23.

29. Aquinas, *Summa Theologiae*, vol. 11, 1a, q.78.4. Thomas's subordination of memory to "instinct," or human cognition, along with his notion of sense-consciousness, does not match with contemporary psychology. However, the point here is not to show up that in the light of modern knowledge certain aspects of his science are naive, which in itself is hardly surprising, but that he attributes to other animals capacities that touch on those of humans, even if the two are distinct.

30. Aquinas, *Summa Theologiae*, vol. 11, 1a, q. 78.4.

31. The ability of rational beings to perceive not just a good end but to abstract and understand what that end means compared with the more specific reflection on particular ends in other creatures is also discussed in *Summa Theologiae*, vol. 17, 1a2ae, q. 11.2.

32. For further work on animal souls and the differences between them and human and plant souls, see Celia Deane-Drummond, "God's Image and Likeness in Humans and Other Animals: Performative Soul-Making and Graced Nature," *Zygon* 4, no 47 (2012): 934–48.

33. *Summa Theologiae*, vol. 11, 1a, q. 80.1.

34. *Summa Theologiae*, vol. 11, 1a, q. 80.2

35. *Summa Theologiae*, vol. 11, 1a, q. 81.4.

36. *Summa Theologiae*, vol. 16, *Purpose and Happiness*, 1a2ae, q. 1–5, trans. Thomas Gilby (1968) (Cambridge: Cambridge University Press, 2006), 1a2ae, q. 1.2.

37. *Summa Theologiae*, vol. 16, 1a2ae, q. 1.3 Thomas also believed that the same physical act may be moral or not, depending on inner purposes.

38. *Summa Theologiae*, vol. 17, 1a2ae, q. 9.3

39. Janet Martin Soskice, *The Kindness of God: Metaphor, Gender and Religious Language* (Oxford: Oxford University Press, 2007).

40. *Summa Theologiae*, vol. 17, 1a2ae, q. 15.3 Also discussed in *Summa Theologiae*, vol. 17, 1a2ae, q. 17.2, where Thomas claims that as soon as other animals perceive something as fitting or unfitting, they spontaneously move toward or away from it.

41. Berkman, "Towards a Thomistic Theology of Animality," 21–40.

42. Thomas Aquinas, *On Truth*, vol. 3, trans. Robert Mulligan (Chicago: Regnery, 1954), q. 25.2.

43. Thomas Aquinas, *On Truth*, vol. 3, q. 24.2.

44. *Summa Theologiae*, vol. 13, 1a, q. 93.2. "It seems that God's image is to be found in irrational creatures" opens this question.

45. By intelligence, Thomas means not the common usage of distinctions among human beings but what distinguishes human reasoning from the mental effort of other animals. Edmund Hill, translator's note, p. 53, note a., *Summa Theologiae*, vol. 13, q. 93. Of course, in the light of recent research since this translation (1963), other animals are also now considered to be intelligent, the subject of "intelligence" no longer being constricted to human persons.

46. *Summa Theologiae*, vol. 13, 1a, q. 93.2

47. *Summa Theologiae*, vol. 13, 1a, q. 93.2.

48. *Summa Theologiae*, vol. 13, 1a, q. 93.6.

49. I am aware that "human nature" raises a number of philosophical questions today about what it might mean. Some may resist the use of evolutionary biology as a starting point, or even the use of it at all. There are ambiguities here, since on the one hand there is an essentialist search for universals among more strident evolutionary psychologists, but on the other hand evolutionary biologists are more aware than they once were of the porosity of species boundaries and shared evolutionary history. Categorizing the human in terms of persons also creates as many problems as it solves. Further, the classical discussion of human nature could be said to be as much about the human condition, in that it is shaped in a particular intellectual culture. In spite of these limitations, I believe that the analysis of dominant conceptions of human nature in the Western world does offer a category that is useful to consider and that, through the concept of image-bearing, human nature can be thought of (for theologians at least) as being in relationship with God.

50. *Summa Theologiae*, vol. 13, 1a, q. 93.6.

51. *Summa Theologiae*, vol. 13, 1a, q. 93.8.

52. Specifically J. Wentzel van Huyssteen, *Alone in All the World? Human Uniqueness in Science and Theology* (Grand Rapids, Mich.: Eerdmanns, 2006), and Wesley J. Wildman, *Science and Religious Anthropology: A Spiritually Evocative Naturalist Interpretation of Human Life* (Farnham: Ashgate, 2009).

53. Frans de Waal, personal comment following public discussion of his lecture on "The Age of Empathy," American Academy of Religion, Atlanta, 2010.

54. Perhaps the most convincing evidence for this is through a recorded video that shows chimpanzees in rapt contemplation of waterfalls, with a commentary by Goodall. While her work has been criticized as over-speculative, it is worth keeping an open mind about the possibility of a latent form of religious instinct, even if, as she admits, it is nonreflective. See http://www.janegoodall.org/chimp-central-waterfall-displays.

55. This is discussed in Jeffrey Schloss and Michael Murray, eds., *The Believing Primate* (Oxford: Oxford University Press, 2009), especially in essays by Michael Murray. See, for example, Michael Murray, "Scientific Explanations of Religion and the Justification of Religious Belief," 168–78. "Games Scientists Play," Alvin Plantinga's essay in this volume, is also useful in this context, 139–67.

56. I have discussed this aspect in more detail in the reply to R. J. Berry: Celia Deane-Drummond, "*Homo Divinus:* Myth or Reality?" in *Darwinism and Natural Theology: Evolving Perspectives*, ed. Andrew Robinson (Cambridge: Cambridge Scholars Press, 2012), 39–46.

57. I do, however, suggest that there are some specific events that require the possibility of special divine impetus, most notably in Christology, where Christ's incarnation and his resurrection on the third day loses their meaning if it is simply merged with human evolutionary history. The difficulty is more precisely how to understand divine participation in the emergence of the human over and above what is already the case for the wider created world. If God is present with the world through divine immanence and is, in a Thomistic sense, the ground of all that is, and if God also acts through secondary causes, what kind of meaning do "intervention" metaphors have in such a context? In other words, I am not convinced that it is necessary to imagine this particular pattern of divine action at the origin of human beings in order for their distinctive aspects to be stressed.

58. R. J. Berry, "Biology Since Darwin," in *Darwinism and Natural Theology: Evolving Perspectives*, ed. Andrew Robinson (Cambridge: Cambridge Scholars Press, 2012).

59. I do concede, however, that theologically it would be worth exploring rather more precisely the relationship between Christology and anthropology in considering the meaning of divine-image-bearing. There is insufficient scope in this paper to do justice to this aspect of the issue.

60. Józef Życiński, "Bio-ethics, Technology, and Human Dignity: The Roman Catholic Viewpoint," *Acta Neurochirurgica* Suppl. 98 (2006): 1–7, http://www.jozefzycinski.eu/.

61. Evidence suggests that human cooperation does have what seem to be genuinely evolutionary elements within it, as suggested by recent research. For recent discussion, see, for example, Stuart A. West, Claire El Mouden and Andrew Gardner, "Six Common Misconceptions about the Evolution of Cooperation in Humans," *Evolution and Human Behavior* 32 (2011): 231–62.

62. For further development of the idea of human flourishing, see Stephen J. Pope, "Theological Anthropology, Science, and Human Flourishing," in this volume.

5. NEUROSCIENCE, SELF, AND JESUS CHRIST
Oliver Davies

1. See, e.g., Rolf Pfeifer and Josh Bongard, *How the Body Shapes the Way We Think* (Cambridge: MIT Press, 2007), and Alva Noë, *Action in Perception* (Cambridge: MIT Press, 2004).

2. Hannah Arendt, *The Human Condition* (Chicago: Chicago University Press, 1958), 294–313.

3. Amos Funkenstein, *Theology and the Scientific Imagination* (Princeton: Princeton University Press, 1986), 12, 290–327.

4. Nicholas Humphreys, *Soul Dust* (London: Quercus, 2011).

5. George F. R. Ellis, "Physics in the Real Universe: Time and Space-time," *General Relativity and Gravitation* 38 (2006): 1797–1824.

6. See, for instance, Joseph Ratzinger's comment that the session marks not the "withdrawal of Christ to an Empyrean which is beyond the world, but is a visible expression for our participation in the mode of his being in the world: through the Spirit, Christ is not absent from the world but present in a new way, as the kingdom of God is realized on earth." Ratzinger, "Himmelfahrt Christi," in *Lexikon für Theologie und Kirche*, vol. 5 (Freiburg: Verlag Herder, 1960): col. 361.

7. *Summa Theologiae*, 3a, q. 57, a. 4, 5.

8. For a discussion of the eucharistic debates of the early Reformation, in which cosmological themes form a continuous background, see Oliver Davies, Paul Janz, and Clemens Sedmak, *Transformation Theology. Church in the World* (London: T&T Clark/Continuum, 2007), 18–29.

9. See Augustine on the exalted Christ as true agent in the sacraments: *Answer to Petilian*, book 2, chapter 7, §15–16, and book 3, chapter 49, §59.

10. See Calvin's remarks on the cosmology of Eph 4:10 in *Calvin's Commentaries on the Epistles of Paul to the Galatians and Ephesians*, trans. William Pringle (Edinburgh: Calvin Translation Society, 1854), 275–76.

11. Dietrich Bonhoeffer, *Christology*, trans. John Bowden (Collins: St James's Place, London, 1966), 47.

12. For a more detailed analysis, see Oliver Davies, *Theology of Transformation: Faith, Freedom, and the Christian Act* (Oxford: Oxford University Press), 2013.

13. David Sloane Wilson, *Darwin's Cathedrals. Evolution, Religion, and the Nature of Society* (Chicago: Chicago University Press, 2003). See also n. 23 below.

14. Michael Tomasello, *Origins of Human Communication* (Cambridge: MIT Press, 2008).

15. Adam Zeman, *A Portrait of the Brain* (New Haven: Yale University Press, 2008), 1.

16. Leonhard Schilbach, Bert Timmermans, Vasudevi Reddy, Alan Costell, Gary Bente, Tobias Schlicht, Kai Vogeley, "Towards a Second-Person Neuroscience," *Behavioural and Brain Sciences* (article is forthcoming).

17. Ibid. See also Bernard Baars, *In the Theater of Consciousness: The Workspace of the Mind* (New York: Oxford University Press, 1997). On freedom and consciousness, see Merlin McDonald, "Consciousness and the Freedom to Act," in *Free Will and Consciousness. How Might They Work?* ed. Roy F. Baumeister, Alfred R. Miele, and Kathleen D. Vohs (Oxford: Oxford University Press, 2010), 8–23.

18. On the evolutionary background to this dynamic of collaboration, see the important evaluation by Stuart A. West, Claire El Mouden, Andy Gardner, "Sixteen Common Misconceptions about the Evolution of Cooperation in Humans," *Evolution and Human Behavior* 32 (2011): 231–62.

19. Bojana Kuzmanovic, Gary Bente, D. Yves von Cramon, Leonhard Schilbach, Marc Tittgemeyer, and Kai Vogeley, "Imaging First Impressions: Distinct Neural Processing of Verbal and Nonverbal Social Information," *NeuroImage*, 60 (2012): 179–88. One of the symptoms of higher-functioning autism is the relative inability to hold these two sources of knowledge together, with a tendency to opt for the "verbal" one.

20. Niklas Luhmann, *Social Systems* (Stanford: Stanford University Press, 1995), 34–36 and passim.

21. Joshua D. Green. "The Cognitive Neuroscience of Moral Judgment," in *The Cognitive Neurosciences*, 4th ed., ed. Michael S. Gazzaniga (Cambridge: MIT Press, 2009), pp. 987–1002. Green insists on a reductionist explanation of this data, however.

22. Oliver Davies, Paul Janz, Clemens Sedmak, *Transformation Theology. Church in the World* (London: T&T Clark International, 2007), 76–86. For a parallel structure around "the uses of error," see also Rowan D. Williams, "Between Politics and Metaphysics: Reflections in the Wake of Gillian Rose," *Modern Theology* 11, no. 1 (January 1995): 3–22, esp. 9–16.

23. Barry Mason, "Towards Positions of Safe Uncertainty," *Human Systems: The Journal of Systemic Consultation and Management* (1993): 189–200.

24. Kathleen R. Gibson, and Tim Ingold, eds., *Tools, Language, and Cognition in Human Evolution* (Cambridge: Cambridge University Press, 1993).

25. Andy Clark, *Supersizing the Mind. Embodiment, Action, and Cognitive Extension* (Oxford: Oxford University Press, 2011), 56.

26. Oliver Davies, *The Creativity of God. World, Eucharist, Reason* (Cambridge: Cambridge University Press, 2004), 137–53.

27. See chapter 6 in this volume.

28. Anthony J. Godzieba, Lieven Boeve, and Michele Saracino, "Resurrection—Interruption—Transformation: Incarnation as Hermeneutical Strategy," *Theological Studies* 67 (2006): 777–815.

29. See Paul Ricoeur, *Oneself as Another* (Chicago: University of Chicago Press, 1995).

30. E.g., Hamann, Marx, and Derrida.

31. This is not, however, the "biologism" that Henri-Jérôme Gagey critiques, for instance, in his chapter in this volume.

6. INCARNATION IN THE AGE OF THE BUFFERED, COMMODIFIED SELF
Anthony J. Godzieba

1. Maurice Blondel, *Action: Essay on a Critique of Life and a Science of Practice,* trans. Oliva Blanchette (Notre Dame, Ind.: University of Notre Dame Press, 2003), 3–4.

2. Ibid., 314.

3. Cf. ibid., 314–29.

4. Maurice Blondel, *The Letter on Apologetics and History and Dogma,* trans. Alexander Dru and Illtyd Trethowan (Grand Rapids, Mich.: Eerdmans, 1994), 161.

5. Charles Taylor, *A Secular Age* (Cambridge, Mass.: Belknap Press / Harvard University Press, 2007), 38–41.

6. Ibid., 323. Another definition: "the ways in which [people] imagine their social existence, how they fit together with others, how things go in between them and their fellows, the expectations which are normally met, and the deeper normative notions and images which underlie these expectations," (Ibid., 323).

7. Ibid., 371.

8. Ibid., 363. Taylor notes that "what is unprecedented in human history [is that] there is no longer a clear and obvious sense that this vastness is shaped and limited by an antecedent plan. . . . Our present sense of things fails to touch bottom anywhere" (325).

9. Ibid., 326–27.

10. Chris Hedges, *The Empire of Illusion: The End of Literacy and the Triumph of Spectacle* (New York: Nation Books, 2009), 26.

11. Ibid., 16, citing Neal Gabler's argument in *Life: The Movie: How Entertainment Conquered Reality* (New York: Vintage, 1998).

12. Hedges, *Empire of Illusion*, 26.

13. Ibid., 190.

14. See Max Horkheimer and Theodor W. Adorno, "The Culture Industry: Enlightenment as Mass Deception," *Dialectic of Enlightenment: Philosophical Fragments*, ed. Gunzelin Schmid Noerr, trans. Edmund Jephcott (Stanford: Stanford University Press, 2002), 94–136. See also Adorno's famous essay "On the Fetish-Character of Music and the Regression of Listening (1938)," in Adorno and Horkheimer, *Essays on Music*, ed. Richard Leppert, trans. Susan H. Gillespie (Berkeley: University of California Press, 2002), 288–317.

15. Daniel J. Boorstin, *The Image: A Guide to Pseudo-Events in America* (New York: Atheneum, 1961); Guy Debord, *La societé du spectacle* (Paris: Buchet-Chastel, 1967); Guy Debord, *Society of the Spectacle*, trans. Donald Nicholson-Smith (New York: Zone Books, 1994); Neil Postman, *Amusing Ourselves to Death: Public Discourse in the Age of Show Business* (New York: Penguin, 1985).

16. Taylor, *A Secular Age*, 770–72.

17. Hedges's only sustained expression of hope comes in the book's concluding pages, and ends this way: "Love will endure, even if it appears darkness has swallowed us all, to triumph over the wreckage that remains" (*Empire of Illusion*, 193).

18. Vincent J. Miller, *Consuming Religion: Christian Faith and Practice in a Consumer Culture* (New York: Continuum, 2004), 179.

19. Terry Eagleton, *The Illusions of Postmodernism* (Oxford: Blackwell, 1996), 39.

20. Congregation for the Doctrine of the Faith, "Letter to the Bishops of the Catholic Church on the Collaboration of Men and Women in the Church and in the World" (31 May 2004) §1, http://www.vatican.va/roman _curia/congregations/cfaith/documents/re_con_cfaith_doc_20047311 _collaboration_en.html.

21. This is traceable in large part to the favorable reception of Blondel's thought within *la nouvelle théologie* and to the influence of more existentialist and phenomenological modes of thinking.

22. *Gaudium et Spes* (Pastoral Constitution on the Church in the World of Today), §36, http//www.vatican.va/archive/hist_councils/ii_vatican_council/ documents/vat-ii_const_19651207_gaudium-et-spes_en.html. For the rela-

tion between autonomy and theonomy, see Walter Kasper, "Autonomy and Theonomy: The Place of Christianity in the Modern World," in *Theology and Church*, trans. Margaret Kohl (New York: Crossroad, 1989), 32–53, esp. 34–37.

23. Cf. the essays in *Augustine and Postmodern Thought: A New Alliance Against Modernity?*, ed. Lieven Boeve, Mathijs Lamberigts, and Maarten Wisse, BETL 291 (Leuven: Peeters, 2009).

24. Michelle A. Gonzalez, "Difference, Body, and Race," in this volume, 132–33.

25. Ibid, 134.

26. Terry Eagleton, *The Idea of Culture* (Malden, Mass.; Oxford, Blackwell, 2000), 64. He continues, "One might define these types more pithily as excellence, *ethos*, and economics."

27. Ibid., 38.

28. Gonzalez, "Difference, Body, and Race," in this volume.

29. For the original idea of the "Court of the Gentiles," see Pope Benedict XVI, "Address to the Members of the Roman Curia and Papal Representatives," §36, December 21, 2009, http://www.vatican.va/holy_father/benedict_xvi/speeches/2009/december/documents/hf_ben-xvi_spe_2009 1221_curia-auguri_en.html. For the first stages of the initiative's developments, see Sandro Magister, "The First 'Court' of Believers and Atheists Will Open in Paris," *L'Espresso* (Milan), June 24, 2010, http://chiesa.espresso .repubblica.it.articolo/134386?eng=yes.

30. The paranoid-critical method views this theological presupposition and the instrumental rationality sanctioned by it as covertly influencing every Catholic argument that attempts to come to grips with modern views of person, society, and the natural world. The fear, then, is that in any dialogue with modernity Catholic theology will necessarily degenerate into a mere rewriting of Feuerbach's *Essence of Christianity*, this time as farce.

31. See, for example, Dupré, *Passage to Modernity: An Essay in the Hermeneutics of Nature and Culture* (New Haven: Yale University Press, 1993); Louis Dupré, *The Enlightenment and the Intellectual Foundations of Modern Culture* (New Haven: Yale University Press, 2004); David Brown, *God and Enchantment of Place: Reclaiming Human Experience* (Oxford: Oxford University Press, 2004). For a theological-aesthetic analysis of Catholic "modernities" of the fifteenth through the eighteenth centuries, see Anthony J. Godzieba, "'Refuge of Sinners, Pray for Us': Augustine, Aquinas, and the Salvation of Modernity," in *Augustine and Postmodern Thought*, 147–65.

32. Blaise Pascal, "Penseés," in *Œuvres complètes*, 2 vols., ed. Michel Le Guern (Paris: Gallimard, 2000), 545–46 (no. 10); *Pensées*, trans. A. J. Krailsheimer (London; New York: Penguin, 1995), 4 (no. 12).

33. *The Oxford Dictionary of the Christian Church*, 3rd ed., ed. Frank L. Cross and Elizabeth A. Livingstone (Oxford; New York: Oxford University Press, 1997), s.v., "Natural Theology," 1132.

34. Walter Kasper, *An Introduction to Christian Faith*, trans. V. Green (New York: Paulist, 1980), 20 (natural "access-point"); Walter Kasper, *The God of Jesus Christ*, new ed., trans. Matthew J. O'Connell (London; New York: Continuum, 2012), 71 (internal reasonableness of faith).

35. What follows summarizes the analysis of experience in *The God of Jesus Christ*, 82–87.

36. Ibid., 81.

37. Ibid., 84.

38. Ibid., 84–85.

39. Ibid., 153.

40. Ibid., 105.

41. Ibid., 154–55. Kasper here combines Boethius's classical definition of "person" as "an individual substance of a rational nature" (naturae rationalis individua substantia [*De persona et duabus naturis*, 3]; Thomas's understanding of human nature "in so far as it is immaterial" as "in some way all things" (Secundum vero esse immateriale . . . est etiam quodammodo omnia [*In libros de anima*, 2.5.5], and Richard of St. Victor's definition of "person" as "an intellectual nature existing incommunicably" (naturae intellectualis incommunicabilis existentia [*De trinitatae*, 2.22.24]) and retrieves them in more contemporary terms (Kasper, *The God of Jesus*, 153–54).

42. Kasper, *The God of Jesus*, 154.

43. Ibid., 155.

44. Ibid., 156.

45. Miller, *Consuming Religion*, 181.

46. Anthony J. Godzieba, Lieven Boeve, and Michele Saracino, "Resurrection—Interruption—Transformation: Incarnation as Hermeneutical Strategy," *Theological Studies* 67 (2006): 777–815.

47. For what follows, see the more detailed treatments in Anthony J. Godzieba, "Incarnation, Theory, and Catholic Bodies: What Should Post-Postmodern Catholic Theology Look Like?" *Louvain Studies* 28 (2003): 217–31; Godzieba, "Knowing Differently: Incarnation, Imagination, and the Body," *Louvain Studies* 32 (2007): 361–82; Godzieba, "The Catholic Sacramental Imagination and the Access/Excess of Grace," *New Theology Review* 21, no. 3 (August 2008): 14–26.

48. See especially Merleau-Ponty, *Phenomenology of Perception*, trans. Colin Smith (1962; rev. reprint, London: Routledge & Kegan Paul, 1978); Maurice Merleau-Ponty, *The Structure of Behavior*, trans. A. L. Fisher (Boston: Beacon

Press, 1963); Merleau-Ponty, *Sense and Non-Sense*, trans. Hubert Dreyfus and Patricia Allen Dreyfus (Evanston, Ill.: Northwestern University Press, 1964).

49. Merleau-Ponty, *Phenomenology of Perception*, 106. Earlier he writes, "Man taken as a concrete being is not a psyche joined to an organism, but the movement to and fro of existence which at one time allows itself to take corporeal form and at others moves towards personal acts" (88).

50. My phenomenological approach to the body and embodiment, with its clear scriptural roots, thus proceeds differently than does the phenomenological approach followed by Pope John Paul II in his *Man and Woman He Created Them: A Theology of the Body*, trans. Michael Waldstein, rev. ed. (Boston: Pauline Books and Media, 2006). John Paul pursues phenomenology in a more transcendental manner (Edmund Husserl via Max Scheler), whereas the approach outlined here (Husserlian intentionality via Martin Heidegger and Maurice Merleau-Ponty) proceeds in a less transcendental and more existential-phenomenological way. My argument also differs greatly from one like David L. Schindler's in "The Embodied Person as Gift and the Cultural Task in America: *Status Quaestionis*," *Communio* 35 (2008): 397–431, where it is presented as a reception of John Paul II's theology of the body and does indeed emphasize relationality, but in trying to secure our "belonging to God and to others, to the entire community of being" as a "filial-nuptial relationality" (431), it eventually dissolves into a blizzard of abstract metaphysical distinctions that are more asserted than proven.

51. See Klaus Hemmerle, *Thesen zu einer trinitarischen Ontologie*, Kriterien 40 (Einsiedeln: Johannes Verlag, 1976), 54 (my translation). See also Kasper, *The God of Jesus Christ*, 306–8; Thomas J. Norris, *The Trinity—Life of God, Hope for Humanity: Towards a Theology of Communion* (Hyde Park, N.Y.: New City Press, 2009), 48–51.

52. Rosemary P. Carbine, "Public Theology: A Feminist View of Political Subjectivity and Praxis," in this volume, 150, 156.

53. Ibid., 158.

54. Cf. Godzieba, "The Catholic Sacramental Imagination and the Access/Excess of Grace," 14–26. For the development of "performativity" as a category for analyzing meaning, see the essays in Peter Gillgren and Marten Snickare, eds., *Performativity and Performance in Baroque Rome: Visual Culture in Early Modernity* (Surrey, UK; Burlington, Vt.: Ashgate, 2012).

55. Bryan S. Turner, "Body," *Theory, Culture & Society* 23, no. 2–3 (2006): 223–29, at 228.

56. Ibid., 223.

7. THE GIFTED SELF: THE CHALLENGES OF FRENCH THOUGHT
Robyn Horner

1. Lieven Boeve, *God Interrupts History: Theology in a Time of Upheaval*, trans. Brian Doyle (New York; London: Continuum, 2007), 30–35. While Boeve locates the emergence of "postmodern sensibilities" within the 1980s, questions concerning the self-identity of the subject have a long lineage. Boeve's work is clearly important in this context as it is at the origin of the conversation that was generative of the present text.

2. See Robyn Horner, "Being Human in Times of Crisis: Rereading *Gaudium et Spes*," *Being Human: Groundwork for a Theological Anthropology for the 21st Century*. Ed. David Kirchhoffer with Robyn Horner and Patrick McArdle (Preston, Victoria, Australia: Mosaic, 2013) 157–72.

3. To make this argument, it is necessary to look not only at what *Gaudium et Spes* actually says about the human person—tracing there a personalist anthropology where "intellect, will, conscience and fraternity are preeminent (61)"—but also at its stated purpose (the desire to dialogue with the modern world) (2, 10) and at its context, together with other conciliar documents (for example, *Dignitatis Humanae*). *Gaudium et Spes*, http://www.vatican.va. For a lucid summary of personalist perspectives from the perspective of Catholic anthropology, see Jan Jans, "Personalism: The Foundations of an Ethics of Responsibility," *Ethical Perspectives* 3 (1996): 148–56.

4. Boeve, *God Interrupts History*, 32.

5. Ibid.

6. David H. Kelsey, *Eccentric Existence: A Theological Anthropology*, 2 vols. (Louisville, Ky.: Westminster John Knox Press, 2009), 81.

7. Joseph Ratzinger, "Part 1, Chapter 1: The Dignity of the Human Person," in *Pastoral Constitution on the Church in the Modern World*, trans. W. J. O'Hara, ed. Herbert Vorgrimler, vol. 5 of *Commentary on the Documents of Vatican II* (New York: Herder and Herder, 1969), 117–18.

8. Jean-Luc Marion, "The Possible and Revelation," in *The Visible and the Revealed*, trans. Christina M. Gschwandtner (New York: Fordham University Press, 2008), 2.

9. Oliver Davies, "Neuroscience, Self, and Jesus Christ," in this volume.

10. *Gaudium et Spes* reasserts that it is possible to know "permanent values" and "realities that do not change" (10); "objective norms of morality" (16); "eternal realities" that can be distinguished from their "changing expressions" (52); "proper forms of culture" (61); and a "right order of things" (72).

11. See, in this volume, the very nuanced appreciation of natural law offered by Henri-Jérôme Gagey, especially in his discussion of the Interna-

tional Theological Commission document *In Search of a Universal Ethic: A New Look at the Natural Law.*

12. On whether this is even an accurate reading of Descartes, see Jean-Luc Marion, *On Descartes' Metaphysical Prism: Constitution and Limits of the Onto-theology of Cartesian Thought*, trans. Jeffrey L. Kosky (Chicago: University of Chicago Press, 1999).

13. Drawing from chapter 4 ("Man as the Event of God's Free and Forgiving Self-Communication") in Karl Rahner, *Foundations of Christian Faith: An Introduction to the Idea of Christianity*, trans. William V. Dych (New York: Crossroad, 1992). While it complicates our current study (in light of the critique of correlation), we take on board Rahner's transcendental perspective to the extent that theology always and already implies anthropology: "To interpret the whole of dogmatic theology as transcendental anthropology means that every dogmatic treatment must also be considered from its transcendental angle, and that one must therefore face the question, what measure of actual material content subsists in the theological subject's *a priori* 'structures' implicit in a particular theological statement?" Karl Rahner, "Theology and Anthropology," in The Electronic Centenary ed., *Writings of 1965–1967*, trans. Graeme Harrison, vol. 9 of *Theological Investigations* (Limerick, Ireland: Centre for Culture, Technology and Values, 2004), 30. See also the comments on pages 39–40, where Rahner attempts to engage the question of whether "the 'modern period' to which this transcendental anthropology is especially adapted is already a thing of the past or in process of decline together with its philosophy" (39).

14. Jean-Luc Nancy, introduction to *Who Comes After the Subject?* ed. Eduardo Cadava, Peter Connor, and Jean-Luc Nancy (New York: Routledge, 1991), 4.

15. Jacques Derrida, *Speech and Phenomena and Other Essays on Husserl's Theory of Signs*, trans. David B. Allison and Newton Garver (Evanston, Ill.: Northwestern University Press, 1973), 60.

16. Derrida, *Speech and Phenomena*, 64.

17. Ibid., 66.

18. "The possibility of re-petition in its most general form, that is, the constitution of a trace in the most universal sense—is a possibility which not only must inhabit the pure actuality of the now but must constitute it through the very movement of difference it introduces. Such a trace is—if we can employ this language without immediately contradicting it or crossing it out as we proceed—more 'primordial' than what is phenomenologically primordial. For the ideality of the form (*Form*) of presence itself implies that it be infinitely repeatable, that its re-turn, as a return of the same, is necessary *ad infinitum* and is inscribed in presence itself." Derrida, *Speech and Phenomena*, 67.

19. Jacques Derrida, "'Eating Well' or the Calculations of the Subject," in *Points: Interviews, 1974–1994,* trans. Peter Connor and Avital Ronell, ed. Elisabeth Weber (Stanford: Stanford University Press, 1995), 274.

20. Ibid., 261.

21. Ibid., 274–76

22. Ibid., 261.

23. See, for example, chapter 3 of Martin Hägglund, *Radical Atheism: Derrida and the Time of Life* (Stanford: Stanford University Press, 2008).

24. Derrida, "Eating Well," 275. John Martis very lucidly traces the loss of the subject, as it is articulated by Derrida and then thought with subtle differences by Maurice Blanchot and Philippe Lacoue-Labarthe. See in particular the final summary in John Martis, *Philippe Lacoue-Labarthe: Representation and the Loss of the Subject* (New York: Fordham University Press, 2005), 225–27.

25. Derrida, "Eating Well," 276.

26. For an investigation of these questions, see Robyn Horner, "Theology After Derrida," *Modern Theology* 29, no. 3 (2013): 230–47.

27. For a helpful discussion as well as a novel solution, see John Martis, "The Self Found Elsewhere: Phenomenological Faith Meets Deconstructive Doubt," *Pacifica* 22 (2009): 198–214.

28. While for Rahner we ultimately remain a mystery to ourselves, "the original and basic concept of knowledge . . . is primarily the being-present-to-itself (*Beisichsein*) of an entity." Karl Rahner, "Some Implications of the Scholastic Concept of Uncreated Grace," in *Theological Investigations,* trans. Cornelius Ernst (Baltimore: Helicon, 1963), 1:327.

29. Jean-Luc Marion, *Reduction and Givenness: Investigations of Husserl, Heidegger and Phenomenology,* trans. Thomas A. Carlson (Evanston: Northwestern University Press, 1998), 204.

30. Jean-Luc Marion, *Being Given: Toward a Phenomenology of Givenness,* trans. Jeffrey L. Kosky (Stanford: Stanford University Press, 2002), 39.

31. Marion, *Being Given,* 196.

32. Jean-Luc Marion, *In Excess: Studies of Saturated Phenomena,* trans. Robyn Horner and Vincent Berraud (New York: Fordham University Press, 2002), 45. We cannot here follow the many questions that arise from Marion's account of the saturated phenomenon and how it might signify. Instead, the reader is referred to the account in Robyn Horner, "Jean-Luc Marion and the Possibility of Theology," *Culture, Theory, and Critique* 52 no. 2 (2011) 335–350. See also the characterization of *l'adonné* and *l'advenant* of Claude Romano in Shane Mackinlay, "Interpreting Excess: Jean-Luc Marion, Saturated Phenomena, and Hermeneutics," in *Perspectives in Conti-*

nental Philosophy, ed. John D. Caputo (New York: Fordham University Press, 2010), 42.

33. It is important to distinguish here between Marion's understanding of the call and that of Derrida. As indicated earlier in the text, for Derrida the call must remain "nonreappropriable, nonsubjectivable, and in a certain way nonidentifiable, a sheer supposition, so as to remain *other*." While Marion's call is similarly not *present* as such, it is given in the response of *l'adonné*, and is given a meaning in the context of that response.

34. Marion, *In Excess*, 49. This "evential" quality enables us to reconcile the alternative readings of "gift" offered by Derrida and Marion, such that the gift may be given but remains unknown as such. See Robyn Horner, *Rethinking God as Gift: Marion, Derrida, and the Limits of Phenomenology* (New York: Fordham University Press, 2001). On the meaning of "evential," see the translator's note to Claude Romano, *Event and World*, trans. Shane Mackinlay (New York: Fordham University Press, 2009), ix.

35. "*L'adonné*, in losing transcendental status and the spontaneity or the activity that this implies, does not amount, however, to passivity or to the empirical me. In fact, *l'adonné* goes beyond passivity as activity, because in being liberated from its royal transcendental status, it annuls the very distinction between the transcendental I and the empirical me." Marion, *In Excess*, 48. For critique on this point, see, for example, Mackinlay, "Interpreting Excess," 22–25; Joeri Schrijvers, *Ontotheological Turnings: The Decentering of the Modern Subject in Recent French Phenomenology* (Albany: State University of New York Press, 2011), 73.

36. See, for example, Jean-Luc Marion, "From the Other to the Individual," in *Transcendence*, trans. Robyn Horner, ed. Regina Schwartz (London: Routledge, 2002).

37. See in particular Jean-Luc Marion, *Prolegomena to Charity* (New York: Fordham University Press, 2002).

38. Jean-Luc Marion, *The Erotic Phenomenon*, trans. Stephen E. Lewis (Chicago: University of Chicago Press, 2007), 29–40.

39. Marion, *The Erotic Phenomenon*, 127.

40. See the discussion in Robyn Horner, "The Weight of Love," in *Counter-experiences: Reading Jean-Luc Marion*, ed. Kevin Hart (Notre Dame, Ind.: University of Notre Dame Press, 2007), 240.

41. With regard to the infinite hermeneutic of the face of the other, see Marion, *In Excess*, 123.

42. For a summary, the reader is referred to Horner, "Jean-Luc Marion and the Possibility of Theology."

43. Marion, *In Excess*, 29. Here we push Marion further than he is explicitly prepared to go, although we read within the spirit of his work.

44. For a fuller discussion on this point, and Marion's understanding, see Mackinlay, *Interpreting Excess*, 187. Robyn Horner, "On Faith: Relation to an Infinite Passing," *Australian E-Journal of Theology* 13 (2009), http://aejt.com .au/__data/assets/pdf_file/0005/158324/Horner_Faith.pdf.

45. Emmanuel Falque, "The Phenomenological Practice of Medieval Philosophy," in *Phenomenology and Theology in Contemporary French Thought: Lectures and Colloquium–Emmanuel Falque and Jean-Luc Marion*, vol. 13 (University of California, Santa Barbara, Department of Religious Studies, Catholic Studies: 2011).

46. The relationship of Derrida's work to theological and philosophical understandings of the fall has been explored in Kevin Hart, *The Trespass of the Sign*, 2nd ed. (New York: Fordham University Press, 2000); J. K. A. Smith, *The Fall of Interpretation: Philosophical Foundations for a Creational Hermeneutic* (Downer Grove, Ill.: Intervarsity Press, 2000).

47. See, for example, Jacques Derrida, "Circumfession" in *Jacques Derrida*, ed. Geoffrey Bennington and Jacques Derrida (Chicago: University of Chicago Press, 1993). See also John D. Caputo and Michael J. Scanlon, eds., *Augustine and Postmodernism: Confessions and Circumfession* (Bloomington: Indiana University Press, 2005). Although he refers to Augustine in a number of places, Marion has recently made Augustine a particular focus in *Au lieu de soi*.

48. Marion, *The Erotic Phenomenon*, 212.

49. "Je m'adviens comme celui qui *se reçoit* lui-même du meme coup que ce qu'il reçoit et afin justement de pouvoir le recevoir—l'adonné." Jean-Luc Marion, *Au lieu de soi: L'approche de Saint Augustin*, 2 ed. (Paris: Presses Universitaires de France, 2008), 144.

50. Ibid., 142.

51. Ibid., 144.

52. Ibid., 145.

53. Ibid., 324.

54. Marion, *Au lieu de soi*, 380, 84, 85, 418. We also recall Marion's analysis elsewhere: "Mystical theology no longer has as its goal to find a name for God but rather to make us receive our own from the unsayable Name." Marion, *In Excess*, 157.

55. Gerard Manley Hopkins, "As Kingfishers Catch Fire," in *Poems and Prose*, ed. W. H. Gardner (Harmondsworth, Middlesex: Penguin, 1963), 51.

56. Marion, *Au lieu de soi*, 420–21.

57. The reference is to Kevin Hart, *Losing the Power to Say 'I': An Essay Celebrating the Four Hundredth Anniversary of the Birth of René Descartes* (Melbourne: Art School Press, 1996).

58. On the nature of the relationship between hope and promise, see Jean-Louis Chrétien, *The Unforgettable and the Unhoped For*, trans. Jeffrey Bloechl

(New York: Fordham University Press, 2002). "Our hope could not be so sure that the gift that it hopes for exceeds us and exceeds all human hope, unless this gift has already been made to that hope, and unless the promise that we receive has already been kept" (117).

59. Robyn Horner, "Problème du mal et péché des origines," *Recherches de Science Religieuse* 90, no. 1 (2002): 63–86.

60. Boeve, *God Interrupts History*, 87.

8. DIFFERENCE, BODY, AND RACE
Michelle A. Gonzalez

1. M. Shawn Copeland et al., "Human Being," in *Constructive Theology: A Contemporary Approach to Classical Themes*, ed. Serene Jones and Paul Lakeland (Minneapolis: Fortress Press, 2005), 79.

2. Michael E. Lee, "A Way Forward for Latino/a Christology," in *In Our Own Voices: Latino/a Renditions of Theology*, ed. Benjamín Valentín (Maryknoll, N.Y.: Orbis Books, 2010), 112.

3. Orlando O. Espín and Miguel H. Díaz, introduction to *From the Heart of Our People: Latino/a Explorations in Systematic Theology*, ed. Orlando O. Espín and Miguel H. Díaz, (Maryknoll: Orbis Books, 1999), 2–3.

4. Maria Lugones, "Playfulness, 'World'—Traveling, and Loving Perception," in *Making Face, Making Soul/Haciendo Caras: Creative and Critical Perspectives by Feminists of Color*, ed. Gloria Anzaldúa (San Francisco: Aunt Lutte Books, 1990), 395.

5. Ada María Isasi-Díaz, "*Burlando al Opresor*: Mocking/Tricking the Oppressor: Hispanic/Latinas' Dreams and Hopes," in *La Lucha Continues: Mujerista Theology*, ed. Ada María Isasi-Díaz (Maryknoll, N.Y.: Orbis Books, 2004), 36.

6. Ada María Isasi-Díaz, "*Mujerista* Theology: A Challenge to Traditional Theology," in *Mujerista Theology: A Theology for the Twenty-First Century*, ed. Ada María Isasi-Díaz (Maryknoll, N.Y.: Orbis Books, 1996), 66.

7. Michelle Saracino, *Being About Borders: A Christian Anthropology of Difference* (Collegeville, Minn.: Liturgical Press, 2011).

8. Ibid., 14.

9. Cymene Howe, Susanna Zaraysky, and Lois Ann Lorentzen, "Devotional Crossings: Transgender Sex Workers, Santisima Muerte, and Spiritual Solidarity in Guadalajara and San Francisco," in *Religion at the Corner of Bliss and Nirvana*, ed. Lois Ann Lorentzen et al. (Durham, N.C.: Duke University Press, 2009), 3–38.

10. Alex Nava, "Browning of Theological Thought," in *Creating Ourselves: African Americans and Hispanic Americans on Popular Culture and Religious Expression*, ed. Anthony B. Pinn and Benjamín Valentín (Durham, N.C.: Duke University, 2009), 184.

11. Ibid.

12. M. Shawn Copeland, *Enfleshing Freedom: Body, Race, and Being* (Minneapolis: Fortress Press, 2010), 7.

13. Ibid., 67.

14. Dwight N. Hopkins, "The Construction of the Black Male Body: Eroticism and Religion," in *Loving the Body: Black Religious Studies and the Erotic*, ed. Dwight N. Hopkins and Anthony B. Pinn (Palgrave Macmillan, 2004), 182.

15. Linda M. Scott, *Fresh Lipstick: Redressing Fashion and Feminism* (New York: Palgrave, 2005).

16. Eleazer S. Fernandez, *Reimagining the Human: Theological Anthropology in Response to Systemic Evil* (St Louis: Chalice Press, 2004), 141.

17. J. Kameron Carter, *Race: A Theological Account* (New York: Oxford University Press, 2008).

18. Manuel A. Vazquéz, "Rethinkng *Mestizaje*," in *Rethinking Latino(a) Religion and Identity*, ed. Miguel A. De La Torre and Gastón Espinosa (Cleveland: Pilgrim Press, 2006), 145.

19. Miguel de la Torre, "Rethinking *Mulatez*," in *Rethinking Latino(a) Religion and Identity*, eds. Miguel A. De La Torre and Gastón Espinosa (Cleveland: Pilgrim Press, 2006), 167.

20. Vazquéz, "Rethinking *Mestizaje*," 150.

21. Ibid., 155.

22. Brian Bantum, *Redeeming Mulatto: A Theology of Race and Christian Hybridity* (Waco, Texas: Baylor University Press, 2010), 7.

23. Ibid., 99.

24. Ibid., 108.

25. Elisabeth A. Johnson, *The Quest for the Living God: Mapping Frontiers in the Theology of God* (New York: Continuum, 2007), 73–74.

26. Alejandro García-Rivera, *St. Martín de Porres: The "Little Stories" and the Semiotics of Culture* (Maryknoll, N.Y.: Orbis Books, 1995), 94.

9. PUBLIC THEOLOGY: A FEMINIST VIEW
OF POLITICAL SUBJECTIVITY AND PRAXIS
Rosemary P. Carbine

1. David Tracy, *The Analogical Imagination: Christian Theology and the Culture of Pluralism* (New York: Crossroad, 1981), 3–46.

2. Ethicist Jeffrey Stout points out that democratic conversation creates the common good via discursive responsibility, or the giving and exchanging of publicly accessible reasons for our views in public discourse. Engaging in dialogical procedures for rational argument, persons participate in a political tradition of practical wisdom that shapes them with democratic virtues. Some of these virtues include charity, justice, temperance, civility, listening

carefully and speaking candidly (sometimes with ad hoc responses), humility, hope, courage, imagination, and luck. Jeffrey L. Stout, *Democracy and Tradition: Religion, Ethics, And Public Philosophy* (Princeton: Princeton University Press, 2004). Religious institutions socialize persons with similar virtues, including freedom, equality, mutual respect, risk, and vulnerability, which in turn form them as responsible citizens for public life. See Ronald Thiemann, *Constructing a Public Theology: The Church in a Pluralistic Culture* (Louisville, Ky.: Westminster John Knox Press, 1991), 29–43; Ronald Thiemann, *Religion in Public Life: A Dilemma for Democracy* (Washington, D.C.: Georgetown University Press, 1996), 85–90, 113–14, 135–41; Ronald Thiemann, "Public Theology: The Moral Dimension of Religion in a Pluralistic Society," *Zeitschrift für Evagelische Ethik* 42 (1998): 176–90; and Ronald Thiemann, "Public Religion: Bane or Blessing for Democracy?" in *Obligations of Citizenship and Demands of Faith: Religious Accommodation in Pluralist Democracies*, ed. Nancy L. Rosenblum (Princeton: Princeton University Press, 2000), 73–89.

3. See J. Bryan Hehir, "Forum: Public Theology in Contemporary America," *Religion and American Culture* 10, 1 (2000): 20–27; Margaret Farley, "The Church in the Public Forum: Scandal or Prophetic Witness?" *CTSA Proceedings of the Fifty-fifth Annual Convention* 55 (2000): 87–101; and R. Bruce Douglass and David Hollenbach, eds., *Catholicism and Liberalism: Contributions to American Public Philosophy* (Cambridge: Cambridge University Press, 1994).

4. Martin E. Marty, *The Public Church: Mainline-Evangelical-Catholic* (New York: Crossroad, 1981), 3.

5. On civil society as a shared space of public debate in democratic societies, see Hannah Arendt, *The Human Condition*, 2nd ed. (Chicago: University of Chicago Press, 1998); Richard J. Bernstein, "The Meaning of Public Life," in *Religion and American Public Life: Interpretations and Explorations*, ed. Robin Lovin (New York: Paulist Press, 1986), 29–52, especially 36–40; and Gary Simpson, *Critical Social Theory: Prophetic Reason, Civil Society, and Christian Imagination* (Minneapolis: Fortress Press, 2002), 131–34. William Dean lays out the "republican" character of public theology in "Forum: Public Theology in Contemporary America," *Religion and American Culture* 10, 1 (2000): 1–8, and David O'Brien associates this kind of civic debate with what he calls "republican Catholicism" in *Public Catholicism* (Maryknoll, N.Y: Orbis, 1996), 33.

6. Rebecca S. Chopp, "Reimagining Public Discourse," in *Black Faith and Public Talk: Critical Essays on James H. Cone's Black Theology and Black Power*, ed. Dwight N. Hopkins (Maryknoll, N.Y: Orbis, 1999), 150–64, and "A Feminist Perspective: Christianity, Democracy, and Feminist Theology,"

in *Christianity and Democracy in a Global Context*, ed. John Witte, Jr. (Boulder: Westview Press, 1993), 111–29.

7. See M. Shawn Copeland, "Reconsidering the Idea of the Common Good," in *Catholic Social Thought and the New World Order*, ed. Williams and Houck, 309–23, esp. 309–16, 322–23. Rather than simply situate a person within multiple communities, including political communities, that shape human identity, *Gaudium et Spes* offers a theological anthropology in which becoming fully human entails political agency and public engagement. "Pastoral Constitution on the Church in the Modern World: *Gaudium et Spes*, 7 December 1965," in *Vatican Council II: The Basic Sixteen Documents: Constitutions, Decrees, Declarations*, ed. Austin Flannery, O.P. (Northport, N.Y.: Costello, 1996), §§24–25, 46, 73–75. All citations of *Gaudium et Spes* in this chapter refer to this version.

8. Linell E. Cady, *Religion, Theology, and American Public Life* (Albany: State University of New York Press, 1993), 67, 68.

9 This phrase is used by W. Clark Gilpin, *A Preface to Theology* (Chicago: University of Chicago Press, 1996), 167–68.

10. Roger S. Gottlieb, *Joining Hands: Politics and Religion Together for Social Change* (Boulder: Westview Press, 2002), 3–23.

11. Edward Farley, "Toward a Contemporary Theology of Human Being," in *Images of Man: Studies in Religion and Anthropology*, ed. J. William Angell and E. Pendleton Banks (Macon, Ga.: Mercer Univ. Press, 1984), 55–78; and David H. Kelsey, "Human Being," in *Christian Theology: An Introduction to Its Tradition and Tasks*, ed. Peter C. Hodgson and Robert H. King, newly rev. ed. (Minneapolis: Augsburg Fortress, 1994), 167–93. For the distinctive contribution of theological anthropology to religious reflection, see Kathryn Tanner, "The Difference Theological Anthropology Makes," *Theology Today* 50, no. 4 (1994): 567–79.

12. Kristen E. Kvam, "Anthropology, Theological," in *Dictionary of Feminist Theologies*, ed. Letty M. Russell and Shannon Clarkson (Louisville, Ky.: Westminster John Knox, 1996), 10–12.

13. The imago Dei should support and protect the full dignity, equality, and rights of all persons, but instead it has functioned to justify and reinforce ideological discourses of domination of women, of all so-called "others" that deviate from an elite white Western norm of humanity, and of the earth. As Mary Catherine Hilkert has argued, the symbol of the imago Dei can be critically retrieved to contest rather than support patriarchal, racist, anthropocentric, and other ideological theologies. Mary Catherine Hilkert, "Cry Beloved Image: Rethinking the Image of God," in *In the Embrace of God: Feminist Approaches to Theological Anthropology*, ed. Ann O'Hara Graff (Maryknoll, N.Y.: Orbis, 1995), 190–205.

14. From the rhetorical analysis of Genesis 2–3 by feminist biblical scholar Phyllis Trible, feminist theologians have well documented a similar connection between sin and the disruption of all relations, in order to demonstrate that patriarchy, or the privileging of certain elite men and women above all "others," is not divinely designed in creation. For a summative account of feminist and womanist approaches to sin, see Sally Ann McReynolds and Ann O'Hara Graff, "Sin: When Women Are the Context," in *In the Embrace of God*, ed. Ann O'Hara Graff (Maryknoll, N.Y: Orbis, 1995), 161–72.

15. Rosemary P. Carbine, "'Artisans of a New Humanity': Revisioning the Public Church in a Feminist Perspective," in *Frontiers in Catholic Feminist Theology: Shoulder to Shoulder*, ed. Susan Abraham and Elena Procario-Foley (Minneapolis: Fortress Press, 2009), 173–92, 241–45, esp. 178–83.

16. Mary Ann Hinsdale, "Heeding the Voices: An Historical Overview," in *In the Embrace of God*, ed. Ann O'Hara Graff (Maryknoll, N.Y.: Orbis, 1995), 22–48; and Donna Teevan, "Challenge to the Role of Theological Anthropology in Feminist Theologies," *Theological Studies* 64 (2003): 582–97.

17. Diana Tietjens Meyers, "Intersectional Identity and the Authentic Self: Opposites Attract!" in *Relational Autonomy: Feminist Perspectives on Autonomy, Agency, and the Social Self*, ed. Catriona Mackenzie and Natalie Stoljar (New York; Oxford: Oxford University Press, 2000), 151–80.

18. Judith Butler, *Gender Trouble: Feminism and the Subversion of Identity* (New York: Routledge, 1989), and *Giving An Account of Oneself* (New York: Fordham University Press, 2005), interpreted by Laura Taylor, "Redeeming Christ: Imitation or (Re)citation?" in *Frontiers in Catholic Feminist Theology*, ed. Susan Abraham and Elena Procario-Foley (Minneapolis: Fortress Press, 2009) 119–40.

19. From within process philosophy, feminist theologians offer a "relational ontology" in which women are not altogether "soluble" but rather are thickly "in-formed" and "in-fluenced" by relationships. See Catherine Keller, *From a Broken Web, Separation, Sexism, and Self* (Boston: Beacon, 1986), and "Seeking and Sucking: On Relation and Essence in Feminist Theology," in *Horizons in Feminist Theology: Identity, Tradition, Norms*, ed. Rebecca S. Chopp and Sheila Greeve Davaney (Minneapolis: Fortress Press, 1997), 54–78.

20. Serene Jones, *Feminist Theory and Christian Theology: Cartographies of Grace* (Minneapolis: Fortress Press, 2000), 22–48. Other examples of feminist anthropologies that offer a constructivist subjectivity include Tiina Allik, "Human Finitude and the Concept of Women's Experience," *Modern Theology* 9, no. 1 (1993): 67–85; Mary Ann Zimmer, "Stepping Stones in Feminist Theory," in *In the Embrace of God*, ed. Ann O'Hara Graff (Maryknoll, N.Y.: Orbis, 1995), 7–21; Mary McClintock Fulkerson, *Changing the Subject: Women's Discourses and Feminist Theology* (Minneapolis: Fortress Press,

1994); Anne-Louise Eriksson, *The Meaning of Gender in Theology: Problems and Possibilities* (Minneapolis: Augsburg Fortress, 1995); and, Elaine L. Graham, *Making the Difference: Gender, Personhood, and Theology* (London: Mowbray, 1995).

21. Linell E. Cady, "Identity, Feminist Theory, and Theology," in *Horizons in Feminist Theology*, ed. Rebecca S. Chopp and Sheila Greeve Davaney (Minneapolis: Fortress Press, 1997), 17–32, at 24.

22. Ibid., 24, 25.

23. In her recent work, Michele Saracino blends postcolonial theories of hybridity, or the plural stories that configure and constitute our personal identities, with postmodern ethical and feminist theories of coming undone, or the ability of another to uncreate and redefine us, in order to elaborate an affective anthropology founded on alterity and relationality. See Michele Saracino, *Being about Borders: A Christian Anthropology of Difference* (Collegeville, Minn.: Liturgical Press, 2011).

24. Elizabeth Johnson, *She Who Is: The Mystery of God in Feminist Theological Discourse* (New York: Crossroad, 1992), 154–56, and Elizabeth A. Johnson, "The Maleness of Christ," in *The Power of Naming: A Concilium Reader in Feminist Liberation Theology*, ed. Elisabeth Schüssler Fiorenza (Maryknoll, N.Y.: Orbis, 1996), 307–15.

25. M. Shawn Copeland, *Enfleshing Freedom: Body, Race, and Being* (Minneapolis: Fortress Press, 2009), 92.

26. Ada María Isasi-Díaz, *Mujerista Theology: A Theology for the Twenty-First Century* (Maryknoll, N.Y.: Orbis, 1996), 64; Ada María Isasi-Díaz, *En La Lucha / In the Struggle: Elaborating a Mujerista Theology* (Minneapolis: Fortress Press, 2004), 2–3, 33; and Ada María Isasi-Díaz, *La Lucha Continues: Mujerista Theology* (Maryknoll, N.Y: Orbis, 2004), 61, 69–91. For a critical commentary on the history and utility of this term in Latino/a theology, see Néstor Medina, *Mestizaje: (Re)Mapping Race, Culture, and Faith in Latina/o Catholicism* (Maryknoll,N.Y : Orbis, 2009).

27. Rita Nakashima Brock, "Interstitial Integrity: Reflections toward an Asian American Woman's Theology," in *Introduction to Christian Theology: Contemporary North American Perspectives*, ed. Rodger A. Badham (Louisville, Ky.: Westminster John Knox, 1998), 183–96; and Rita Nakashima Brock, "Cooking without Recipes: Interstitial Integrity," in *Off the Menu: Asian and Asian North American Women's Religion and Theology*, ed. Rita Nakashima Brock et al. (Louisville, Ky.: Westminster John Knox, 2007), 125–44. Living in and cultivating the interstices of our identities does not separate us from our relations with or our responsibilities to multiple groups. The quest for interstitial integrity—for a meaningful self-identity amid multiple group identities—is not romanticized, isolationist, or individually therapeutic but

takes place against the theological horizons of solidarity and social justice. Brock, "Interstitial Integrity," 191–92.

28. Arendt, *The Human Condition*, 175–81, 183–84.

29. Paul Ricoeur, *Oneself as Another*, trans. Kathleen Blamey (Chicago: University of Chicago Press, 1995), 107, 161.

30. Ibid., 54, 22; also 111–12, 143–48.

31. Karen Baker-Fletcher, *A Singing Something: Womanist Reflections on Anna Julia Cooper* (New York: Crossroad, 1994), 188–206. As quoted by Stephanie Mitchem, *Introducing Womanist Theology* (Maryknoll, N.Y.: Orbis, 2002), 122.

32. Cady, *Religion, Theology, and American Public Life*, 162.

33. Ibid., 66–68, 85.

34. Jane Kopas, "Something Particular: Women's Self-Narratives as a Resource for Theology," in *Themes in Feminist Theology for the New Millennium (I)*, ed. Francis A. Eigo (Villanova, Pa.: Villanova University Press, 2002), 1–34, especially 8, 13.

35. M. Shawn Copeland, *Enfleshing Freedom: Body, Race, and Being* (Minneapolis: Fortress Press, 2010), 29–38, 56–57, 65–66.

36. Ibid., 81–83. For a ritual re/membering of the body of Christ with personal and political implications, see 51–53.

37. J. Bryan Hehir emphasizes these paragraphs as hermeneutical keys to understanding Vatican II's view on the Church's role in public life; J. Bryan Hehir, "The Social Role of the Church: Leo XIII, Vatican II, and John Paul II," in *Catholic Social Thought and the New World Order*, ed. Oliver F. Williams and John W. Houck (Notre Dame, Ind.: University of Notre Dame Press, 1993), 29–50, at 36–38. While beyond the scope of this chapter, Mary Hines has examined the (dis)connects between the Church's public discourse about the right to political participation and its inner institutional structures that lead to a less than fully participatory Church for women and that more recently failed to protect men and women affected by clergy sex-abuse scandals. Mary E. Hines, "Ecclesiology for a Public Church," *CTSA Proceedings of the Fifty-fifth Annual Convention* 55 (2000): 23–46, esp. 25–26, 40.

38. Feminist theologians cannot easily follow the "anthropological turn" in *GS*, to Christology, in which Jesus embodies the image of God, the primary model of discipleship, and the paradigm of redeemed humanity. As Elizabeth Johnson has argued, the myopic focus on the maleness of Jesus in Christology carries an "effective history" that raises questions about women's ability to image the divine, to imitate Christ, and to be saved, which ultimately relegate women to the status of second-class citizens in the body of Christ and in the body politic. Johnson, "The Maleness of Christ."

39. See Michael Stogre, "Commentary on the Pastoral Constitution on the Church in the Modern World," in *The Church Renewed: The Documents of Vatican II Reconsidered*, ed. George Schner (Lanham, Md.: University Press of America, 1986), 19–36, esp. 25–27; Walter Kasper, "The Theological Anthropology of *Gaudium et Spes*," Communio 23 (1996): 129–40, at 129; William C. McDonough, "The Church in the Modern World: Rereading *Gaudium et Spes* after Thirty Years," in *Vatican II: The Continuing Agenda*, ed. Anthony J. Cernera (Fairfield, Conn.: Sacred Heart University Press, 1997), 113–33, esp. 122, 125–26; and, John J. Markey, *Creating Communion: The Theology of the Constitutions of the Church* (Hyde Park, N.Y.: New City, 2003), 84–99.

40. The council fathers failed to attend to or to contest the anthropocentric mastery and domination of nature but rather took it as basic to theological anthropology, assuming the creation of only humanity in the image and likeness of God (*GS*, no. 9, 12, 15, 33, 34, 57). Mary Catherine Hilkert, "*Imago Dei*: Does the Symbol Have a Future?" *Santa Clara Lectures* 8, no. 3 (2002).

41. My reading of *GS* in this essay centers especially but not exclusively on community as a major interpretive concept. John Markey argues that community is one of "three heuristic keys" to interpreting this conciliar document, alongside pneumatology and sacramentality; see Markey, *Creating Communion*, 94–8.

42. Christine Firer Hinze, "Straining Toward Solidarity in a Suffering World: *Gaudium et Spes* After Forty Years," in *Vatican II: Forty Years Later*, ed. William Madges (Maryknoll, N.Y.: Orbis, 2006), 165–95, esp. 170–75.

43. As Peter Phan states, "Eschatology is anthropology conjugated in the future tense on the basis of Christology." Peter Phan, "Contemporary Context and Issues in Eschatology," *Theological Studies* 55, no. 3 (1994): 507–36, at 516.

44. Hilkert, "Cry Beloved Image," 195–96.

45. Hilkert, "*Imago Dei*: Does the Symbol Have a Future?" 15, 18 (my italics).

46. Iris Marion Young, *Inclusion and Democracy* (Oxford: Oxford University Press, 2000), 65, 70–77.

47. The following paragraphs expand on the definitions of these types of praxis outlined in Rosemary P. Carbine, "Claiming and Imagining: Practices of Public Engagement," in *Prophetic Witness: Catholic Women's Strategies for Reform*, ed. Colleen M. Griffith (New York: Crossroad, 2009), 176–85, 259–62.

48. Chopp, "Reimagining Public Discourse," 152.

49. Testimonies "have criticized and reshaped who 'we' are, as a social public and as Christianity, by making public the memories of suffering and giving public hearing to new voices, experiences, and expressions of life, while calling into question essentialist and hegemonic definitions of these publics." Chopp, "Reimagining Public Discourse," 154, cf. 160–63.

50. Ibid., 157.

51. See Arendt, *The Human Condition*, 50–51, 57–58; María Pía Lara, *Moral Textures: Feminist Narratives in the Public Sphere* (Berkeley and Los Angeles: University of California Press, 1998), 5–6, 14–17, 35–44, 59, 70; Marshall Louis Ganz, "The Power of Story in Social Movements," August 2001, http://www.ksg.harvard.edu/organizing/tools/toolshome.shtml; and Mary Doak, *Reclaiming Narrative for Public Theology* (Albany: State University of New York Press, 2004), 19–23, 159–71.

52. Rosemary P. Carbine, "Turning to Narrative: Toward a Feminist Theological Understanding of Political Participation and Personhood," *Journal of the American Academy of Religion* 78, no. 2 (2010): 375–412, esp. 386–96, on the contributions of women's-liberation theologies to the theo-political importance of narrative for political subjectivity.

53. Michael J. Himes and Kenneth R. Himes, *Fullness of Faith: The Public Significance of Theology* (New York: Paulist, 1993), 4. The Himeses derive their take on public theology from David Hollenbach, "Editor's Conclusion," in "Theology and Philosophy in Public: A Symposium on John Courtney Murray's Unfinished Agenda," *Theological Studies* 40 (1979): 700–15, at 714.

54. Moral cohesion is one of the primary goals of this praxis of public theology. Robin Lovin, "Religion and American Public Life: Three Relationships," in *Religion and American Public Life*, 7–28.

55. Himes and Himes, *Fullness of Faith*, 61–62. See also J. Milburn Thompson, *Justice and Peace: A Christian Primer*, 2nd ed. (Maryknoll, N.Y.: Orbis, 2003), 92–102.

56. Cady, *Religion, Theology, and American Public Life*, 51–56, 62–64; and Linell E. Cady, "H. Richard Niebuhr and the Task of Public Theology," in *The Legacy of H. Richard Niebuhr*, ed. Ronald Thiemann (Minneapolis: Fortress Press, 1991), 107–29.

57. Gilpin, *A Preface to Theology*, 173–83, especially 182; cf. 129–31, 147. Religious symbols communicate "who a human being is, what the good life for a human being ought to be, and what kinds of relationships among human beings promote the good life." Michael Himes, "Public Theology in Service to a National Conversation," in *Religion, Politics, and the American Experience: Reflections on Religion and American Public Life*, ed. Edith L. Blumhofer (Tuscaloosa: University of Alabama Press, 2002), 138.

58. Cady, *Religion, Theology, and American Public Life*, 99–109; Himes and Himes, *Fullness of Faith*, 55–61.

59. *Economic Justice for All: Pastoral Letter on Catholic Social Teaching and the U.S. Economy: A Catholic Framework for Economic Life* (1986; Washington, D.C.: U.S. Catholic Conference, 1997), §§15–19.

60. *Economic Justice for All*, §§13–15; cf. chap. 2, §§28, 31–34.

61. Pontifical Council for Justice and Peace, *Towards Reforming the International Financial and Monetary Systems in the Context of Global Public Authority*, October 24, 2011, http://www.news.va/en/news/full-text-note-on-financial -reform-from-the-pontif. See also Mark J. Allman, ed., *The Almighty and the Dollar: Reflections on Economic Justice for All* (Winona, Minn.: Anselm Academic, 2012).

62. Walter Brueggemann, *The Prophetic Imagination*, 2nd ed. (Minneapolis: Fortress Press, 2001), 1–19.

63. Mark Lewis Taylor, *The Executed God: The Way of the Cross in Lockdown America* (Minneapolis: Fortress Press, 2001), 117. Going beyond the performing arts, Taylor's more recent work probes the political significance of other creative arts—e.g., painting, literature, music/song, poetry, sculpture, and textiles. See Taylor, *The Theological and the Political: On the Weight of the World* (Minneapolis: Fortress Press, 2011), 114, 136. Taylor explores the ways in which the artful practices of dominated and marginalized peoples carry a "symbolic force" that gives voice to oppressed peoples, who resist and flourish via that art and who "are enabled [by that art] to weigh in to create the world anew." Taylor, *The Theological and the Political*, 12–4, 114; cf. chap. 3.

64. Maria Cristina Garcia, "'Dangerous Times Call for Risky Responses': Latino Immigration and Sanctuary, 1981–2001," in *Latino Religions and Civic Activism in the United States*, ed. Gaston Espinosa, Virgilio Elizondo, and Jesse Miranda (New York: Oxford University Press, 2005), 159–73.

65. Yvonne Abraham and Brian R. Ballou, "350 Are Held in Immigration Raid," *Boston Globe*, March 7, 2007, http://www.boston.com/news/ local/articles/2007/03/07/350_are_held_in_immigration_raid/; and Louis Sahagun, "*L.A. Church in Forefront of Sanctuary Movement*," *Los Angeles Times*, March 23, 2007. For more about the impact of U.S. policy and practices on immigrant families, see Kristin Heyer, *Kinship Across Borders: A Christian Ethic of Immigration* (Washington, D.C.: Georgetown University Press, 2012), esp. chap.3.

66. For profiles of undocumented mothers and children in sanctuary, see Sasha Abramsky, "Gimme Shelter," *Nation* 286, no. 7 (February 25, 2008): 24–25.

67. Alexia Salvatierra, "Sacred Refuge," *Sojourners* 36, no. 9 (2007): 12–20. See also James Barron, "Churches to Offer Sanctuary," *New York*

Times, May 9, 2007; and Saul Gonzalez, "Immigrant Sanctuary Movement," *Religion and Ethics Newsweekly,* June 15, 2007, http://www.pbs.org/wnet/religionandethics/week1042/feature.html.

68. For more on the emergent notion of citizenship in this movement that is theologically rooted in the imago Dei, see Rosemary P. Carbine, "The Beloved Community: Transforming Spaces for Social Change and for Cosmopolitan Citizenship," in *Women, Wisdom, and Witness: Engaging Contexts in Conversation,* ed. Rosemary P. Carbine and Kathleen J. Dolphin (Collegeville, Minn.: Liturgical Press, 2012), 237–58.

69. Cady, *Religion, Theology, and American Public Life,* 111.

10. DESIRE, MIMETIC THEORY, AND ORIGINAL SIN
Wilhelm Guggenberger

1. James Alison, *The Joy of Being Wrong: Original Sin through Easter Eyes* (New York: Crossroad, 1998), 25.

2. An example for that is the modification of Girard's understanding of the use of the term "sacrifice" in a Christian context. See René Girard, "Mimetische Theorie und Theologie," in *Vom Fluch und Segen der Sündenböcke,* ed. Jozef Niewiadomski and Wolfgang Palaver (Thaur: Kulturverlag, 1995), 15–29.

4. The actual mythological text may for the most part hide the reality of what was happening at the beginning of a culture. That is why we have to read these texts in a proper way and analyze the structure of the text or narration very attentively. See René Girard, *The Scapegoat* (London: Athlone Press, 1986), 117–24.

5. See René Girard, *The Girard Reader,* ed. Games G. Williams (New York: Crossroad, 1996), 268.

6. Jonah Wharff, "Bernard of Clairvaux and René Girard on Desire and Envy," *Cistercian Studies Quarterly* 42, no. 2 (2007): 1.

7. The question of humanization in an evolutionary sense is discussed in René Girard, *Things Hidden Since the Foundation of the World: Research Undertaken in Collaboration with Jean-Michel Oughourlian and Guy Lefort* (London: Athleon Press, 1987), 84–104; and Raymund Schwager, *Erbsünde und Heilsdrama: Im Kontext von Evolution, Gentechnologie und Apoklyptik* (Münster: LIT Verlag, 1997), 62–73.

8. See René Girard, *Celui par qui le scandal arrive* (Paris: Desclée de Brouwer, 2001), 17.

9. Michael Kirwan, *Discovering Girard* (London: Darton, Longman and Todd, 2005), 14.

10. See René Girard, *Deceit, Desire, and the Novel: Self and Other in Literary Structure* (Baltimore: John Hopkins University Press, 1976), 15–17.

11. Jean-Michel Oughourlian, *The Genesis of Desire* (East Lansing: Michigan State University Press, 2010), 31.

12. Oughourlian, *Genesis of Desire*, 34.

13. Scott R. Garrels, "Imitation, Mirror Neurons, and Mimetic Desire: Convergence between the Mimetic Theory of René Girard and Empirical Research on Imitation," *Contagion* 12–13 (2006): 47–86. See Oughourlian, *Genesis of Desire*, 88–95.

14. The German biologist and psychiatrist Joachim Bauer argues along these lines, criticizing particularly Richard Dawkins theory of "the selfish gene." Joachim Bauer, *Das kooperative Gen: Abschied vom Darwinismus* (Hamburg: Hoffmann und Kampe, 2008).

15. I think that even Adam Smith recognized this problem. But after having eliminated every possibility of basing moral norms on something transcendent to human interaction, he could not find a satisfactory solution to the problem. It was for that reason, I think, that he moved to the concept of the invisible hand of Providence. See Wilhelm Guggenberger, *Die List der Dinge: Sackgassen der Wirtschaftsethik in einer funktional differenzierten Gesellschaft* (Wien: LIT Verlag, 2007), 261–73.

16. Thomas Hobbes, *Leviathan: Revised Student Edition*, ed. Richard Tuck (Cambridge: Cambridge University Press, 1991), 97.

17. See Peter Sloterdijk, "Erwachen im Reich der Eifersucht: Notiz zu René Girards anthropologischer Sendung," in *Ich sah den Satan vom Himmel fallen wie einen Blitz: Eine kritische Apologie des Christentums*, ed. René Girard (München: Hanser, 2002), 250.

18. Michael Kirwan, *Girard and Theology* (London: T & T Clark, 2009), 24.

19. See René Girard, *Battling to the End: Conversations with Benôit Chantre* (East Lansing: Michigan State University Press, 2010), 198.

20. Kirwan, *Discovering*, 49.

21. In the scapegoat mechanism, the aspect of it that most has to be concealed is "the arbitrary selection of the victim, its essential insignificance, which contradicts the meaning accumulated upon its head by the scapegoat projections." Girard, *Reader*, 22.

22. This is shown by the example of Oedipus in René Girard, *Violence and the Sacred* (Baltimore: John Hopkins University Press, 1977), 85–88; cf. Wolfgang Palaver, *René Girard's Mimetic Theory* (East Lansing: Michigan State University Press, 2013), 155–57.

23. Raymund Schwager, *Must There be Scapegoats? Violence and Redemption in the Bible* (San Francisco: Harper and Row, 1987), 26.

24. Girard, *Reader*, 21.

25. In *Mimetische Theorie und Theologie*, Girard uses the phrase "paradoxical unity of all religious," which means that the difference between biblical or Abrahamic revelation and other religious traditions is huge and important but not a complete break (27).

26. Raymund Schwager, *Jesus in the Drama of Salvation: Toward a Biblical Doctrine of Redemption* (New York: The Crossroad Publishing Company, 1999), 135.

27. Alison, *Joy*, 29.

28. Willibald Sandler, *Der verbotene Baum im Paradies. Was es mit dem Sündenfall auf sich hat* (Kevelaer: Topos, 2009), 79: "Gott *kann* dem Menschen nicht schenken, dass der Mensch das, was er von Gott hat, nicht von Gott, sondern *ausschließlich* aus sich selbst heraus hat."

29. Søren Kierkegaard, *Sickness unto Death* (Redford: A & D Publishing, 2008), 15: "That self which he despairingly wills to be is a self which he is not (for the will to be that self which one truly is, is indeed the opposite of despair); what he really wills is to tear his self away from the Power which constituted it."

30. See Girard, *Deceit*, 53–55.

31. Schwager reflecting on the subject of the mystery of iniquity thinks that it is not to us to decide finally the question of whether there are angels, fallen angels, and like spiritual beings. Theology must address such topics seriously even if answers are not likely to be forthcoming. But to explain what is going on within human societies and to understand the dynamism of rivalry and violence, we do not need to revert to supernatural demonic beings. See Schwager, *Erbsünde und Heilsdrama*, 176–82.

32. Alison, *Joy*, 208.

33. "Katechon" means the restraining power referred to in 2 Thessalonians 2:6–7. This power, which is not divine, restrains lawlessness, the man of sin, and the satanic chaos itself but also the final coming of Christ. See Palaver, *Girard's Mimetic Theory*, 252; Kirwan, *Theology*, 96–99.

34. René Girard, *I See Satan Fall Like Lightning* (New York, Orbis, 2001), 84.

35. Girard, *Violence and the Sacred*, 72.

36. See Lieven Boeve, *Interrupting Tradition. An Essay on Christian Faith in a Postmodern Context* (Louvain: Peeters Press, 2003), 120–34.

37. Robert J. Daly, "A Phenomenology of Redemption?" in *For René Girard: Essays in Friendship and Truth*, ed. Sandor Goodhard et al. (East Lansing: Michigan State University, 2009), 106.

38. Nikolaus Wandinger, "Impulses for a Systematic Concept of Sin," *Milltown Studies* 47 (2001): 9.

39. Girard, *Satan*, 147.

40. Girard, *Reader*, 284.
41. Kirwan, *Girard and Theology*, 84.
42. Alison, *Joy*, 117.
43. Girard, *Things Hidden*, 225.
44. Girard, *Battling*, x.
45. Schwager, *Drama of Salvation*, 142–143. The importance of the Spirit is highlighted by Girard as well. See Girard, *Satan*, 189–90.
46. Schwager, *Drama of Salvation*, 144.
47. Alison, *Joy*, 45.

TURTLES ALL THE WAY DOWN? PRESSING QUESTIONS FOR THEOLOGICAL
ANTHROPOLOGY IN THE TWENTY-FIRST CENTURY
David G. Kirchhoffer

1. This contribution originated as an attempt to capture the most pressing issues identified at the Anthropos seminar—Exploring Anthropos: Theological Anthropology for the 21st Century—held in Leuven in April 2011. In addition to the presentation of versions of the chapters of this book, a final plenary discussion took place there. This chapter makes reference to oral communications in the context of that final discussion by naming the participants who during the discussion contributed the ideas discussed here.

2. The story is recounted in various versions in recent literature. See, among others, Kevin Hart, *Postmodernism: A Beginner's Guide* (London: Oneworld, 2004), 29; Cheryl Hunt, "Travels with a Turtle: Metaphors and the Making of a Professional Identity," *Reflective Practice* 7, no. 3 (2006): 315–32.

3. Henri Bergson, *Creative Evolution*, trans. Arthur Mitchell (New York: Holt, 1911).

4. Peter Singer, "Speciesism and Moral Status," *Metaphilosophy* 40, nos. 3–4 (2009): 567–81.

5. See Niklas Luhmann, *Soziale Systeme: Grundriß einer allgemeinen Theorie* (Frankfurt am Main: Suhrkamp, 1984).

6. See, for example, Charlene L. Muehlenhard and Leigh Ann Kimes, "The Social Construction of Violence: The Case of Sexual and Domestic Violence," *Personality and Social Psychology Review* 3, no. 3 (1999): 234–45.

7. See, for example, Simone de Beauvoir, *Le deuxième Sexe*, 2 vols. (Paris: Librairie Gallimard, 1949).

8. See, for example, K. Anthony Appiah and Amy Gutmann, *Color Conscious: The Political Morality of Race* (Princeton: Princeton University, 1996).

9. See, for example, Gary Francione, *Animals as Persons: Essays on the Abolition of Animal Exploitation* (New York: Columbia University Press, 2008).

10. See Julie Clague, "The Historicity and Progress of Morality. Some Catholic Contributions," *Louvain Studies* 35, nos. 1–2 (2011): 200–15.

11. We owe this idea to the Leuven liberation theologian Jacques Haers.

12. See, for example, James Gilligan, *Violence: Reflections on a National Epidemic* (New York: Vintage, 1997).

13. See, for example, Sandra Waddock, "Mindfulness and Integrity: The Ongoing Challenge of Leadership Development," in *Business Ethics: New Challenges for Business Schools and Corporate Leaders*, ed. Robert A. Peterson and O. C. Ferrell (Armonk, N.Y.: M. E. Sharpe, 2005), 98–114.

14. Systematic theologian Erik Borgman emphasized this point during the final discussion of the seminar.

LIEVEN BOEVE teaches fundamental theology and serves as dean of the Faculty of Theology and Religious Studies, KU Leuven, Belgium. He is the coordinator of the research group Theology in a Postmodern Context and cofounder of the interdisciplinary research group Anthropos. His focus is on theological epistemology, the relation between theology and continental philosophy, and theological anthropology. His publications include *Interrupting Tradition: An Essay on Christian Faith in a Postmodern Context* (Peeters/Eerdmans, 2003), *God Interrupts History: Theology in a Time of Upheaval* (Continuum, 2007), and the coauthored volume *The Ratzinger Reader* (Continuum, 2010).

ROSEMARY P. CARBINE teaches at Whittier College and specializes in historical and constructive Christian theologies, with a focus on comparative feminist, womanist, and Latina/*mujerista* theologies, theological anthropology, public/political theology, and teaching and learning in theology and religion. She has coedited *Women, Wisdom, and Witness: Engaging Contexts in Conversation* (Liturgical Press, 2012) and *Theological Perspectives for Life, Liberty, and the Pursuit of Happiness: Public Intellectuals for the Twenty-First Century* (Palgrave Macmillan, 2013). She has served as convener of the Theological Anthropology panel within the Catholic Theological Society of America.

OLIVER DAVIES teaches Christian Doctrine in King's College London. His publications include *A Theology of Compassion: Metaphysics of Difference and the Renewal of Tradition* (SCM Press, 2001), *The Creativity of God: World, Eucharist, Reason* (Cambridge University Press, 2004), and *Theology of Transformation: Faith, Freedom, and the Christian Act* (Oxford University Press, 2013).

CELIA DEANE-DRUMMOND teaches at the University of Notre Dame. Her focus is on theology and ethics and their intersection with the biological sciences. She has been director of the Centre for Religion and the Biosciences (Chester University, UK). Her publications include *The Ethics of Nature* (Blackwell, 2004), *Ecotheology* (DLT, 2008), *Christ and Evolution* (Fortress, 2009), and *Human Nature, Evolution, and Other Animals* (Eerdmans, 2014).

YVES DE MAESENEER teaches fundamental theological ethics at the Faculty of Theology and Religious Studies, KU Leuven, Belgium. He is the coordinator of Anthropos, an interdisciplinary research group of theological ethicists and fundamental theologians developing a renewed theological anthropology. He is coeditor of *Religious Experience and Contemporary Theological Epistemology* (Peeters, 2005).

JOHAN DE TAVERNIER teaches theological ethics at the Faculty of Theology and Religious Studies, KU Leuven, Belgium. He is director of the Centre for Science, Technology, and Ethics (Science, Engineering, and Technology Group, KU Leuven). His research interests include the personalist tradition, food ethics, engineering ethics, and animal ethics. He is the editor of *Responsibility, God, and Society: Theological Ethics in Dialogue* (Peeters, 2008) as well as of books published by the Centre for Peace Ethics (Leuven).

HENRI-JÉRÔME GAGEY teaches fundamental theology at the Catholic Institute of Paris and serves as director of the research group Christian Anthropology. His research interests include political theology, communitarianism, and the practical implications of Christian faith. Among his publications is a recent book *La vérité s'accomplit* (Paris, Bayard, 2009), on theological truth in a postmodern context.

ANTHONY J. GODZIEBA teaches fundamental and systematic theology at Villanova University and specializes in the theology of God, Christology, theological anthropology, and philosophical theology. He is currently doing research on the intersection of art, music, theology, and spirituality in early modern Catholicism. He is the author of *Bernhard Welte's Fundamental Theological Approach to Christology* (Peter Lang, 1994) and coeditor of *Christology: Memory, Inquiry, Practice* (Orbis, 2003).

MICHELLE A. GONZALEZ teaches systematic theology at the University of Miami. Her research interests include Latino/a, Latin American, and feminist theologies, and she does interdisciplinary work in Afro-Caribbean studies. Her publications include *Afro-Cuban Theology: Religion, Race, Culture, and Identity* (University Press of Florida, 2006), *Created in God's Image: An Introduction to Feminist Theological Anthropology* (Orbis, 2007), *Embracing*

Latina Spirituality: A Woman's Perspective (St. Anthony Messenger Press, 2009), and *Lived Religion in the Americas: A Critical Study of Liberation Theologies* (New York University Press, 2013).

Wilhelm Guggenberger teaches Christian social ethics and serves as dean of Theological Studies at the University of Innsbruck. He is a member of the interdisciplinary research group Politics-Religion-Art and of the international Colloquium on Violence and Religion. He has published books in German on the sociological theory of Niklas Luhmann vis-à-vis with Catholic social teaching, fundamental ethics, and business ethics.

Robyn Horner is associate dean for the Faculty of Theology and Philosophy at Australian Catholic University. Her interests include the works of Jean-Luc Marion, Jacques Derrida, and Emmanuel Lévinas, as she explores the intersections of theology and poststructuralist philosophy. Her publications include *Rethinking God as Gift: Marion, Derrida, and the Limits of Phenomenology* (Fordham University Press, 2001) and *Jean-Luc Marion: A Theo-logical Introduction* (Ashgate, 2005).

David G. Kirchhoffer teaches theological ethics at the Australian Catholic University in Brisbane. His focus is on the meaning and relevance of the concept of human dignity and on contemporary understandings of the human person in contemporary ethics. His publications include *Human Dignity in Contemporary Ethics* (Teneo Press, 2013), and he is co-editor, with Robyn Horner and Patrick McArdle, of *Being Human: Groundwork for a Theological Anthropology for the 21st Century* (Mosaic/Wipf and Stock, 2013).

Stephen J. Pope teaches fundamental moral theology and social ethics at Boston College. His research interests are Christian ethics and evolutionary theory, love and justice in contemporary Christian ethics, and charity and natural law in Thomas Aquinas and Roman Catholic social teachings. His publications include *Human Evolution and Christian Ethics* (Cambridge University Press, 2007) and *The Fullness of Life: The Science of Well-Being and the Ethics of Virtue* (Georgetown, forthcoming).

Ellen Van Stichel is a postdoctoral researcher at the Faculty of Theology and Religious Studies, KU Leuven, Belgium. In 2010 she defended her dissertation "Out of Love for Justice: Moral philosophy and Catholic Social Thought on Global Duties." She is a member of the research group Anthropos, and her research interest lies in care ethics, Catholic social thought, and social and biomedical ethics.

act: Christian, 5, 6, 84, 90, 93, 95, 96; ethical, 89, 91, 93, 95–97, 100; of feeling, 45; human, 29, 84, 93; of liberation, 105, 178; of loving, 14, 45, 95, 125; of meaning-giving, 121; of piety, 178; of power, 138; of receiving, 121; of understanding, 15, 66; unity of human, 45; of willing, 15, 45
action: collective, 161, 162; embodied, 111; free and responsible, 42; master of, 44; nonviolent, 179, 180; political, 150, 152; sacramental, 113; volitional, 46
Action Française, 44, 45
Adam and Eve, 16, 17, 18, 25. *See also* original sin
adaptation, 49, 51, 58, 166
Adorno, Theodor, 103
affectivity, 23
African American, 142, 160
Agacinski, Sylviane, 38
agency: animal, 63–65, 73; human, 5, 64, 69, 73, 186, 189, 190; moral, 24, 121, 186; political, 149, 150, 151, 154, 155, 159, 160, 163
aggression, 26, 48, 55, 169
Alison, James, 165, 178, 181
altruism, 28, 49, 99, 167–168; in animals, 72; and evolutionary theory, 21, 47; of God, 21; as imitation of God, 26; kin, 50, 51, 55, 57; reciprocal, 50
altruistic behavior, 50, 72
American culture, 6, 102, 103
authenticity, 15, 63, 72, 84, 210
animal: continuity with humans, 47, 62, 74; discontinuity with humans, 47, 74; distinctiveness of human beings, 4, 5, 60, 62; instrumental value or use of, 61, 63, 74; intelligent, 13, 15, 16, 23, 63, 67, 69; moral status of, 61; nonhuman,

14, 64, 75; rational, 2, 15, 16, 66, 187; reasoning, 36, 66, 67; self-seeking, 23; social (animals), 47, 65, 67, 72; social (human beings), 23, 36, 93
animality, 37, 39, 55, 66
Anna, Gabriele De, 52
anthropocentrism, 16, 19, 42, 45, 61, 64, 117, 185–187
appetite: concupiscent, 68; intellectual, 67; irascible, 68; rational, 67; sensitive, 23, 58, 67
Aquinas, Thomas: causality, 17; definition of natural law, 2, 3, 14–16; divine likeness, 4, 62, 75; divine persons, 37; exalted Jesus, 82; Genesis, 66; God as Father, 84; human capacities, 5, 57, 66–70; human reason, 63, 66; image of God, 4, 69, 75; image-bearing, 61, 62, 69, 74, 75; nature, 2, 3, 14–16, 49, 55, 57; passions, 58; personhood, 43; rational and intellectual appetite, 67, 68; relationship between humans and other animals, 62–69, 74, 75; soul, 58, 67; subsistent form, 15, 37, 109; virtue, 57, 58
Arendt, Hannah, 80, 155, 160
Aristotle: distinction between matter and form, 38, 39, 43; *Nichomachean Ethics*, 49; *scala naturae*, 46; teleology, 29, 62
Arnhart, Larry, 49
art, 36, 83, 113
artificial intelligence, 187
atonement, 28, 30
Augustine, 23, 43, 68, 69, 125, 139
authenticity, 6, 102, 104
authoritarianism, 24
authority, 20, 49, 98, 140, 142, 203
autonomy, 24, 45, 53, 105, 106, 111, 117, 152, 172, 190

experience, 6, 21, 24, 35, 46, 51, 55,
57, 70, 73, 83, 85, 97, 99, 104, 105,
107–111, 113, 114, 119, 121, 122,
124–126, 134, 135, 146, 165, 171, 173,
174, 177, 180, 181, 189, 190, 192

faith, 5, 18, 40, 41, 70, 72, 93, 97–100,
106–108, 110–113, 117, 124, 133, 136,
145, 148, 192
Fall, 7, 17, 18, 23, 25, 28, 30, 124, 173,
174, 177, 185
Falque, Emmanuel, 124
family, 15, 44, 161
Father, 83, 92, 126, 138, 170, 171, 177,
180
female, 35, 133, 140
feminist anthropology, 153, 156, 157
feminist public theology, 8, 151, 156
feminist theological anthropology, 151,
152, 155–157
feminist theology, 146, 150, 154, 155,
157, 158
Fernandez, Eleazer S., 142
Fichte, Gottlieb Johann, 82
free will, 42, 44, 48, 52, 53, 55, 58, 64,
67, 166, 171
freedom: Christian, 96, 98, 99; as creativity, 63; finite, 34, 35; of God, 73;
human, 6, 37, 58, 63, 64, 66, 73, 74,
81, 82, 96, 97, 98, 117–119, 154, 164;
Kantian, 43; positive and negative, 63;
religious, 19, 180
Funkenstein, Amos, 80

Galatians 2:20, 26
Galileo, 17
game theory, 50
Ganz, Marshall, 160
García-Rivera, Alejandro, 164
Gaudium et Spes, 1, 6, 19, 20, 34, 105,
113, 115–118, 123, 124, 157, 189
Gehlen, Arnold, 166
gender, 22, 133, 137, 139, 142, 143, 149,
151–154, 157–159, 188
genes, 13, 23, 65, 81, 113
Genesis: 1:26, 13, 23, 25; 5:1, 14; 3,
18, 23, 25; 3:5, 172; 9:6, 14; divine
command in, 60; Thomas Aquinas on,
66
gift: of creation, 20; of creaturely life, 74;
God's gift of relationship, 112; Jesus'

sacrificial, 138; logic of, 7; of self, 21,
122, 125, 181
gifted self (*adonné*), 6, 115, 121, 122, 125
Girard, René: anthropology, 165; on collective human behavior, 169, 170, 172,
174; on collective memories, 165; on
desire, 166; on mythological narratives,
165, 170; on Western culture, 165, 173
globalization, 103, 135, 157, 188
God: children of, 142; Father, 83, 92,
126, 138, 170–171, 177, 180; glory
of, 139; intervention, 17, 70, 72;
relational, 7, 112, 145, 161, 188. *See
also* Holy Spirit; image of God; Jesus;
Trinity
good: Thomas Aquinas on, 67, 69; common good, 21, 24, 113, 149, 150, 156,
158, 160, 163, 176; good of human
beings, 30, 58; good life, 24, 55, 56;
good of the other, 95, 113, 191; goodness of creation, 56; goodness of God,
126; human good(s), 15, 24, 25, 27, 29;
within natural law thinking, 20, 29,
34; nonmaterial goods, 67; as opposed
to evil, 4, 25, 26, 29, 46, 56, 175, 178;
public, 162, 163; true good, 167
grace, 6, 9, 20, 23, 27, 106, 112, 120, 126,
180; divine grace, 1, 22, 30, 74, 114,
181, 192; perfecting nature, 59; and
salvation, 6, 106; sin and, 2, 8, 33, 152,
171, 177
group loyalty, 4, 47
guilt, 50, 53, 169, 170, 176, 179, 180

Hebrews 1:3, 21
Hedges, Chris, 6, 102–104
hegemony, 105, 106
Hemmerle, Klaus, 112
hermeneutic circle, 33, 39, 107, 110
hermeneutics, 2, 4, 28, 108, 111, 113,
122, 124, 134
Hilkert, Catherine Mary, 159
Himes, Kenneth, 160
Himes, Michael, 160
Hispanic theology, 135
historicity, 3, 31, 32, 186, 188, 189
Hobbes, Thomas, 49, 55, 168
Hollenbach, David, 160
Holy Death (Santissima Muerte), 137
Holy Spirit, 6, 20, 22, 43, 74, 92, 98–99,
144–145, 180